Praise for *12,000 Miles in the Nick of Time:*

"Jacobson takes us on an inner trip with wry social commentary and ruminations on the nature of a family as it navigates the cross-generational divide, and what it means to be a parent."
—Nancy Paradis, *The St. Petersburg Times*

"An amusingly chronicled and appealing ride."
—Elizabeth Einstein, Newsweek.com

"An alternately enthralling and maddening book about a family of hardcore individualists and eccentrics whose search for something more than snapshots from their travels reminds us of how exhilarating and difficult this world really can be."
—*Creative Loafing*

"Jacobson achieves his ultimate goal—for his children and the reader—by demonstrating the sublimity of the world."
—Leah Ourso, *Memphis Flyer*

"Very funny . . . History presented as a grand adventure. Makes you want to chuck everything and head for far-flung places."
—David Pitt, *Booklist*

12,000 Miles in the Nick of Time

Also by Mark Jacobson

Gojiro
Everyone and No One

12,000 MILES
IN THE NICK OF TIME

A Semi-Dysfunctional Family
Circumnavigates the Globe

Mark Jacobson
with additional commentary by Rae Jacobson

Grove Press
New York

Published simultaneously in Canada
Printed in the United States of America

FIRST GROVE PRESS EDITION

Library of Congress Cataloging-in-Publication Data

Jacobson, Mark.
    12,000 miles in the nick of time : a semi-dysfunctional family circumnavigates the globe / Mark Jacobson ; with additional commentary by Rae Jacobson.
        p. cm.
    ISBN 0-8021-4138-2 (pbk.)
    1. Jacobson, Mark—Journeys.   2. Voyages around the world.   I. Title:
Twelve thousand miles in the nick of time.   II. Jacobson, Rae.   III. Title.

G440.J23 2003
910.4'1—dc21   2003041821

Grove Press
841 Broadway
New York, NY 10003

04 05 06 07 08   10 9 8 7 6 5 4 3 2 1

For our children's grandparents, here and departed.

CONTENTS

12,000 Miles in the Nick of Time

Burning Is Learning

It is easy to get lost in the mucky dung-strewn back alleyways in Varanasi's Holy City, but finding the Burning Ghat is never a problem. You just follow the corpses.

Some dead bodies, wrapped round and round in snow-white gauze, sit upright like solitary commuters in the backseat of slowly pedaled bicycle rickshaws. Others, swathed in bright orange, lie on garland-decked pallets that are borne high by crowds of weeping relatives. They all will lead you to the river, the Holy River Ganges. Failing that, you can follow your nose, pick up the smell of incense or, if the wind is right, charring flesh.

So there we were, the world travelers, watching dead people on fire.

It was a rare chance to stand at a sacred crossroads of existence, I told the children. The Infinite Round of Being was playing out before us. A billion believing Hindus dreamed of coming to this very place, to die and be cremated. To have one's body burned here, the ashes tossed into the Holy River, was to assure a good burial, a release from the endless karmic cycle of birth and rebirth. Here, it was possible for souls to attain nirvana, which was the goal of all souls.

In deference to these vast, humbling forces, we should be quiet and respectful at the Burning Ghat, I said.

Not that the locals appeared to be observing such decorum. An argument had broken out near one of the three ten-foot-high pyres. A family was screaming at a fat middle-aged man in a deeply soiled dhoti. Pointing at a clipboard, the man screamed back.

It was a fight over money. After all, it takes more than three tons of wood, cut into one hundred-pound railroad tie–size pieces, to properly burn a body. Lumber is not cheap. With the deforestation crisis throughout the Gangetic Plain, it was getting more expensive all the time. The lumber has to be lorried in from the south, or floated down the river from Himalayan foothills in ominous, black-hulled boats. Aware of this ever-rising cost, Hindu pilgrims save for years for their funeral pyres. Apparently the particular pilgrim currently on the fire had not saved enough. Head and torso blackened but still intact, the fuel for his trip to heaven had run out.

If the cremation was to continue, the man with the clipboard, who identified himself as "the captain of the Burning Ghat," said he would require further payment. Otherwise, he told the deceased's weeping, railing relatives, he would have no choice but to remove the half-incinerated body and replace it with another, of which there was no shortage, corpses being stacked up in several places on the steps leading to the river. The dead man's sons and daughters were claiming extortion, screaming they had already paid the agreed amount.

So it was a negotiation, still another subcontinental bargaining session. Here, even the transmigration of souls did not have a fixed price. Ah, India. Just when you feel you've weathered today's onslaught of the bizarre, things ratchet up one more notch. What a country! They didn't have this back in Brooklyn.

Still, I could tell, the Burning Ghat was not making it as a family fun destination.

The kids were not digging it. It was only a few weeks ago that they'd visited the Tuol Sleng Genocide Museum in Phnom Penh, Cambodia, the one-time high school where Pol Pot's Khmer Rouge tortured and killed twenty thousand people. At the great temples of Angkor, they'd walked by the armless, legless beggars. In Thailand there was that bus at the bottom of the ravine, dried blood on the broken windows, little boys in rags prying off the tires with their bare hands. But now, a month and a half into our circumnavigation of the globe, the Burning Ghat was the last draw.

"This is horrible! Disgusting!" critiqued the then-sixteen-year-old, Rae.

"Bad," chimed in twelve-year-old Rosalie.

"Really bad," assented Billy, nine at the time.

The three of them were united on this point. They were all going to throw up if we didn't get out of there immediately.

The really dumb thing was: I wasn't positive about Tuol Sleng, but I really thought they were going to like the Burning Ghat.

Nattering like some ninny Chevy Chase, I'd told my wife: you'll see, the Burning Ghat is going to be a pick hit. Knock their unchanged socks right off. As it turned out, of all the places the children professed to hate in our three-month spin about the planet, the Burning Ghat, and India in general, was the most hated.

It wasn't just the heat and filth. Back in New York, Rae had no compunction about lying around on the cruddy sidewalks of the East Village with her skin-pierced, semi-no-account friends. Indeed, all three of our children were born while we lived in a fourth-floor walkup on St. Marks Place, the East Village's famously disreputable bohemian promenade. They had more than a passing acquaintance with the phantasmagoric, not to mention stench.

But this was different. True, in New York they might have subway leerers and backpack snatchers, but they didn't clutch at you all the time. In New York you didn't have to stay at places where whirring fans crashed from the ceiling like downed helicopters in the middle of the night. In New York you didn't have to eat *mutter paneer* every other meal and brush your teeth with orange soda lest giant parasites burrow into your bone marrow. In New York, they didn't bargain over whether or not to throw half-burned dead people into the river, not every day anyway. And if they did, you didn't have to watch it with *your parents.*

"I'm breathing through my mouth, Dad," hissed Rosalie, gagging on the thick black smoke from the funeral pyre. "I've been breathing through my mouth for days. . . ."

On a global jaunt, the whine was equally global. They didn't simply want to go back to the Vishnu Guest House, the two-dollar "traveler's" hotel we'd spent an epic hour trying to find soon after our arrival from Kathmandu, dodging massive piles of cow dung up and down the rabbit warren maze of blind alleys in Varanasi's Old City. Certainly there was some fun to be had sitting on the Vishnu balcony above the Holy River watching surly French backpackers study their Lonely Planet guides while attempting to ignore incursions of monkeys that swept down from the hotel roof to steal banana pancakes from their greasy dinner plates. It was even more fun, especially from the point of view of Billy, the scampish World Wide Wrestling Federation fan, to shoot pebbles at those same monkeys with slingshots provided by the harried but ever-amused hotel staff.

Wham. Right in the red-colored butt, you see that shot? Fun. But the kind of fun that only went so far.

No, the children wanted greater distance from the Burning Ghat than simply returning to the humid rooms of the Vishnu Guest House and their squat toilets. A one-way ticket out of India, and Asia itself, would not even suffice. What was called for was a little teleportation. A zap back to that nice little spot on the couch in our current Brooklyn abode, a bowl of Cocoa Puffs on the table, the cordless phone at the ready and a third rerun of some particularly moving episode of *Buffy the Vampire Slayer* on the box. That sounded like the proper degree of separation from the Burning Ghat.

Well, *tough*.

We'd come all this way to escape the enveloping ersatz of the fetid American cultural experience, traveled long and hard to be at one with The Real. And we were going to partake of that real, goddammit. The world was a bigger place than what the anti-Christ popular culture said it was. The world was bigger even than some foul, smoky club on Houston Street where everyone dressed in black. Bigger than Michael Jordan and *Behind the Music*. If it took the Burning Ghat to prove it, well, *tough*.

It was *for their own good*.

In the context of the Great Round of Existence, the Burning Ghat connoted a specific familial symmetry. The Burning Ghat spoke of The Eternal Return.

It was here that my wife and I spent our honeymoon. There wasn't any choice. Niagara Falls was all booked up. Or at least that was my standard reply when asked why, twenty years before the current journey, we decided to drop out, mid-career so to speak, and travel around the world for a year with knapsacks on our backs, *val-da-ree, val-da-rah*.

Originally we had what Pan American Airways, then still struggling to present air travel as the 1939 World's Fair equivalent of a stately Cunard passage across the Atlantic, referred to as an "Eighty Days Around the World" ticket. It was the forerunner of the exotic multicountry deals they sell nowadays under modernist rubrics NY–LA–TKY–HK–BKK–DEL–BAH–ATH–LON–NY, with perhaps a MAD or JOH substituted for a DEL or BAH. Except nowadays they throw in a free web page so you can spam unsuspecting surfers with tedious accounts of your run-ins with Russian customs.

In the path of Jules Verne and David Niven, we took our eighty days and traveled west, making Bali by the seventieth day, which is less than halfway around and was not going to work out math-wise. We sold our tickets to some Germans and went overland, which is how the hippies used to do it, before the Ayatollah and sundry Taliban loosed fundamentalism and bad water upon all the good dope cities. Back then, an extra nine months on the road didn't seem excessive, especially with time off for a few bouts of dengue fever. Somewhere in the middle we pulled into Varanasi, and, following the bodies, found our way to the Burning Ghat where, suddenly, we found our future on the line.

Taking pictures of the Burning Ghat is forbidden. Everyone knows this. Liberal ethnographical pluralist/internationalists then as now, we respected that. At least that's what we tried to tell those boys, some preteen Fagin's army, who came out of nowhere to surround us, claiming unforgivable sacrilege.

"No pictures of the Burning Ghat," they bum-rushed, demanding that my wife hand over the unused camera sticking out of her bag.

We'd been warned about this, in the "scams and cons" section of one guidebook or another. The "offended" parties demand the film, then run off with the camera: a fairly standard shakedown, nothing to get pent-up about. But these kids got too close. Voices were raised, a crowd began to gather and a moment later, rocks were flying. A nice little entry for the honeymoon scrapbook: stoned to death, at the place of death.

But then, conveniently, a policeman appeared. He hit the kid who had thrown the first stone with his bobby's baton, opening a cut on the young hooligan's head. The kid shouted and the cop knocked him down and kicked him in the ribs. Shocked by such brutality, we, being respectful pluralist/internationalists, attempted to intercede on behalf of our erstwhile attacker. Heeding these pleas for mercy, the cop got in one more good shot to the gut, then stopped. The kid got up, spit at us through bloodied lips, and hobbled away.

"This man has helped you," said a man in the crowd, indicating the mustachioed cop, a strong and silent type in his nifty brown and red uniform. "Without this man you could have been seriously hurt, even killed. Those boys are evil. Maximum bandits. He has saved your future for you."

There was no mistaking the next bit of business. *Baksheesh* was a way of life upon the subcontinent, we well knew. But how much? How much was the future worth to two honeymooning Americans traveling God's great hippie highway?

"I would say fifty rupees," the onlooker suggested.

About six bucks in 1980. Then, it seemed like a deal.

So now we were back at the Burning Ghat, with The Future in tow, the three of them.

What more accurate accounting of the future could there be? What else has really happened in the twenty years between then and now?

For my part, there were a few books written, none immortal. Some movies written and rewritten. The range of experience was wide, often very rewarding, in a city-boy journalist sort of way: there were games of one-on-one with Dr. J., a joint with Bob Marley, two-mile descents beneath the ground with South African gold miners, midnight sails with caviar poachers in the Caspian Sea, a playful swat in the arm from John Gotti, a kiss on the cheek from the Dalai Lama.

But what, in the end, are these things worth? What is the DNA of experience? How do you package it, send it along? How many times can you tell those same moldy stories?

No, when I look at my particular life, all that I have accomplished and not accomplished, when I draw a bottom line beneath the debits and credits, the most tangible, irrefutable sum is: them.

The three of them.

"You are wise to have brought your children to the Burning Ghat," said Mr. Sen, who had appointed himself our guide, elbowing aside any number of other unsolicited dispensers of spiritual and logistical information. In Varanasi, we had steered clear of such individuals, making exceptions only for "Goldie people" i.e., those who claimed to be close friends of Goldie Hawn, of which Varanasi offered a surprisingly large contingent. Indeed, upon hearing that we were Americans, many people assumed that we "knew Goldie," who apparently is something of a collector of "Benares silks," the spectacular brocades for which the Holy City is famous. As "friends of Goldie," we were asked back to several houses to drink tea in rooms displaying large, autographed pictures of the former star of the seventies comedy show, *Laugh-in*.

The dark-eyed Mr. Sen was no Goldie person. With his wooly-haired coif and frumpy, frayed sport jacket he suggested a former student radical, an embassy-occupier perhaps, gradually gone to seed and blurred apocalyptic vision. He was determined to extend cultural enlightenment to the naive and hopelessly self-satisfied Americans in his midst.

"Burning is learning," Mr. Sen declared.

"Huh?"

"Burning is learning. Cremation is education." This was Mr. Sen's most effectively rhymed tourist mantra. One didn't have to be a Hindu, or even an Indian, to come away from Varanasi a changed person, Mr. Sen made clear. "You can be a Christian, or any manner of pagan. . . ."

Originally from a small village outside the industrial city of Kanpur one hundred miles east, where his health was "ruined by terrible pollution and the amorality of money," Mr. Sen came to Varanasi three years ago because, as "a follower of Lord Shiva . . . there was nowhere else to go."

Varanasi has always been Shiva's city, Mr. Sen said, ever since the God decapitated Brahma and wandered through all of India with the bloody head stuck to his palm. In Varanasi, the skull finally came loose, rolling from Shiva's hand. The god decided he liked Varanasi and decided to make it his home. To this day he hasn't left, which is the reason the city is referred to as *Avimutka,* or "the unabandoned."

Indeed, without Lord Shiva, whom Mr. Sen described as "the one thousand-eyed creator and destroyer of the universe, Lord of Dance, keeper of the cosmic time upon his drum," there would be no Holy City, nor Holy River.

To buttress this contention, Mr. Sen directed us to the Puranas, Hindu scripture, where it says the Ganges once flowed through heaven, its waters as clear as white light. It was the desperate prayers of a million saints that brought the river to earth. The baleful gaze of sage Kapila had set fire to the sixty thousand sons of King Sagara. The saints hoped the celestial waters of the Ganges would purify the ashes.

The Ganges, however, was not happy to leave heaven. Angry at its fall, the river sought to drown the earth on impact. It was only Lord Shiva who prevented the disaster. Craning his neck, the god caught the plummeting Ganges amid the furrows of his infinite brow. Even now, uncounted eons later, the river-bed of the Ganges conforms to those contorted curves that guide the now silty, turbid waters along its 1,560-mile course from the Himalayan glaciers, across the broad plains of Uttar Pradesh and Bihar, to the Bay of Bengal.

It was in this way that Shiva, who set the boundaries of things, separated the water from the land, just as he divided the night from the day, Mr. Sen told us. It was in these transitional places where any conscious being must pay special heed, Mr. Sen said, "because there is no simple line between things." There was always "a zone of change," a threshold "like the twilight" where whatever was became something else. These in-between places, called *tirthas*, were Shiva's realm, his and his alone.

As world travelers, journeying through foreign lands, "where life is different from one place to another," our little family should pay extra attention to *tirthas*, Mr. Sen implored. "You will go past many borders, and you should pray for Shiva's aid in cross-ing them." Safe passage was never assured, for Shiva was a will-ful god, a trickster. Humanity had no choice but to suffer his capricious whims.

This appeared to be the case at the Burning Ghat. The Burning Ghat was paramount among *tirthas*, Mr. Sen said, for it was here that "life became death and life again." As it was, the transitional journey of the pilgrim currently on pyre was not pro-gressing smoothly. As the dead man's relatives continued to protest, several workers were removing the body from the cre-mation pile with long sticks, in preparation for tossing the par-tially charred remains into the river. Nothing was left but a blackened torso, a skull and the stump of a single arm. The pilgrim's eyes had been dissolved in their sockets, a sight I attempted to shield from the kids' view.

In search of The Real, it was important to screen out the Too Real.

"This is terrible. Can't we just give them the money?" exclaimed Rae, horrified at the proceedings.

The other kids took up the cry. Only moments before, they expressed no other desire than to get away. If Hindus wanted to throw their dead mothers and fathers on the fire like a Memphis barbeque, that was their business. Now, the tune had changed.

"It's their father! We can't stand here and allow that to happen to their father! How much money do they need? Why can't we just give it to them?"

Mr. Sen looked surprised. He said he was unsure whether the course of a burial could be changed at this late juncture, especially due to the intervention of a stranger, a non-Hindu. "Do you have money?" he asked the children.

"*He* does!" the kids exclaimed, pointing at me. Kids. They're always putting the touch on you for something.

Regardless, it was too late now. The body was thrown into the river. *Splash.* The pilgrim's relatives stood stock-still and mute, watching the ripples in the water. Already attendants were bringing down another stiff, wrapped in white gauze.

This about concluded our sight-seeing expedition to the Burning Ghat. We'd already turned to go when Mr. Sen grabbed my arm.

"You are a lucky man," he said softly. "Your wife is a lucky woman. To have these children . . . they are very generous. They wish to help. That is very lucky."

It was the presence of children that, more than anything, brought human beings into close contact with the Divine, Mr. Sen said. As each death opened a *tirtha*, so did every birth. Each time a child came into the world, the boundaries of reality were pierced, the status quo irretrievably altered. It was something to celebrate, since it was by this process that existence was furthered, Mr. Sen said, suddenly looking very sad. For a moment it appeared as if he would begin weeping.

"I have no children, my wife and I could not. . . . It was a great disappointment to us. Because of this we are no longer together. . . . So I am alone, marooned here in this brutal world. I have come here to wait to die. To escape this place, since there is nothing for me here."

Back in Brooklyn, even in the so-called "breeding grounds" of our Park Slope neighborhood, it was not unusual to hear couples bemoan their inability to conceive. There were many tales of drugs ingested, operations undertaken, and then, eventually, journeys to far-off lands where children would be adopted, gathered up from poverty and despair, given loving homes. It seemed a function of the modern world, the barrenness and the adoptions both.

It was another matter altogether to hear of infertility here, amid the multitudes of The World's Largest Democracy. Just that week the *Hindustani Times* was reporting the birth of the billionth Indian. My heart went out to Mr. Sen, follower of Shiva, spirit of the reproductive principle, in whose puissant honor men constructed Shiva *lingas*, wood and stone phalluses, some as much as fifty feet tall.

Beside the Burning Ghat, the family stared at the river where what was left of the pilgrim's body had disappeared. There was nothing there now, just a swirl of muddy water. It was starting to rain, the cremation pyres sizzling under the falling droplets.

"It is good to have children," Mr. Sen commented as we made our way from the Burning Ghat. "That way, when you die, there will always be someone to pay for your funeral."

* * *

Then we were on the river, the Holy River.

It was shortly after dawn, and we were going downstream, thinking of Huck and Jim, stars of one of our favorite books. Years before, on one of our many car trips, we had started reading the great Finn up in Minnesota, at the source of the Mississippi, the Father of Waters, near a little town of about one hundred people called Jacobson. Jacobson, Minnesota—a Jewish Jacobson with an *o*, not even a Swedish Jacobsen, with an *e*.

Excited by this marvelous synchronicity, we entered a bait and tackle shop, announcing our namesake. When the man in the Valvoline cap finally looked up, he said his name was Demming, and once he happened to drive through Demming, New Mexico, "a little dump full of railroad bums," so he knew exactly how we felt.

We kept reading Mark Twain all the way down the great river to New Orleans, always a favorite travel destination, owing to the shabby sexual allure of the French Quarter, which the girls, despite our constant assertions that the place was nothing but a frat boy tourist trap, found irresistible.

If I'd had the presence of mind, I'd have brought a copy of *Huck Finn* to intone as we plied the Ganges, thereby consecrating Shiva's river in some typically solipsistic Brooklyn manner. Twain had been this way himself, 140 years ago, following the equator on his own round-the-world journey. Even then, he said, Varanasi was "as old as tradition, as old as history and looks older than both of them put together."

Our boatman wasn't exactly recent issue, either. Ochre-toothed and hollow-cheeked, his turban unraveling like the frayed dressing from a festering battle wound, we'd seen him standing on the ghat outside the Vishnu Guest House.

"Boat . . . boat . . . cheap price," he said over and over, his voice barely audible. There were other boatmen, offering similar cheap prices, but we appreciated the historical dialetic represented by this particular mariner's craft. This owed to the fact that despite the age and decrepitude of most of the Ganges rowboats, the majority of them sported freshly painted ads for Coca-Cola on their otherwise weathered sides. It was a fairly recent advent. When my wife and I came here, Coca-Cola was not sold in India. The Indira Gandhi government was following a protectionist economic course, and Coke, which had refused to turn over the details of their so-called secret formula to local bottlers, was banned from the country. Instead, everyone drank bicuspid-dissolving sugar solutions like Thumbs Up and Campa-Cola, which sported a logo remarkably similar to the "real thing." But times had changed. Indira was dead, a deal was made. Now Coke was guzzled in India, just like everywhere else.

Therein lay the uniqueness of our boatman's craft. While the right flank of his boat was decorated with the ubiquitous Coke logo, the left retained a faded but still discernable ad for Campa-Cola. Whether this was due to oversight, sloth or design mattered little. The fact that this particular boatman alone among so many others (the rest of the boats had Coke on both sides) had chosen a mid-course between long cherished singularity of the nation-state and the inevitabilities of global capital struck us a fitting straddle of past and present.

The rain that had started at the Burning Ghat was coming down harder now. Winds pushed against the thick, claustrophobic humidity. Flat and placid only a few moments before, the Ganges grew choppy, turbid brown water smacking against the boat's rutted gunwales. A storm was coming in, thick black clouds scudding across the wide plains from the west.

It was the monsoon, and about time, too. According to reports, the previous weeks had been unbearable in the Holy City. Few could remember a hot season quite so hot, so filled with dust and sweat. The afternoon temperature rarely dipped below forty degrees Celsius. The evenings were little better. To simply sleep for more than an hour at a time was impossible. The heat was such that the cows lay down on the stone streets, refusing to move sometimes for days, tempting harried taxi and rickshaw drivers to kick them out of sheer frustration, which would have been a sin.

The monsoon brought relief. Every year, as the heat built along the plains, people waited for the monsoon. Sometimes it came sooner than other times. Now, finally, it was here.

But the monsoon would not be an unmixed blessing. The downpour, which would banish the heat and replenish the haggard land, eventually would also saturate the ground. The swelling Ganges, held in place by Shiva's dreadlocks no more, would breach its banks. By August everything would be flooded, the grand Moghul-style buildings along the ghats inundated, water filling the lower rooms to the ceilings. After this would be the months of stench and mildew, along with the leeches and inevitable outbreaks of disease, which had only grown worse due to the close quarters. Almost two million people lived in the Varanasi now, more than double the number here twenty years ago.

But what was the use of complaining? Every year it was the same; it was the cycle of things. The wet always followed the heat, just as night preceded day. This was the way of things, the form to the world, more evidence of the immutable Great Round of Being. Besides, no one came to Varanasi for the weather.

The boatman squinted upstream, into the oncoming storm. The dark clouds were closer now, looming up beyond the railway bridge. Was it auspicious to be upon the Ganges at the exact moment when the dry shifted to the wet, to find oneself and one's family present at the moment of change, smack inside one of Mr. Sen's *tirthas*? It wouldn't do any good to ask the boatman. He was as silent as Charon, steadily rowing.

In fact, no one in the boat had said a word since pushing off from the Burning Ghat. An accusatory quiet had come over

us. The girls were mad, again. They had told us they didn't want
to go to the Burning Ghat, we'd made them go, and what did
they get out of it beyond another nightmare? Ostensibly desperate to get home to curl up with their gloomy suicide CDs,
from Joy Division on down, they were teenagers, content to play
footsie with the angel of death. They wanted it like an Anne Rice
vampire book, full of spike-haired bloodsuckers melted on the
floor like ice cream in the sun, but still a way cool-looking puddle.
As for the actual shear of loin and limb, the corruption and can-
kering of bodies, they wanted no part of that, and who could
blame them?

They were a long way from compulsively scanning *The
Times* obit pages like me. In the Great Round of Being, with its
twin *tirthas* of birth and death, they were a lot closer to the
former than the latter. Or at least this was the hope. Who needed
all this mortality, this endless reminder of the perishability of
the Now?

Their own unremitting distaste for this whole circum-
navigatory journey only served to depress them further. All the
complaining, the bleats about homesickness, the tantrums over
food and dirt, made them feel like ungrateful wretches. They
were embarrassed by the shock of their own provinciality. They
were supposed to be the hip kids from New York City, minds as
open as the ocean.

Yet here they were in The World, and it was driving them
crazy. It was a degree of self-hatred they deftly repackaged and
shipped back our way, a vicious little circularity, proving yet again
that families don't need to be holed up in some Eastern European hovel or rambling about like less financially advantaged
Cheever characters in a Connecticut split-level to turn in on
themselves, rip each other to shreds.

The storm was coming quick now, a deep thrum of thun-
der and cascades of rain. Muddy slog no more, the river was alive,

churning up from underneath. Holy water arched high, drench-
ing our REI miracle-fiber travel shirts, soaking the kids' daypacks.
Wind lifted the sand on the opposite river bank. Unlike the town
side, with its dense buildings and thousands of death cult pilgrims, the other shore was undeveloped, seemingly devoid of
activity. It appeared as a bone-white stretch of desert, empty
except for the occasional apparitional figure bouncing along on
the back of a camel. But now, in the throes of the gale, the entire sandy slope appeared to be rising. Up it went, hovering for
an instant above the river like a giant white cowl, or a diapha-
nous spacecraft.

The smell of ozone filled the air, followed by lightning,
electric daggers serrating the sky. Then the wind shifted, scat-
tering the hovering sand. The shoreline disappeared. In the
blowing rain, we couldn't see more than five feet. Suddenly, it
was as if we were there by ourselves; us and the impassive,
unspeaking boatman, on the river fallen from heaven.

For once, no parental prattle about the beautiful danger of
"nature" or some such other idiocy filled the space between us.
We reached out for each other, the five of us, holding hands. It
wasn't the first time on this trip that disaster seemed close. In
the previous month and a half we'd been on nearly a dozen air-
planes, some big, others small and coughing. Every time one of
these off-brand planes left the ground we chanced massacre,
total destruction, the end of our line. All five of us, gone, in
one screaming descent, only to reappear one more time in that
dreaded, dead passenger manifest.

Jacobson, M.
Jacobson, R.
Jacobson, R.
Jacobson, W.
Cardozo, N.

Our names, one on top of another.

Alone on the Holy River, there was a kind of intimate, inexorable fatalism to it. It all seemed out of our hands.

It is one of the magic attractions of the Ganges, and rivers in general—the Jordan, the Mississippi, the Rubicon and a hundred streams from mythologies known and long forgotten. Unlike lakes and oceans and other bodies of water imagined to be holy, unlike the peaks of mountains that ascend beyond the layer of obscuring clouds, no river is so wide that whatever lies beyond is not within reach. The other side is always visible. Here, in the reasonable imagination, it is possible to cross over. Except now, in the draping onrush of the monsoon, we could not see the river's edges. Both shores were obscured.

The random flashes of lightning brought a high relief to our faces. For the millionth time, I could study the physical features of my children, puzzle who had gotten what from whom, the way Rae's eyes came from my mother, and Rosalie's skin coloring so closely matched my wife's. How come Billy had blue eyes and blond hair and he looked like me, anyway? The mix and match of Mendel's tic-tac-toe board never ceased to turn up one more permutation, a roll of dots on dice. The collective genome was filled with chute and ladder helixes that predated places called Russia, Romania, Spain and Newfoundland, a mess of Jews and Catholics, too. Double, toil and trouble, our batch was poured from an unknown mash of biology, volition and lust. Who knew which buttons my wife and I pushed to produce the trio of children in this boat. Three big bangs. First inside my wife's body, then too big for that, then too big for cribs and baby clothes, then too big for coloring books, then too big for first grade, the second and the third, too big for our all-consuming care. Eventually, too big for our conception of who and what they are: the ever-expanding universe of them.

We were lucky that way, as the somber, childless Mr. Sen pointed out. Linking hands in a leaky boat on a holy river, we were each other's *tirtha,* a boatload of multidirectional, many vectored *tirthas.* We, the older generation, looked at them, the youthful offspring, and tried to make sense of what was to come, at least most immediately. Likewise, they looked at us, when they could bear to look at us, and groped toward a vision of where they came from.

The world that came before us was back home in the good ol' U.S. of A., locked up inside the frames of a few fading, scratchy photographs, images of other, vanished worlds—the Cardozos thrown out of Spain in 1492, the assorted Jacobsons, traveling steerage from Russia and Romania. These pictures, gathering dust in basements, pressed flat between old atlases full of countries swept away by vicious history, would soon fade to imperceptibility, as unknown as the future beyond them.

What remained was us. Little us, nuclear us. For the moment, the entropy that inevitably flings things and people apart was suspended. The force field of our own making ruled the day, a most favorable kind of gravity. We were together. The will by which we created life in our family, this fleeting passage during which we lived under the same Brooklyn roof, rode in the same Toyota Camry station wagon, and got on the same airplane to go on this trip that had landed us, currently, in the city of the Hindu dead, remained in control. That's really what this trip was, a grand, somewhat nutty gesture, a tribute to the ephemera of our lives together. Even if everything went perfectly, in the middle class way of thinking of things—them doing well, going off to college, getting really swell jobs, et cetera—we'd never be as close as we'd been over the sixteen years since Rae came on the scene, followed by her sister and brother. Arrows on the dartboard; for now we'd landed here.

It was like those rare times, in the red-floored kitchen of our often indifferently regarded home in Brooklyn, when, for no particular reason, someone called "family hug" and we grabbed each other, just because we were in the same room and we could. You had to get it while you could, put aside a million mixed feelings, because those moments were irretrievable. It had been a big juicy chapter, this time of us being together, this invention of us. In no small way, we were all just passing through, tipping our hats like any Lone Ranger, here today and gone tomorrow. It was hard to say where we would go next. With the next lightning strike, it could be over. Sometimes things just fell apart.

The deal was to horde the here and now. What was known only to us. The shared knowledge, the inside jokes. And so our eyes went to the flying purple shirt.

Long sleeves flapping, it came out of the enveloping mist like a brightly dyed kite, skimmed the roiling surface of the river and soared directly overhead. Only moments before, almost certainly, the shirt had been nothing more than a humble piece of washing, jumbled in a pile, ready to be beaten senseless against a flat rock by one of a hundred laundry *wallahs* working along Mir Ghat or Gai Ghat.

Twack!

Twack. Twack. Twack. The sound of wet cotton against flat stone was just another bit of ambient noise in the Holy City. The purple shirt likely blew away in the storm, too bad for the laundry *wallah*, but good for us, since now we could raise our collective eyes and see it cartwheel upward into the low-hanging clouds: one more memory held in common by us and us alone, one more tiny distinction that set us off from all the other families in the world, some smarter and more loving than us, some white-trash sons of bitches smacking each other in the supermarket. Eight thousand miles might be a long way to see a shirt fly across a river, but considering the stakes, it was worth it.

The shirt had barely disappeared when we heard a thump against the side of the boat.

We'd run into something. It was a body. We could see an unmistakably human form barely below the murky surface of the river. We knew, from Mr. Sen, that certain individuals could not be cremated at the Burning Ghat. Mr. Sen had given us a handy mnemonic, B-A-C-T-M-L, pronounced "backmelt," so we might easily remember those—the Beggars, Ascetics, Children, Thieves, Men bitten by snakes and Lepers—whose karmic fate was to be banned from cremation on the Burning Ghat. Many of these unburned bodies later washed up on sandbars, where they were sometimes eaten by Varanasi's roving packs of wild dogs. It was a good reason to keep moving. If you stayed too still, the dogs thought you were food.

"Oh, no," said Rosalie, when the body thumped against the side of the boat once more. She had a nasty thought: the body in the water might be the half-burned corpse of the dad we'd seen removed from the pyre for nonpayment.

But it wasn't. It wasn't a dead body at all. It was some kid, very much alive, just fooling around. We'd seen him earlier, walking along the ghat, selling garlands. He was about ten, tall and thin, with a big smile. Now he stuck his head out of the river, smiled, spit some holy water against the Campa-Cola side of the boat and dove beneath the surface again.

A few minutes later we were back onshore, climbing up the steps of the ghat to the Vishnu Guest House once more. The rain had come through the windows and our mattresses were soaked. No problem, the hotel people said after congratulating us as if our arrival had been instrumental in the onset of the quenching monsoon. If our mattresses were wet we should turn them over to the dry side and put on the fan. It was more of the usual cycle, more than a bit of the Great Round of Being here in the Holy City. They always flipped the mattresses over when one side got wet.

We did this and went out onto the balcony. Despite the rain, the French backpackers still sat at their tables. They appeared not to have moved. They were still seated on the porch smoking their sooty cigarettes, thumbing through their Lonely Planet guides. Monkeys were jumping down from the roof, sticking their paws into cups of tea. Whether the French people condoned this monkey behavior or simply didn't notice, we never found out. They never looked up.

Row 66

It figured that our last meal in the U.S. of A. would be at McDonald's. Mickey D's was the only place to eat in the Japan Airlines terminal, where they should at least have sushi. The usual mess came to $45 for the five of us, the most I'd ever spent at a McDonald's. I'd thought they all had the same prices, that this was the selling point, the deadening identicalness. Then again, on the extreme off chance you might be flying to a locale where there was no McDonald's, the central office probably wanted to make sure they got to stick it to you one last time.

This was just the sort of crap, I explained to the children, that made this trip essential: the reason we Jacobsons, loyal and patriotic Americans deeply in favor of the Bill of Rights and especially freedom of speech, had no choice but to leave these same shining shores so many other Jacobsons before us had risked life and limb to reach. Things were just too dumb here, currently.

I mean, burgers, fries and shakes are fine, but they're for kids, right? Kids' taste buds only register sugar, salt and fat. It is a physiological fact. Only later does the full range of taste become accessible, resulting in the expansion of consumable options and with it, human creativity, culinary and otherwise. That was the crime of McDonald's, the addicting arrestment of sensual growth, the infantilization of the national palate. Like the cigarette makers, they got you early, held on.

This was the essence of the trouble afoot in this formerly great nation of ours, I told the kids. If fifty-year olds ate the same food as twelve-year olds, saw the same movies as twelve-year olds and had the same politics as twelve-year olds (i.e., no politics) that sure simplified the demographic. The biggest swindle in the history of the species was underway right here in the U.S.A. Corporate social engineers, closet Mengeles every last one of them, had dismantled the stages of human development.

This was the way it was now: First you're born, doted over in some little wham-bam simulacrum of what used to be known as childhood. If you get enough toys, you get to remember yourself as a happy kid. If not, well, you know who to blame. This stage lasts from three to four years. Then comes the longest phase of existence, teenagehood, which takes up the next fifty or sixty years depending on how popular you are. Postpuberty is key here, owing to the fact that this period generates maximum anxiety and personal dislocation, the state of mind most receptive to all forms of advertising. Life is pretty much over after this, since by now you likely have some hideous disease that didn't exist prior to the onset of the modern world. But you don't die. The doctors get to torture you for the next fifteen years out of spite since they're mad they were so much richer before managed care. Then you die. This was the new life cycle.

I brought up these scenarios not to unsettle the children but to elucidate what the world could come to if we didn't take action. They rolled their eyes and thought they'd heard it all before, which wasn't true. I had plenty more where that came from, and no amount of groaning and covering their ears was going to stop me from attempting to enlighten them.

A lot of it came down to the popular culture, once friend to humankind but now its implacable enemy and oppressor. Back in my glorious day, pop culture, disseminated as a series of mysterious, deeply miscegenated broadcasts sent by DJs like Murray the K, arrived in my little transistor radio as a secret language of liberation. Growing up in civilservant Queens, amongst the American Dream lockdown of cops and firemen, what came out of the radio, and even television, had the air of subversion. Primitive but powerful, it showed another way, a delicious alternative to parental authority.

Forty years later, the roles of control between the culture and parents have been reversed. Souped up far beyond Freudian prophesy, the TV world has commandeered the function of the superego in the addled psyche of its virtual offspring, who just happen to be my children. The electro-techno universe charts Orwellian borders for the newest edition of the receptor class, zealously bringing them ever closer to its malign bosom. By age four or so, the parent, the erstwhile control figure, has usually been reduced to the status of remote, defrocked creator god, a blustering but sketchy outsider, a low resolution fallback system in case the cable is down.

Herein was the paradigmatic shift in the structure of the American family. Yet, with the reduction of old-fashioned parental influence in favor of cathode domination also came opportunity, the potential for recasting old authority roles in the mold of the romantic outsider, the secret *agent provocateur*. If the hand was played right, the moldy old Dad—that is, me—could become the Promethean bringer of *outré* knowledge, the revolutionary fly in the monolithic culture/matrix ointment. That's what this trip was all about, I told myself, a journey on a new kind of underground railway, another version of the transistor radio under the covers, a pirate station beaming the message that would, if not bring down the kingdom, at least put a kink in its suffocating concept.

Like Moses, I would lead my children from pop bondage. Because it wasn't enough to sit around congratulating ourselves because half Rosie's school was Russian and Billy's class list contained names like Omar, Juan, Natasha, and Amidou. Brooklyn was full of names, multi-kulti hues; that's why we liked living there. But in the U.S. of A. everything was just a matter of time. With each passing moment it mattered less which far-off land these kids came from. They were playing Wrestlemania 2000 and collecting Pokémon cards like everyone else. Their parents were probably doing the same.

This is what I told the kids. Nothing less than the transference from the realm of childhood to moral, intelligent adults was at stake. Every nanosecond spent under the spell of the corporate "them" was not only making us stupider and more provincial but also more secure in that stupidity and provinciality.

For inspiration, I turned to Montaigne, especially his essay, "On the Education of Children." The fact that Montaigne lived in the sixteenth century, before teenagers were even invented, and that he had no offspring of his own, mattered little. When attempting to enlighten a child, Montaigne said, "it was sheer motion that allowed for absorption of what could not be gleaned standing still." This was the true purpose of "going around." It "stretched the imagination" by allowing the traveler to experience himself or herself as not only "seer of foreignness" but also as "the foreign." This was the real path to knowledge, "the chance to rub up against others . . . to rub and polish our brains through contact."

The "rubbing against," the "polishing of brains," this was the Trip Manifest, the highly focused Vision Quest behind the decision my wife and I made to take the family, and most of the money we had in the bank, to go around the world.

It was something to think about, battling through a hel-
lacious traffic jam on the rise of the elevated Brooklyn–Queens
Expressway, driving to the airport. From up here, high above the
Gowanus Canal, which was built in the 1850s and smells like it,
you get a primo view of the Statue of Liberty, her torch raised
over New York harbor.

Lady Liberty. Sometimes, and I don't have to be feeling
particularly sentimental, the mere sight of her is enough to bring
tears to my eyes. I put myself in the mind of my own grandmother,
smuggled out of Romania in a potato sack, recall the hallowed
family story of her passage, six weeks in steerage, dumped out onto
the rough shore of Ellis Island without knowing a word of English,
and I'm awash with utopian emotion yet again.

My wife is the same. After all, she is a Cardozo, member of
the giant, extended family forced to sail the ocean blue (and
bloody) in 1492, after kindly Queen Isabelle and King Ferdinand,
Columbus's imperial bankrollers, helped chase them from Spain
at the height of the Inquisition. Some went to Holland and
Brazil, others came here. They're one of the oldest families in
the country. Indeed, it was one of my wife's cousins, Emma
Lazarus, who wrote the famous sonnet, "The New Colossus,"
which is engraved upon Lady Liberty's pedestal. In the fourth
grade, growing up in Flushing, Queens, my whole class, nearly
all grandsons and granddaughters of immigrants, were made
to memorize the stirring lines about the tired, the poor, the
huddled, tempest-tossed, masses yearning to breathe free.

Even now it was true, I knew, yearning to breathe free of
the stench of the Gowanus where the filtration system broke in
1967 and hasn't been fixed right since. Even now, America was
a beacon, a golden door.

A case in point was Ahmed, a twenty-seven-year-old Algerian
employee of the Legends Car Service, who piloted the minivan
that brought us to JFK. After growing up in a "large and poor"

family in a "difficult" section of Algiers, Ahmed, a handsome man with deep green eyes, first went to Marseilles, then Paris, where he studied biophysics, before arriving in Bay Ridge, Brooklyn, where he presently shared a one-bedroom apartment with six other car service drivers. Soon, he said, he planned to marry a woman he'd met the previous New Year's Eve. Just that day Ahmed had looked at a three-room apartment in the shadow of the Verrazano Bridge. The rent was high, but maybe not too high. With some paint and a new refrigerator it would be "an okay place to start a family."

Since he came to America on a plane, not a boat, Ahmed did not see the Statue of Liberty for nearly a year after his arrival. "I didn't know where it was," he remarked. Now, however, often stuck in traffic two and three times a day on the Brooklyn and Manhattan Bridges, he sees the statue all the time and it always brings him joy.

"I look at it and I know I am not in Algeria," he said.

It was awful in his homeland now, Ahmed said. "Everyone hates everyone else." Only a year ago "gangster" government forces, dressed up like the opposition Islamic fighters, massacred several hundred people in a desert village where his brother lived. "They came with masks covering their faces, no one knew who they were," Ahmed said. Even now, with prejudice against Muslim people rising, America was not violent like this, Ahmed said. "In Brooklyn, there are no land mines," he noted.

"It was not a good feeling" to turn your back on your home. "But sometimes your home turns its back on you," Ahmed sighed as he abruptly lurched across several lanes of traffic, barely avoiding a truck performing a similar move. Ahmed cursed softly in Arabic, then in French. The value of speaking several languages was something his grandfather, who had fought against the French in the colonial war, instilled in him. Ahmed spoke five: French, Arabic, Spanish, German and English.

"How many languages do you speak?" Ahmed asked, turning around to ask the kids. They looked at each other and shrugged. Well, Rosalie allowed, she had just finished her first year of French at school.

In the ensuing silence I got to berate myself yet again for my pathetically lax parenting practices. Other children, the ones who were going to get ahead in this world, spoke more than one language. Some even went to the Lycée—where, not yet fourteen, they'd already read Proust in the original, or so the brochures claimed. If our kids weren't keen on picking up another tongue, which they resolutely were not, they should have been beguiled, or tricked, or forced to do so. But this never happened.

Of course, I spoke no foreign languages myself, having barely passed the Spanish regents in high school. To me, pushing a button other than "English" at the ATM seemed impossibly exotic. It was the same with music lessons—lots of screaming about practicing from me, not much playing from them. Again, I gave them little to emulate. Despite being a former music critic for several national magazines, I played no instruments, bailing out of the saxophone after three weeks, and quitting piano, too.

"You speak only English?" Ahmed asked the kids, breaking the silence.

"Well, that's good, very good," he said, smiling. "America is such a big country, who cares about other languages? English is the king of languages." He imagined that his own children might learn Arabic, because his wife often spoke it, but he had no intention of speaking anything but English around his new apartment.

"English is enough," he said again, another happy American yearning to breathe free.

*   *   *

Japan Airlines gave us seats C through G, Row 66.

Row 66. Oh, the sweet synchronicity. Once upon a time, like the song says, you could get your kicks on Route 66, winding "from Chicago to L.A.," through St. Louis, down to Missouri; Amarillo; Gallup, New Mexico; Flagstaff, Arizona; and don't forget Winona. They made a TV show about it, with George Maharis and Martin Milner tooling up and down the über two-lane blacktop in a Corvette Stingray. Every week they went to another town, had another adventure. I liked the show, and didn't know what to make of it when Mickey Agabagian, the biggest hitter in the fourth grade, said, "Those guys are just a pair of homos."

Nowadays, except for a couple of snippets around Tucumcari, New Mexico, Route 66 winds no more. The road is basically defunct, replaced by I-40, which just goes straight. Route 66 has been retired to the mythscape, along with the honest P.I. About the only place you can see those old bullet-hole-ridden US 66 signs are in nostalgia-milking theme restaurants with names like the Roadkill Cafe, with things like "diesel-tire-tracked chicken breast" on the menu.

Yet the notion of the long highway, the long passage to somewhere, anywhere but here, retains its power. Row 66 was our Corvette, our chariot in the sky, our means of global circumnavigation, at least as far as Bangkok, Thailand. It seemed important to follow the grand circle, to "go around," as Montaigne said. It was a good thing the world was round, not flat, we thought, especially in the time of Y2K, with so much loose talk in the air. Everywhere you went, people, preachers, politicians, environmentalists, media men were envisioning the end of this, the end of that. Images of fiery pits of hell, a world on the brink, abounded. The loom of the apocalypse, never out of fashion, rose like a giant drowning tidal wave, poised at its crest, a cobra ready to strike. It was a wonder the bad popes and other fearmongers had been able to sell such bad science of a flat earth for so long.

People were suckers for this sort of brinkmanship. The idea of a beginning, a thundering of "let there be light" and an end, that point where either through divine decision, heedless human violence or simply not looking where you were going, you could fall off the edge into nothingness, suited the human need for paranoid resolution.

So it was a good thing the world was round and we were going around it. This was the true state of things: the eternal churn on the axis, the dependable return of day and night. Continuum, we were all about continuum. The continuum, that was the basis of family life. In the end we would come back to where we started. JFK was both the first and last airport rubric on our tickets. This was the whole point of circumnavigation, returning to where you began, because while plying the immutable rim of the circle, nothing remained the same. The traveler was always changed by the journey. It would be up to us to compute the emotional math of what the sum of that change was.

In 1513 it took Magellan, the first of the circumnavigators, more than a year to get halfway around the world before running into the Polynesian chieftain Lapu-Lapu, who killed the robber baron with a spear and who remains a national hero in the Philippines to this day. Shoehorned into Row 66, it would only take us twenty-three hours to get to Bangkok, half a planetary turn away. But still, twenty-three hours is a long time to be on a plane.

Twenty-three hours. Yessir, it is a stretch . . . gives a man time to lean back and catch up with things, size up the situation.

You must know this trip didn't come out of the blue. We have always been a traveling crew. Planes, trains and rented automobiles, sleeping in tents under three-hundred-foot-tall redwood trees, heading across the desert with less than half a tank, we've done this and much, much more. For us, nothing beats driving through the bayous and Cajun prairies of southern Louisiana, sucking heads off crawfish, tossing leftover *boudin* to the gators, their teeth glinting in the vapor lights of passing truckers. We love beat-up places like Mamou, Louisiana, with its fourteen storefronts, nine of them bars. The only place to stay is the old Cazan Hotel, with its outsized radiators and swayback beds, each one a fine moldering spot for the decaying corpse of Willy Loman. The first time we went to the Cazan, not knowing the routine, we called ahead to reserve the room with a credit card.

"Credit card? Oh, just tell me your first name. We got plenty of room," the man on the line told my wife. When we got there, no one was around. Everyone was at the bar downstairs, Hank Williams (so help me God) playing low.

"Why, you must be Nancy," the bartender said to my wife when we walked in, and proceeded to kiss her hand. Rosie's and Rae's, too. All the other drunks did the same, each bow more filled with flourish than the last. Good ol' Cazan, they'll even wake you up at seven on Saturday morning so you can catch the bands playing live on the weekly Cajun radio show across the street at Fred's Lounge where the announcer does the home mortgage commercials in French and the only rule is "no standing on the jukebox."

So many of our best times happened on the move. One time we went out to the South Dakota Badlands to look for fossils, spending all day digging in the dirt with tiny dental tools. A mess of bikers, bellies out to there, roared in from the rally at Sturgis, kicking up dust. Dark goggled, colors reading "Cement City, Michigan," they stopped and asked what we were doing in the pit.

"Looking for bones," Rae said.

"What kind of bones?" asked the biker.

"Archaeotherium," replied Rae and Rosalie simultaneously. "Sort of like a giant pig, from thirty-three million years ago."

"A big pig from thirty-three million years ago," the biker said. "From around here?"

"Yeah. They lived all over this area, in the Oligocene Era."

"The Oleo what?" The biker reached out. "Let me see one of those." Rae handed him a foot bone, encased in a plastic bag. The biker examined it, held it up to the sunlight. "This bone is thirty-three million years old? No shit?"

The kids nodded.

"Far out," the biker said. Somewhere deep into his late forties, he'd been reaching back for his youth as a longhair Harley rebel, a hellbent if somewhat blown-out American icon. He was, at least in own self-regard, a man who took up *space*. Now, peering about the timeless Badlands landscape, he could only shake his head.

"I'm just a goddamned speck, ain't I," the biker said. Then, seemingly sobered by this reminder of his true place in the cosmos, the biker turned to Rae and Rosalie, said, "Thanks, girls," and throttled off, disappearing into the sandstone hills.

This is the stuff of treasured lore in our family. We were always going somewhere, driving down to the Everglades, an all-time favorite, or across the country to Yellowstone, to L.A. and Joshua Tree, where we loved to swim under the date trees at the Twenty-Nine Palms Inn. I could say these trips kept us together, but that would be wrong because back then being together was not an issue. We *were* together.

That was the problem. Prior to departing for The World, our togetherness was somewhat sketchy. The previous several weeks, months actually, had been far from a breeze. It wasn't nearly as bad as 1995, the plague year, when my father died and my wife got cancer. I remember the afternoon when the bomb dropped, only a few days after New Year's. She'd had a test. But she had lots of tests. The doctor was in her early thirties, kind of sexy I thought, her skirt riding up above her knee. She had a way of extending her words, separating the syllables. So it took a minute to put it all together.

Ma-lig-nant, she said. They don't say can-cer. They say ma-lig-nant.

Three weeks after her surgery I was in the same hospital having my lung chopped up. My chest X ray looked funny, the doctor said. They stuck tubes down my throat but weren't satisfied, so they decided to do a lung biopsy, on an "exploratory" basis, which is sort of like giving Columbus a switchblade except he never finds the New World, just keeps cutting. After the operation and several days in the hospital, they said "sorry," maybe I was okay after all. I never told anyone I was in the hospital, not right after Nancy. No reason to let that out. People might think we were cursed, like we did something to deserve it.

Rae was twelve then, and very much afraid. She had bad dreams. In one we were all in a car headed for a bridge that was washed out. The car sank to the bottom, then surfaced, but we—the parents—were gone. Rosalie, eight, said little, but her teachers thought she seemed distracted, they wanted to know what was up. Apparently she never told them. That was like her, always headstrong. If she was going to be an orphan it was nobody's business, she said.

But we got through that, the chemo, the recovery, all of it. My wife was very brave. We brought her lots of flowers and ice cream sodas. When she felt better we went back to the Badlands, where we got stuck in a storm, 110-mile-an-hour winds, out of nowhere. It got so bad we had to abandon the tent, spend the night in the rocking car watching other people's tents blow away, rising up into the night sky as if blown to Oz. Not that we were worried, even for a moment. We were *together*, you see.

Prior to taking off for The World nothing like that happened. No one was sick. The city marshals, those vultures, hadn't towed away the car for unpaid tickets. There were no floods in the basement. Yet there was an unmistakable sense of distress, a gathering cloud clamping down on our Brooklyn homestead. We were not together. It was the Year of Living Cluelessly.

Much of this baffled angst centered on the older daughter. She was flunking out of high school, failing every class, no snap for someone with an off-the-chart IQ. This was especially true in the current version of the New York City public schools. Usually, not sticking a syringe into the teacher's neck was good enough for at least Bs, if not honor roll.

The situation was at least as disconcerting to the oldest girl child as to the parental units. After a few years at a private school in Brooklyn Heights, majoring in the management of peer pressure and downtown fashion, she'd gotten into La Guardia High School, on Manhattan's West Side, which was, as the administration never tired of telling everyone, a "special" place, home to the elite of the city's artistically inclined, venue of the chosen few. Out of every eighteen who auditioned for the "vocal music studio," the school took one. One of those was Rae. Not that it was that big a shock. She really can sing, when she feels like it. Once, when she was eleven, she was called out of an audience to do a duet with Phoebe Snow on a bunch of Sam Cooke songs. Chuck Jackson, also performing on the show, whose "Any Day Now" was one of those secret missives I used to listen to under the covers in my parents' house, clapped me on the shoulder and said, "Talented little girl you got there."

Yes, everyone said, La Guardia was a good thing, a fabulous opportunity. I was tickled. Once upon a time, when I was growing up in the New York public schools, La Guardia High School was called Music and Art. It was in Harlem, near City College in a tottering but beautiful old Gothic building. There were other "special high schools," Bronx Science and Stuyvesant, which were for "the brains." But for Queens boys like myself, Music and Art was the ultra bohemian fantasy. On winter mornings, walking through the dreary civil servant streets of Flushing on the way to the hopelessly unromantic Francis Lewis High School, I would sometimes pass Carol R., notable unrequited object of my desire. She'd gone to our junior high, where the English teacher, obviously likewise smitten, put her *Catcher in the Rye* paper up on the bulletin board. Now she was a Music and Art girl, waiting for the bus, holding her guitar case, bundled in her outsized pea coat, long woolen scarf wrapped about her neck.

God, I was crazy about her. What had she done the night before? Seen Bob Dylan sing "Who Killed Davey Moore" at Gerdes Folk City? Maybe Dylan had even noticed her, sitting there in the front row, puffing on a Pall Mall, and invited her to the Kettle of Fish on MacDougal Street. Or even back to his room, above the Folklore Center on Sixth Avenue. Just killed me, Bob Dylan, my hero, betraying me like that, making it with Carol R.

Back in 1963, anything could happen to a Music and Art girl. Music and Art girls were a breed beyond cool. Now my own daughter was a Music and Art girl.

Except she wasn't really; she was a La Guardia girl, which was too bad, because she would have made a great Music and Art girl in her long black velvet coat, her gleaming raven hair down to her waist. In the thirty-odd years since my mooning after Carol R., some changes had been made. Music and Art's old Harlem building, deemed far too scary and decrepit for "special" school status, had been abandoned for La Guardia's giant brick box behind Lincoln Center on 65th Street, a far more utilitarian zone. Now, owing to the Hollywood movie that would forever alter the ethos of the place, La Guardia was "the *Fame* school," the place where Irene Cara sang of going "to live forever." Here, you learned how to become a professional, to blow up, get big.

Well, La Guardia was a disaster. I couldn't figure it. So what if those black girls with the big gospel voices had been tearing it up in church for years? So what if she didn't want to become a backup Broadway singer, which it seemed the program was aimed to make her? So what if she really hated to go to theory at 8:10 A.M.? She could still cruise through. It wasn't like the other classes, the supposedly academic ones, were so tough. English and history, she'd already read all the books, she could do that in her sleep. In fact, she would have had to do it in her sleep, because that's what her teachers claimed she was doing in class, when she showed up.

"What's with you?" I demanded, for the hundredth time. These conversations were getting to be a drag. All this hectoring, all this resistance. "A chimpanzee can pass these classes."

"Well, then go get a chimpanzee," she retorted. "Because I'm not doing it."

"But . . ."

"But what? Get off my back."

"But—"

"Look, I'm not talking about this."

"What can I do to help?"

"Nothing!"

"Listen . . ."

"No!"

Then she'd just scream and run out of the room.

My little girl . . . where had that person gone? That sweet-faced expectancy, all those kisses?

I remember the day she was born, at St. Luke's-Roosevelt Hospital on Sixtieth Street, on a bright, cold Wednesday morning in January 1983. We were living on the Lower East Side then, in our St. Marks walkup. Our friend Jonny, who would become loyal godfather of all our children, drove us to the hospital. Somewhere around Times Square my wife started to go into what's called the "transition" stage, which means showtime, almost. It was about then that Jonny, uncharacteristically rattled, almost ran into a hansom cab, one of those horse and buggies in which tourists ride around Central Park. The buggy driver cursed loudly at us.

"My wife is having a baby!" I shouted.

"Big fucking deal, everyone gets born!" the horseman yelled back.

A couple of weeks before the blessed event, it occurred to me that I should film the proceedings. Start those home movies off right, begin at the beginning, so to speak. I got the idea from childbirth films they showed us each week at Lamaze class, to give us a general idea of what to expect. One movie was from France. Everyone was crying. The mother, the father, the grandmother, the doctor, the nurses, all of them sobbing uncontrollably. When the baby started yowling, everyone cried even harder. There was another one from Italy, which was more of the same, except with more crying. Then we saw a film shot in Utah, by Mormons. In this one the doctor and the husband stood over the wife wearing surgical masks, each one of them barking out orders throughout: birth as Marine drill. When the baby was born the nurses whisked it away and swaddled it heavily, then handed it to the father. The last one was British. This consisted of a doctor sitting at a desk explaining the birth process. Every once in a while he pointed at a diagram of the birth canal on a blackboard. That was it—no Mom, no Dad, no baby.

Our film would be more artful, an emotionally significant record of the miracle of life, I told my wife. It would be something in the manner of Stan Brakhage, an underground movie artist, whose deeply fixated flickers I'd seen back in the early 1960s at Jonas Mekas's filmmaker's co-op on West Forty-first Street, a dump where the label reading "7UP" on the soda machine had been replaced with a handwritten placard saying

"LSD-25," a mystery substance with which, at age fifteen, I was not yet familiar. Brakhage documented the birth of his child, getting up close and personal, cervix-wise, smearing placental fluid on the lens of his wind-up Bolex 16mm as a low-tech FX.

No way I was smearing her placenta on a Bolex, my wife said.

"Come on, it'll be great," I told her. "We can dub the kettle drum part from *Thus Spake Zarathustra* to accompany the snipping of the umbilical cord . . . bomp, bomp, bomp . . ."

"Do what you want, but leave me out of it," was the reply.

So there was no movie of the arrival on this earth of Rae Cardozo Jacobson. Most of what remains is the memory of an argument with the midwife, which was followed by a vague, glorious haze from the moment the water broke. Centimeter by dilating centimeter, the passage that Mr. Sen would later inform us was called a *tirtha,* opened. We knew the biology, of course, but what did that tell us? The key to every theory of existence, the closest we'd ever get to sacred, was emerging from my wife's body.

After she was born, at the soonest possible opportunity, when I felt she'd been alive long enough to understand my question but not long enough to forget where she'd been, I asked Rae what life had been like on the other side.

"Where'd you come from, Rae?" I asked.

"I just comed," she replied, ever the coquette; but then again, she's always been able to keep a secret.

It rained the night we made Rae. We were living in Jensen Beach, Florida, at the time, a redneck/old folksville fifty miles north of what the locals call "the Palm Beaches."

Even before we met, my wife and I had a thing about Florida, although not the Miami Beach/Fort Lauderdale/Jeb Bush part. To us, Florida was at once the most beautiful and defiled of states.

Florida was the first place we ever went together, over Thanksgiving, in 1979. We slept in a tumbledown motel near the Cork-
screw Swamp and woke up with a big box turtle at the foot of
our bed. For Thanksgiving, we ate at the diner on US 1, outside
of Homestead. The jukebox kept playing "Heaven's Just a Sin's
Away" by the Kendalls, which was our waitress's favorite song,
and the turkey was served with hush puppies instead of sweet
potatoes.

We were living in Jensen Beach because my wife was trying to finish college at The Florida Institute of Technology, a
school that, true to her academic ethic, she had found out about
from an ad in the back of *Skin Diver* magazine. Not yet totally
subdivided and malled up like so much of the rest of the state,
there was a doomed poetry about Jensen; it wasn't gone, but it
was going. Every day something disappeared. Like that hundred-
acre stand of mangroves on the road out to the beach where, for
eons, loggerhead turtles came to lay their eggs, except now when
the babies hatched they were attracted by the condo lights and
crawled out into the road and were crushed. Every day I ran past
those mangroves, watched the swirl of tannic water flow through
the spidery roots. Then, one day, they were gone, every single
last one of them. Asked about it in the local paper, the devel-
oper, a local, said he was sorry, but the clearing made sense; the
fine, about $1,000, was "inside the budget."

Things sure were shiftless down in the so-called Sunshine
State. One morning we contracted a boy up the street to mow our
lawn. When he came back the next day a houseguest friend of ours
answered the door. "Oh," the boy said, with disappointment. "The
lady and man who used to live here . . . said I should mow their
grass." He thought we'd moved out since we'd talked with him.

On this unsolid ground, my wife and I would forward the
reproduction of the species. We'd been preparing for some time.
Since we returned from our trip, really. Only weeks before there'd

been a visit to the local hospital where a doctor wielding a laser pencil had erased a contentious patch of endometriosis. We'd outfitted ourselves with the paraphernalia of premeditation, the ovulation thermometer and the rest. Like the rent, we knew what time of the month it was. But on that night none of this was needed.

Now, there is lovemaking and there is lovemaking. There is that first time, balled up in a finished basement on Bell Boulevard in Queens with "Love Love Me Do" playing in rechanneled stereo. There are the ones in cars, in hammocks down in Mexico, the weird ones in weird places, like Pittsburgh. But there is no lovemaking like consciously trying to make love; that is, making a person, someone to love, out of nothingness. These are not accidents. There is nothing relative about lovemaking like that, no discussions about whether it was good or bad. It either works or it doesn't. That is the miracle of it.

Thinking of this makes me dream, about the night my parents made me.

I can see the scene now. He'd been back from the war a year or so by then. The steamer trunk and corrugated boxes would still be piled up on the oak floor, since they'd just moved to 174th Street, to the bottom floor of the house owned by my aunt Kate and uncle Sam. Counting back nine months from May 12, 1948, the big night would have occurred sometime at the end of August or the beginning of September 1947, the late summer breeze coming through the sheer white curtains.

Did they know, that night, when they undressed in their new half of a house, that this time, when they lay down, that this time would be the time? You wonder. Or at least I wonder.

Like I said, it had been raining that night in Jensen Beach during the spring of 1982.

It had been raining for days and the cat was plumb tuckered from dragging the corpses of palmetto bugs around our tacky little rental house. It could get thick down there, so heavy that you didn't want to do anything and just walking along was like parting a curtain. But that's how we liked it, the wet Gulf Stream air torpid in the breezeway, seeping through the jalousie windows. Through the thickness, you could hear the train whistles and the thump the grapefruits from the tree behind the clothesline made when they hit the ground.

That was the night. I could tell by the way she looked at me, a bit surprised, a bit amazed, but mostly serene, as if what was meant to be had happened, at last.

A couple weeks later we left Jensen and came north, a little Swedish caravan, my fifteen-year-old Volvo following my wife's ten-year-old Saab. On I-95 we stopped to buy apricot nectar, which was supposed to calm pregnant tummies. Eventually the Winn-Dixies and Publixs gave way to IGAs and A&Ps; finally to Sloans, Gristedes, and the Puerto Rican bodega on the corner. Jensen Beach was a good place to be, for a while. You could jog stoned by the nuke plant up toward Fort Pierce, stop to laugh at the high-rises the fools built out of beach strand. Ka-blooey, who cared? We were already living in Florida, at least halfway to oblivion. But things had changed. We were on the edge of permanency. We were going home.

My wife was twenty-nine and I was thirty-four. It had been plenty of time to be young. Not a bad deal at all.

"It has a face!" This comment, spoken by her father, is the first thing Rae claims she heard upon exiting her mother's womb and taking her rightful place among the living of this earth.

Even if it is highly unlikely (as she admits) that Rae actually recalls my exclamation as her marvelous, if a bit bluish, head emerged that fateful morning at the Roosevelt birthing room, there is no doubt that I did utter the phrase. I deny, however, Rae's charge that my use of the pronoun "it," rather than the more specific "she," reveals any dehumanizing attitude on my part toward her, "from the very beginning."

At the point when I made the comment in question, Rae's gender was not yet known. She was only halfway out. Of course, had my wife and I been more modern, not such Luddites, we would have already known the proper pronoun. Most people know the sex of their child months before the actual birth, on account of amniocentesis. It is considered somewhat gauche to withhold this information from yourself, I have been told. What can be known, should be known. The stupid doctors knew, why not you? I guess we just like surprises; there's always time to tell the people who are hung up on it whether to buy pink or blue.

Right then she was still an "it." What else was there to call this mystery we had created, this life form that had grown inside my wife? Nothing was usual. Even the hospital, all those gleaming, antiseptic surfaces that are supposed to assure us young moderns things are indeed under control, imbued its own unknowability, the blipping of monitors like a soundtrack from deep space. A split second from completing her journey from wherever to here, Rae remained totally, wholly Other.

Nearly seventeen years later, the phrase "It has a face" reentered our lives. "It" walked, or rather slouched, among us, once again. "It" snarled. "It" got pissed off. "It" stalked out of the room. "It" was: a Teenage Frankenstein.

Things really hit the fan in the season of Columbine (it figured those Beavis and Butthead killers, Klebold and Harris, would let McVeigh's April 19th homage to Waco go by, and shoot up their school on the 20th—our anniversary—but then again, serves us right for getting married on Hitler's birthday). Seeing our kids stare at the coverage, it was easy to track back thirty-six years to when Kennedy was shot and another group of teenagers sat stunned before images of Oswald, Ruby and the rest. All hell breaks loose in different ways for different generations. Littleton, Colorado; Jonesboro, Arkansas; Springfield, Oregon—these podunk hells where kids went postal were far from Brooklyn. Yet, to the extent that youth cements a bond, these children, shooters and victims both, were our children's confederates. Their people.

High school, and the hatred thereof, cuts through class, clique and geographic lines. Rae understood, she too was going to a massive high school, full of theater people, the La Guardia version of jocks. She'd strode those endless corridors to classes she would have rather done anything else than attend. She knew the terrors of the place and how it played on your insecurities, put you on edge, drove you mad.

At La Guardia, where the post-Columbine graffiti in the bathroom read "15 Jocks Got Killed in Colorado and All I Got Was This Lousy Trenchcoat," the other shoe had dropped. A visit to open school night proved sobering. After waiting an hour to see the Spanish teacher, the woman seemed to have only the fuzziest notion who Rae was.

"Hmm . . ." the teacher said, "it looks like she's fallen down on her homework a little bit." I looked at her book. There were twenty-two homework assignments; Rae had handed in one.

"One out of twenty-two . . . that's falling down a *little?*"

"Well, she certainly can improve."

Heck, yeah, she could *improve*! She could have handed in two, or maybe even three. Truth be told, almost everyone in our family is somewhat lacking in what the shrinks call Executive Functioning, i.e. staying on top of the mess on your desk and in your head. But this was a new standard in underachievement. I'd sucked at Spanish too, way worse than Rae, but at least I was guilty enough to turn in the homework. From looking at the woman's book, Rae wasn't alone. Hardly any of the young

Mozarts at this "special" high school had handed in half the stupid homework. The mind reeled. Something had to be done! But what?

You know: you won't find a bigger supporter of public education than me. I went to New York City public schools from grades one to twelve, and knew a lot of people who'd graduated from city colleges, too. They were hard then, and cost nothing; CCNY was known as the Harvard of the subways. I didn't know one kid who went to private school, outside of the Catholic ones, and it wasn't like old St. Kevin's, where the nuns beat my buddies black and blue, was a garden spot. To me it is part of the utopia: good public education, the mix of people, backgrounds, ideas.

La Guardia helped cure me of this ideal. Every other day, sometimes at seven in the morning, sometimes after midnight, the phone would ring and this garbled electronic message with these punch-in voices came on. "Your son . . . *or daughter* . . . Rae Jacobson . . . has been reported absent . . . *or cutting* two . . . *or three* days this week. Please call extension 2314 . . . *or Mrs. Jackson* for further information." Alas, the mailbox of . . . *Mrs. Jackson* was always . . . *full.*

It would remain like that, to the bloody end. After Rae finally got out of La Guardia to attend another school, the calls kept coming. Sometimes she was absent three times a week, sometimes four. The thing we couldn't understand was who was marking her "present" on the days she was supposedly in school. A while later, after not attending the school for six months, Rae's first semester report card arrived in the mail. It was kind of impressive to note that even if she never attended a single class, her grades hadn't suffered that much. She'd managed to pass two classes. Several teachers did write, however, in the little standardized computer rubric that appears beside the grades, that she needed to "participate more in class."

Somehow, even now, I find this less than funny. I suppose this is why most memoirs of family life are written by children. The kid perspective just has more leeway, more room for irony, responsibility-free complaint. Few parents feel they can talk as openly about their children as their children talk about them. Issues of accountability and complicity in failures undercut the parental memoirist. Probably this accounts for the meager number of titles in the parental memoir genre, and the large percentage of whitewash jobs among those. If psychoanalysts depended on parents talking about the shortcomings of their children, the couches would be even more empty than they are. If you're not bragging, sticking those Wesleyan stickers on the rear window of your car, there is not all that much to say comfortably. If you don't love them enough and they don't love you enough, is that something you really want to admit? A few years ago, *Granta* ran a group of pieces dealing with the writers' parents. The cover, done in stark typography like the old *Time* magazine "God Is Dead" issue, said only "They Fuck You Up." If the magazine had decided to do a follow-up of parental memoirs of children (which, of course, they didn't) the title would have been "You Fuck Them Up."

Throughout Rae's entire school traumas, I never got it, what was going on. In between the yelling and groundings, I gave what I imagined to be reasonable advice; for example, didn't she realize how much less hassle it would have been for everyone, mostly her, if she'd just show up, sleaze through? So what if she didn't perform like her Brain friends? Not everyone has to do well in school, your hand up in the air, fitting into whatever mold the overlords decree. She'd always been so sharp, the sweetest and the smartest. Everyone said so. She had her own way about her, hip from birth. One of the stories I always delighted in telling was how, when she was about three, we brought her for some testing thing at Hunter, the city program designed to identify geniuses and reward them with free, super-enriched programming all the way through to college. It seemed worth a shot. The tester reeled off some numbers and told Rae to say them "backwards." Rae said okay, turned around, faced the other way and repeated the numbers. The tester, noting that she'd never seen a kid do that before, said Rae was "truly an unconventional thinker." We thought this was tremendous compliment (and still do), almost better than actually getting into the school. It was almost as if my beloved daughter had realized from the very start exactly how to truly please me. Be *my* kid. But, as I would soon find out, this kind of "unconventionality" would become *a problem,* especially in the context of the Delany-card-ruled realm of New York City public education, the teetering, electronic message–sending bureaucracy I regarded with such dim utopian nostalgia.

I truly didn't get it.

"It has a face!"

Yes, it did. And a beautiful face it was, even half covered by smudgy black makeup. A beautiful face, with soulful deep brown emphatic eyes, luminous skin, and a strange half smile in the Da Vinci mode. No one smells better, even when she sneaks cigarettes.

Except now the face was mad, anguished, exasperated. For one thing, Rae announced, there was no way she was blowing her entire summer on some demento trip around the world. She had other, as yet unrevealed plans and not one of them included spending three months with her parents.

"Oh, yeah, what plans?"

"Plans."

"Hanging out at the Cube and watching TV?"

"You're rude. You know that? You're really rude."

"Oh, sorry. Maybe I'll send you an engraved invitation. Big, raised gold letters. Oh please, come with us on this hideous trip around the world. I know it is an awful imposition but please humor us with your presence."

"Rude! Rude! Rude!"

What was this? Hadn't we always had fun on our trips? Didn't we have fun in the Glades? She was two, maybe three, the cutest thing you ever want to see singing "Take Me Out to the Ballgame" while standing on top of a cypress stump in her yellow-and-red-striped dress. What about the Galapagos? All those blue-footed boobies, blubber-backed walruses mooning on the beach? What about the landslide?

The landslide was legend. Rae was five, Rosie one. We'd just come back to the mainland from the Galapagos and thought, being in the neighborhood, we'd better explore the Amazonian headwaters, get down there in the bush. We caught a bus in Quito, took a particularly hair-raising ride through the Andes, and went to Baños, a little town where a hundred-foot-tall waterfall surged out of the mountain, people washed their clothes in giant natural springs and munched on tiny barbecued guinea pigs called *cuy*. One fine morning Rae and I hired the kindly-seeming Vicente and his musty old Impala to take us down the road, thirty or forty kilometers in, to the spot where we could walk across the quarter-mile-long, three-foot-wide suspension bridge that spanned the Rio Pastaza. We stood on the rickety, swaying bridge watching the river's two branches, the Blanco, which was clear, and the Negro, which was muddy, come together. How great was that, being in there, the jungle all around? We'd never seen anything so green. But then it got hot, and we got hungry. We told Vicente we'd better start back.

It didn't seem right, all those cars and trucks coming in the other direction, a near traffic jam on the one-lane dirt road. Vincente stopped one of the truck drivers to find out what was up. Something had happened up the road. The only word I could make out was "rompio."

"Rompio?" I inquired.

"*Rompio.* Broken. *Muy malo,*" Vicente said, gunning the motor.

Only two hours before we'd driven down that road; now the mountain above had collapsed, sending down a massive landslide (it was only later we would find out the road was sometimes called *el puerto del cielo*—the door to heaven—on account of the number of people killed there). Cursing, Vicente said it could take at least a week to clear away the debris and the only other way back to Baños was by way of Puyo, up toward Lago Agrio, a two-day drive.

We came around the bend and saw the slide. It was huge, with boulders and dirt everywhere. We got out to check out the scene, walking a few steps before we heard Vicente rev the car engine. He was pulling away!

Hey! I ran after the car. He stuck his head out the window and shouted, *"A pie,"* pointing to the landslide, indicating that we should walk over it. *"A pie . . . es mejor . . . you go,"* he yelled again and drove away.

With the Impala gone, there was no sound except the creaking of the tree branches in the light breeze. What were we supposed to do now? Nancy and Rosie were at the hotel back in Baños. We were stranded in the jungle.

We did the only thing we could. I held the camera, Rae held her blanket, Stripey, and we started climbing. The pile of debris was at least fifty feet high, full of giant rocks. No big deal, I told Rae. We'd gone over bigger hills than this. Way bigger! Once we walked to the top of the Statue of Liberty! What was this compared to that? This was going to be *fun*!

Except the mountain wasn't quite finished falling down. With each step we took, something came loose. Rae stepped on a soft spot, fell, smacked her knee. The fun part was now officially over. I picked her up, started carrying her across the rocks. We could make it. No way we couldn't make this. We were the Dad and the Rae, we could get over. Nothing could stop the Dad and the Rae.

We were doing all right until I dropped the camera. It was wedged between some rocks. A couple of larger-sized stones tumbled by. I was thinking this could get hairy when the Indian ladies arrived, looming up from the other side of the hill. There were two of them, with flat noses, leathery faces and gold teeth beneath bowler hats. One held out her arms and said, *"la niña."* We knew she meant us no harm. The woman put Rae's arms around her neck and started walking, fast, over the pile. I followed, trying to keep up.

By the time I got to the other side, Rae gave me that look, like, what took you so long? One of the Indian ladies let her wear her bowler. It is one of those pictures I carry of my children, not in my wallet, in my head, along with so many others. After a while a tourist bus from Baños pulled up. Some traveling Argentines wanted to see what a fallen-down Ecuadorian mountain looked like. They drove us back to the front door of our hotel. When my wife asked us about our ride to the jungle, Rae and I looked at each other, shrugged and said, "Ah . . . it was okay."

So, yeah—What about the landslide? I asked the teenage Frankensteinette who had hijacked the body and soul of my little girl.

What about Raoul—Raoul, our special, personal transportation system? In real life Raoul was a patriotically angry statue of an eagle in Battery Park. Businessmen ate their lunch on his pedestal, pigeons crapped on his head. But in the dream life Rae and I worked up, Raoul was our friend, our personal carriage to parts unknown. On special nights Raoul would leave his lonely perch in Battery Park and fly up to our window on St. Marks Place. We'd jump on his back and go everywhere, even to outer space.

"Stop it," Rae demanded. I could tell by her look that she thought bringing up Raoul was dirty pool, since Raoul was a special thing, sacred between us, and it wasn't fair to bring him into this crummy argument. Besides, Raoul and the landslide were *then*. This was *now*.

What was the big deal if she didn't go? It was a couple of months. What was a couple of months? She could stay home, walk the dog, take out the garbage. Someone was going to have to do it, right? Surely we could trust her to be on her own in the house for a couple of months? What did we think, she'd have wild parties, throw the beer bottles into the washing machine, and become a crackhead? Burn down the house?

"That's not the point."

"What's the point?"

"The point is . . . the point is . . ."

"What!"

"The point is . . . *the point is this is a family trip and you're part of the family. The point is we don't want to go unless you go. The point is we love you.* . . ."

This, of course, tore it, because, blackmail or not, it was true. We really didn't want to go without her. And we did love her. *I* loved her. In the beginning, when she was the only kid for those first four years, I don't think I ever loved anyone the way I loved her. It was a whole other thing, different from how I loved my parents, different from how I loved my wife. For her part, I was her father and that was more than enough. The Dad and the Rae, nothing, not rain, or sleet, or snow, or landslide stopped us.

But, like she said, that was then and this was now. We still loved each other and all, but something had slipped, broken along the way. It wasn't simply the usual teenage tripe, the codified battles of adolescence. I mean, it was, but it was more. Neither one of us knew exactly what, but Rae felt it first, and most acutely. Once, when she was twelve, we were driving across the country and stopped at a KOA campground in Minnesota. We got out and set up the tent, but Rae was nowhere around. Later I saw her in the car, crying.

"What's up, sweetie?"

It took a while, but what was up was that she felt that things had changed between us. This kind of stunned me. I tried to rationalize, you know, before there was only her, and now there were Rosie and Billy, and, yeah, it was true, I'd been busy a lot, working. She *knew* it would be different when the others were born. She understood that. Even if before she had been "The Princess of All," which was one of her many, many honorifics, she was happy to be "princess of some." No, it wasn't that. It was me. I didn't look at her the way I used to. I didn't touch her the way I used to. She didn't make me happy the way she used to.

It was a horrible moment, these loud kids from the giant RVs parked next door screaming and playing Frisbee. It was horrible because she was right, something had changed. A lot of it had to do with school. I was on her case, screaming about her being lazy, not trying. For all my hot air about sneaking through the back door of the consensus culture, her lack of conventional achievement ticked me off. Expectations (especially the ones you won't even admit to yourself you have) can be fatal.

I could try to be more supportive, I said. We could go out more, like before. That would be good, she said, but that wasn't exactly it. Then what was? She didn't really know. Neither did I. There were many tears, the two of us crying together, because we both knew, whatever was missing, whatever we needed to do to put it back right: it wouldn't be easy.

Four years later, you couldn't say things had taken a turn for the better. She was as sweet as ever, as loving as ever, as cool as ever. But that space between us had only gotten bigger. Sometimes we couldn't even hear each other speak, except when we were yelling, of course. As for this trip, the one I hoped might paper over the gap, she knew she was "passing up the chance of a lifetime."

That's what everyone told her, every grown-up, at least. Going around the world, that's the chance of a lifetime. There was no arguing that. The world was a big place, and she was a curious girl. But there was something about these so-called chances of a lifetime, they have a good chance of coming up again.

It got bad. Before, when we fought, it always blew over. This wasn't blowing over. I was fixated, careening between telling myself I didn't care if she came and the truth, which was that I was desperate for her to come. Here we were supposed to be sitting around reading guidebooks, planning fabulous itineraries, jumping out of our skins with expectation, and there was this sad battle of wills.

People noticed. "Hey, you're going around the world, why so glum?" asked my neighbor Bill Flood, watching me trudge down the street.

Salt of the Brooklyn earth, Bill Flood. He was born in the house where he still lives with his wife and two kids. The Mayor of Eleventh Street, some of the new people in the neighborhood called him, in the patronizing way of those with no time, no time at all, to sit on the steps of their property and study the surroundings. Not that Bill cares what the yuppies think of him. He's canny, secure in his own skin. He happily lets people like me move in—thereby pushing up his real estate values—and then makes sport of their smug assumptions about the kind of guy he must be.

"That's good, the world," Bill said. "We're going to the Poconos . . ." He gave a knowing shrug, the way he does when he's about to try to get under your skin. "Three, four hours in the car and I'm there. Enough's enough. Know what I mean?"

Yeah, I knew what Bill meant. The World? Did I really think that $10,000 check written to Ticket Planet, the "global travel expert," would give me the inside track on the Dad of the Year race? Who needed The World when you had a pool in your back-yard and a cover to keep the leaves and bird poop off? As for the kids, did they really care?

"Poconos. Three, four hours," Bill Flood repeated. "Lake, cabin . . . what do you got to kill yourself for?"

Right. What was I really trying to prove here? Maybe it would have made more sense if I'd just followed the course of the Springsteen song about having a wife and kids in Baltimore, Jack, going out for a ride and never coming back. Or adhered to a similar sentiment in a tune by my all-time fave Steve Earle, in which the protagonist talks about how he "threw the car seat into the dumpster and headed out into the night." There was a whole literature based on the idea of how when the going got tough you should get the hell out. Blow the pop stand, fade into the bush, rent the double-wide, split. The World was a big enough place to hide. But you weren't supposed to bring them with you, fool! What was the use of that?

The truth was, I felt the cold winds of entropy blowing through the atoms of our little nuclear setup and it scared me. Some bonding time, that's what we needed. Some bonding time —*in India.*

With the departure date getting close, the pressure built. I got a little distracted. One night a few weeks before we were due to leave, after one more argument with Rae, I went out to walk the dog, tripped and went flying. It is amazing how much damage you can do to yourself smacking into a sidewalk. I frac-tured my wrist, smashed up my kneecap and got the biggest black-and-blue mark I'd ever seen. Deep purple, it was, across my back, from rib cage to rib cage. Every day it seemed to grow, an expanding prune-colored map of the distance between my daughter and myself.

It was only the Storm King Mountain School that solved the problem. My wife saw the place in the camp ads in the *New York Times Magazine*. They offered summer courses in what was described as a "disciplined" environment: attentive but orderly. It sounded perfect for the serial non–homework doer. A summer school with bars. And there was room, plenty of room.

The day the application arrived, Rae regarded it warily. What was this? she inquired. Her potential summer, she was informed.

She sat down to read the brochure. By this time she'd given up the idea of staying in the house by herself, or living with various buddies. That was out, she knew that. So this is what it came down to, the Storm King Mountain School or The World. Put that way, she chose The World. Not that she would go happily.

Interlude:
Talkback/Backtalk # 1

by Rae Jacobson

A h. That year. I remember it in that particular way people do when they get nostalgic about a certain song coming on the radio. Just the good parts of a bad time. Mostly a haze of cut classes, St. Marks Place days and dancing. I suppose a typical-day description is in order.

A Friday, for instance: Wake up way too early, munch a bowl of cereal (Cocoa Puffs, Lucky Charms, whatever was sweet and not horribly stale), jump on the ever-slow F train, switch to the A and hop off at Fifty-ninth Street, mill around the area for a bit, look for some friends to provide me with entertainment. These people, my academically inept brethren, offered countless amusements. These ranged from walking in circles around the corner pushcart until the bagel guy began to bounce and scream inside his little metal box, to serenading dog walkers and old ladies with our vast repertoire of cartoon theme songs. Should none of this prove stimulating I'd reluctantly opt to then go into school for my third-period Global class.

My actual schedule was period two through nine but I chose to shorten my day to three to eight with breaks in between. During these breaks I went to the only place I really could, the disgusting, smoky, roach-infested, beautifully awful seventh-floor bathroom, quintessential center of the La Guardia screwup's social life.

The bathroom was school-bus yellow and constantly being repainted to cover up all the crap we wrote on the walls. On good days it was possible to stay in there for three periods straight without getting kicked out or taken to the dean by one of the infamous roving security guards hired to police us into obedience and make us go to class. I'd sit there with friends or just random bathroom acquaintances, have a cigarette maybe or chitchat about silly high school gossip. If you listened to everything that was said in that room I guarantee you'd know at least something about almost every clique in school. Another thing about the bathroom is that it was neutral territory. All conflicts needed to be put aside because there simply wasn't enough room. During lunch periods it could get so packed you'd be sitting back-to-back with a motley crew of ravers, goths, all varieties of affected dressers plus a few stupid trendy girls who didn't inhale their cigarettes and basically just took up space. Sometimes the room would be so smoky you could hardly see your hand in front of your face. Once when we got busted, literally twenty girls piled out in an enormous cloud of smoke. The guard was amazed. "How many can you fit in there?" he asked incredulously. So that was the middle of my days, but toward the end, I'd get what I refer to as "school panic syndrome" (S.P.S.). I'd just have to get out—collect whoever I could to join me and simply slip past the desk guards. I frequented a few classes, such as English, Global and the ever-popular New Music Singers, but that was about it.

Now don't get the idea that I didn't care about messing up in school. It was the opposite. I was constantly freaked and upset. Fighting with my parents and feeling guilty were also perpetual effects of my lack of respect for the fascist school regime. It wasn't that I didn't want to learn, I love learning, but school felt like prison and it practically hurt to be there. It was like being trapped both mentally and physically—we were actually locked into the building until our day was over. If we left we ran the risk of being chased down the block by one of the many security men or women, all of whom daydreamed about being real police officers instead of spending their time busting grungy high schoolers who just would not go to class.

La Guardia held a sort of prestige. It was the *Fame* school; they were selective and supposedly they turned out stars. I was a vocal major by the school's definition. Part of the chosen few. This was supposed to make us feel elite, we were on our way to becoming the next singing stars of America!

The only problem was that I didn't want to be a star, in fact I get awful stage fright and I don't like singing in front of other people. I have a decent voice but it's nothing compared to the others that were there, competitive, belting, nine-billion-octave-range voices that were more than slightly intimidating, especially to someone who had primarily been a shower singer before. I wasn't even coordinated enough to do the hand signals that were supposed to accompany the scales. Most of all, though, I really didn't want to be a singer. I was failing and generally miserable. I did not suffer alone, however. Many of my peers were equally or more pained than myself. These were my morning buddies, my lunchtime conversation providers and my partners in high school crime. It was just a waste of time and at that point I felt like there really wasn't much time to be wasted.

Of my closer friends in this group, one has by now dropped out and gotten his G.E.D. after deciding high school "just wasn't for me," two have been sent to boarding school, two to rehab, and more than I'd like to admit have turned to drugs or just plain disappeared. Not to be overly fatalistic, however—many have cleaned up their acts and become actual students, maybe by switching schools like I eventually did or just by giving in a little bit and trying. I remember at one point toward the end of the year a friend and I got together and made a list of everything we needed to do to be academically sound and just generally happier. I don't know how much of it we actually got through but both she and I started doing some better, so I guess that's a positive spin on it all.

Through all of this I held on to one thing: my social life. It was great.

I lived for Friday night St. Marks treks and Saturday night dancing at our favorite club, The Bank. In actuality The Bank was pretty much our *only* club option due to the fact that they didn't ID. On Saturday nights we'd all get Gothed up and trek down to Houston and Avenue A. The place was pretentious and most of the people there were incomprehensibly silly in their capes and gowns, but we thought it was fantastic and the music suited us (a mix of eighties new wave, industrial and goth pop). We loved dressing up and dancing as we trotted around through billows of clove smoke, bumping happily into brooding attractive Goth boys, all of whom seemed to harbor the aspiration to be Robert Smith when they grew up.

The girls were beautiful for the most part and we'd watch them in awe as they swished around the dance floor in their outrageous outfits. To be there and to just let yourself go and dance is to feel like you truly belong somewhere. The club is long gone now and though the nightlife we loved has moved to a new place (same DJ, and for the most part same people), but it won't ever be the same. Part of the whole Bank experience was the tiny moment of panic right before you walked in. You didn't know if they'd realize you were underage. The new spot—Downtime—always IDs, so we all have fake ones, but it does take away some of the fun. The familiarity that was so reassuring seemed to get lost during the move and it really is a loss, maybe more for me than for my friends, because however much I griped and complained, it was the only place I felt really free.

On the topic of dancing, I actually went to the La Guardia Senior Prom, with a friend of a friend, this six-foot-two homie named Melvin who carried a little stuffed animal Taco Bell dog in his pocket. His girlfriend had backed out at the last minute and the ticket was nonrefundable, so they gave it to me. It was fun, I guess, mostly getting all dressed up and dancing, but I almost felt sad because I knew I didn't deserve to be there.

By this point my parents had informed me that we were going around the world, mainly Southeast Asia but parts of Europe and the Middle East, too. I couldn't believe it—I was going away to foreign countries with just my family for three months during summer vacation. In other words (or at least the words I heard), I was going to miss my sixteen-year-old summer and everything that could have happened during it to go on a trip I had no desire to be on, alone with my family.

One thing I must add here is that generally I love family trips. Never mind the whole backseat bickering and "Don't make me pull this car over" type of stuff (there is plenty of that); our trips were pretty much always fun. This one, however, was a different story. I was going to miss the entire summer, go ridiculously far from anyone and *everything*. All I wanted to do was relax and calm down after a year of tension and angst, that last word being the common adult generalization for any negative feelings teenagers could possibly have. But no luck. I was being shipped off to God knows where and I was not pleased.

This provided a new problem. I was torn between my adult-logic side that said, "Go, this is a once-in-a-lifetime chance. You have to, you'll regret it forever if you don't." And my teenager social butterfly insecure side that said, "God, if you go you'll miss everything, you'll be separated from all your friends for three months, this is supposed to be the time of your life. The year has been so miserable, you need a good summer," and so on. I'd dreamed of it throughout the whole year—the summer, my escape from my life and my little social world, from all the gossip and drama. My escape from school, from *everything*. But when it was all said and done I just did not want to go. I fought bitterly with my parents about it, but in the end the aforementioned "adult" logic and my desire to explore won out and this is how I found myself on the plane to Bangkok.

And did I mention I hate flying?

Esteeming the Chance Booty

Yeah, twenty-three hours is a long time to be on a plane. But at least Japan Airlines was up to date. National carrier to the land that invented Donkey Kong and porno comix, they knew their lemming customers. Even we coach travelers were provided the use of the "home entertainment" TV screens, which were embedded right into the seat backs, affording an eight-inch screen-to-eye throw, at least until the person in front reclined quickly and violently. Several movies were on the program, almost all starring Meg Ryan, who must really do it for the fellas back in Shinjuku. Also available were twenty different video games, about half of which Billy had beat by takeoff. But that is the magic of the virtual; you can always beat the games again. And again.

We landed in Bangkok after midnight, but right away, it was obvious that things had changed since my wife and I had been in the Thai capital. For one thing, the traffic was a lot worse. True, even twenty years ago, there was no way to stay outside in the thick, sour air for more than an hour without getting a splitting headache. Even then the place was a more awful L.A. gone amok.

But at least they hadn't started building that hideous elevated highway that now shrouds Sukhumvit Road halfway to the

Cambodian border. Back then it didn't take two hours to drive the ten miles from the airport to Khao San Road at one o'clock in the morning.

Definitions of the good old days are always relative.

In the wake of the Vietnam War there were hundreds of cheap hotels in Bangkok. There was the Thai Son Greet, which sounds like a Yul Brenner number from *The King and I* but was actually the lowest of the bunch, a classic of sleazedelia. Across the street from the railway station, "The Greet" was run by a balding seventy-year-old Thai lady with an eye patch and no teeth. Once she had a canary, which sang very sweetly. This kind of offset the general ambiance, but then the canary died and the lady let it lie dead in its cage for several days. It was best to bring your sleeping bag because either the sheets had never been changed, or were black to begin with. The walls of the common bathroom were pocked with peepholes, a beady eyeball behind every one. There were tales of travelers ramming chopsticks through the holes, giving those voyeurs a real eyeful, but these stories were considered apocryphal.

"You look, you vomit, you leave," said this Aussie guy about The Greet—the perfect Zagat's entry, for sure.

Now The Greet was gone and our personal favorite, the old Malaysia, home to many R&R GIs during the war, was fixed up and expensive. So we bunked into the Veng Thai Hotel on the outskirts of the Bang Lan Phu backpacker zone. *Arthur Frommer's Budget Travel* magazine, our cheapskate Muse, said it was the best deal in the "moderate category, with pool," which sounded fine except that when we booked the place over the net, the e-confirmation contained the then notorious "Happy exe" virus. Upon arrival, we asked the uncomprehending desk clerk about the virus message.

"Happy?" he said. "Yes! Very happy!"

It was two-thirty in the morning by the time we checked in, but we were wired. It wasn't like we were about to chug right off to sleep, not on our first night in The World.

Luckily, Khao San Road, the tourist strip around the corner, never closes. The battery of noodle women were still frying the street version of Pad Thai in greasy woks, still charring their stunted little ears of corn on black-caked grills. Piles of cheap clothing filled tables, picked over by sallow teenagers. Even the Chahad-Lubavitcher was still open with three or four Hasidim inside, their long black coats buttoned to the top, beads of sweat hanging from their *payes* in the sultry tropical night. Two of them were from Brooklyn, a few subway stops from our house. Asked what they were doing in Bangkok, the Lubavitcher named Mel said he came to Thailand because "it was cheap. It was always cheap," he said, when you "traveled on God's ticket."

The kids took it in stride. After months of hype, foisting *National Geographic*s on them as if the magazine was a magic-lantern portal to the grand exotica they would soon enter, Khao San Road seemed strange. But hardly more so than a midnight stroll down Mott Street in New York's Chinatown. In New York, on hot summer nights, the teem of the Orient was only a few smelly blocks away. After midnight you could watch the mob-run private carting services throw the pungent refuse into giant dumpsters. Sometimes, a blue crab, miraculously still alive, skittered from the fish market trash, only to be crushed against the ruddy sidewalk beneath the heel of a sanitation worker's heavy boot.

But the kids had seen all that before.

This was the double-edge sword of growing up in New York. The most urbane of cities, it showed you a slice of this, a slice of that. Your parents were always after you to eat piles of meat in Brazilian restaurants in Jackson Heights with the soccer game blaring. Or drink those strange Taiwanese fruit shakes with the tapioca balls as big as marbles rattling up through half-inch-wide straws. In the big city you didn't get to sit in front of the TV in the living room of the split-level waiting for your parents to drive you to the mall. If you happened to live on St. Marks Place, where we did for years, entertainment might be as simple as peering out the fourth-floor window (with the newspaper stuffed in the jambs to keep out the winter wind) and watching a man with a kitchen knife chase another up the block. When the would-be killer dropped the knife as the cops approached, you joined the other people leaning out the window shouting, "It's behind the garbage can!"

Later on, you could get on the bus, or the subway, and probably never have to learn how to drive, if you didn't want to. You had that kind of autonomy. By the time Rosalie was in the sixth grade, she was taking the train every day, changing from the F to the A, making all connections. When you're raised in the city, you are always traveling, moving through time and space, through good neighborhoods and bad. You didn't have to look fourteen layers beneath the surface to find the true naked weirdness that lurked all around.

On the other hand, growing up in the Big City cut into the general awe. So little escaped the cultural sprawl of the grand metropolis. Probably, in New York, you could even buy those cute-as-silk-pants boxing shorts hanging from sticks on Khao San Road, the shiny orange ones with the green Thai letters splashed across the front that the vendor claimed translated to, "Oh, enemy, you too will perish before my power." To the kids a fried noodle was a fried noodle, on whatever continent.

On that first night in The World, the main thing our little rootless cosmopolitans found remarkable were the cyber cafes. There were half a dozen of them, open twenty-four hours, lining the street, each pumping techno music. Inside, "travelers" were banging the Hotmail, keeping in touch. If it wasn't for the standard-issue Indonesian drawstring pants—obligatory casual wear for all Southeast Asia wanderlusters—they might have been back at home, faces glued to screens, Josef K. office workers toiling away in their little cubicles.

We fell right in, typing away. Eight thousand miles away and a couple of keystrokes brought you back to Brooklyn again. After all, we'd been gone since Tuesday morning. Who knew what we might have missed?

E-mail. Fuck e-mail.

Back when the world was big, bigger than big, there was no such thing as e-mail. To get a letter you had to go to some huge and drafty post office, past sleeping guards, AK-47s balanced on their laps, to the Poste Restante box, where foreign missives sat in a series of trays. The mail was supposed to be arranged alphabetically according to addressees, each wooden box affixed with a hand-drawn letter. But this was a joke. Due to language difficulties, sloth, spite or whatever, finding a *J* letter in the *J* box was a haystack-needle deal. A *J* letter could be in the *G* box or the *R* box. It could easily have fallen on the floor where it might lie for a month or so, with the imprint of a flip-flop or combat boot on the envelope. It could have been knocked out of view by the occasional passage of a push broom; it could have been ripped to shreds by locals foraging for stray dollar bills or unfranked stamps.

You never felt safe unless you looked through all the mail, in every letterbox. If you were in Bombay, or Istanbul, that could be several thousand pieces. In this process you'd often pass through dog-eared, soiled missives, sometimes as much as two and three years old. "Emergency!" "Please Call Immediately," "Hold For Arrival. Important!" would be written on the envelopes, in red, underlined. There were the love letters, too, addressed in blotty Bic pen, S.W.A.K., drenched in French perfume by the sender, but now smelling of mildew, like everything else in the hall. There they'd sit, edges curling, the deadest of dead letters.

The cyber cafe represented just one more increment in the erasure of twentieth-century romance. Didn't seem the same, Bogey saying e-mails of transit were in Sam's piano. How rinky-dink the cyber world seemed. Time and space were too close together. The world was choking on its own proto-dystopic networking. Closeness brought sameness, linguistical standardization. The Internet was the new Tower of Babel. The last time everyone tried to talk to themselves in the same language, God, the paranoid Yahweh of the Pentateuch, shredded human aspiration to a thousand tongues, incomprehensible to each other. He could do it again. He could start right here in this funky Bangkok cyber cafe, huff and puff and crash asunder this Esperanto of typing. Or at least blow it back to DOS.

I checked out the website of The Wilsons, my new arch-enemies; "the fantastic Wilsons," we'd taken to calling them. They were going on a similar trip to ours, albeit on a somewhat more grandiose scale. A pair of doctors and their three brilliant towhead children, they had dropped out of the "rat race" and were already into their sixth month of traveling. There were other families who'd done the same, and even written books about it, but they traveled in Land Rovers, with a full complement of porter/nannies. The Wilsons eschewed such easily lampooned amenities. Obviously a heartier, bolder crew, The Wilsons planned to stay away for "a year, maybe two." This we knew from their website, which they scrupulously maintained from the road, complete with digital photos of their tanned and marvelously blond offspring climbing the Mount Bromo volcano in Indonesia and throat-singing with Tuvan yak herders.

There was no need for The Wilsons to get home in time for school. The Wilsons were homeschooling, or as they so cleverly referred to it, "home away from home schooling." It was "better" that way, said Tom, the levelheaded but warmhearted dad and webmaster of the clan (although everyone got a chance to do their postings, so it was possible to follow the altogether engrossing musings of your favorite Wilson). The Wilsons had "always" homeschooled, Tom wrote. Traveling was simply part of the program. To them, "life was the curriculum." The Wilson kids never whined about the "quite rigorous" homework he gave them, Tom wrote. They were "two to three grade levels" ahead of where they would have been if they'd stayed home.

According to the most recent entry, they'd just reached the Seychelles, where they planned to "cool out" for a while. Wendy, the mom, planned to use the time to finish the quilt she was making of the various materials she'd gathered on their journey. "What else would someone do on an island in the middle of the Indian Ocean but finish a Yankee quilt," Wendy noted, with wry humor. Those Wilsons, they sure were fantastic. Who else but them would think of folding hundreds of origami ornaments to stick on a baby palm tree after hitting Bali on Christmas?

Where we dreamed of going, the Wilsons went; what we dreamed of doing, the Wilsons did. The Wilsons were the real us, the us of our dreams. If only we could be more like them, bring out our inner Wilsonness. We could homeschool. I could set aside a room in the house. That would be the learning lab. The children would look forward to our many hours in that hallowed sanctum, the lot of us falling in love with the most marvelous works our species has yet produced. Over time we would cease to see ourselves as this scuffling little scrap of humanity, cut off and alienated from life's mortal core. We would become powerful, paragons of human feeling, walking advertisements for true family life.

Fat chance. As soon as I mention homeschooling, the kids begin to roll their eyes and make jokes about hording cans of tuna fish in the basement, as if I'm signing them up for the Branch Davidians. Besides, did any of us really want to spend *that* much time together? There was no escaping it. We were not Wilsons. We didn't have their rigor, their vision, their website. Then again, it could all be lies. There were a lot of lies on the Internet. Every day formerly rational people like Pierre Salinger were floating a harebrained theory some idiot believed. Maybe the Wilsons weren't so wonderful. Maybe they were staying in Hiltons or Oberois. Had whole armies of bearers whom they undertipped. Maybe the Wilsons never left home at all. They could be nothing but a bunch of bad-toothed ex-hillbillies, living in a tract house south of Chattanooga, or maybe just the dream obsession of one nutty recluse, not a family at all.

Either way there was no use getting all bent out of shape about it. The Wilsons were the Wilsons, we were us and there was not much to be done about it, I told myself, logging off the website.

Really, what was the big deal if the kiddies spent their first night in The World listening to Snoop Dogg and instant messaging their friends? At least they'd be practicing their typing. Besides, it was late. Across the street the noodle makers were stowing their woks. The boxing-trunks guy folding his satin shorts bathed in the blinking neon from a shuttered pharmacy. The location of an Asian pharmacy is always good to note. They don't have prescriptions; you just go in and ask for what you want. Right now the blinking neon said, PROZAC . . . PROZAC . . . PROZAC.

No, I told myself. There was no rush. The World was all around us. We'd find it soon enough.

Outside of checking out the gemstone-studded temples downtown, taking a ride on the mighty Chao Phrya River, skulking through weird food stalls of Chinatown, and tooling about in the smoke-billowing, three-wheeled *tuk-tuks* (Bill, the transport maven, rated them primo), Bangkok is not what you'd call kid friendly. They even threw us out of the lobby of the Oriental, the town's grand old hotel. Years ago, you could stay in a hippie rathole next door and go over to the Oriental for a swim, a tiki drink and a Thai ballet show on the grass. But now the security guards immediately suss out the freeloaders, even those using their children as a cover. It was another new thing. White people used to be able to get away with anything in Southeast Asia.

Even so, touristwise, Bangkok is still mostly about sex. Of course, it is not like it was. Back in 1980, my wife and I went over to Patpong District, then the main sex zone. Action was easy enough to find. Three steps down the road and we were accosted by a kid with snaggly teeth who handed us a wrinkled note saying, "You see smoke ring come out of pussy, you see fish in pussy, you see pussy make kiss and fart noise . . . follow this boy."

The "Sexy Club" was a red-and-black vinyl joint down a back alley filled with the usual Axis-power German and Japanese businessmen. After a cheesy Farfisa organ solo that could have been played by Question Mark and the Mysterians, a young woman came out from behind a curtain (how old was she? Sixteen?) and walked slowly (was she drugged, sick, or simply so, so tired?) over to the fattest German in the place. She got up on his table and straddled herself over his beer glass. Then, with a small swiggle, a Ping-Pong ball came out of her vagina and fell into the beer, plop, splashing the German and his equally red-faced compatriot.

That about did it for my wife, who suggested we leave. The check, however, was a problem. After being told our Cokes would cost one hundred baht a piece, the price had increased fifteenfold, for a total of three thousand baht, or $150. Calling attention to this discrepancy led to much heated yelling and demands for payment. A couple of big guys appeared, glowering. We tossed three hundred baht on the table and headed for the exit. Unfortunately, due to the murky lighting in the club, we opened the wrong door and found ourselves inside a broom closet, which was immediately locked behind us. This somewhat compromised our position in the ensuing negotiations, but we soon slipped a hundred more baht under the doorjamb and were allowed to leave.

With some necessary deletion, we told the kids this story, which they found highly amusing. But most likely they would never have guessed what was really up with Bangkok tourism if they hadn't come upon a manuscript on the floor in the hallway of the hotel. The author, a Brit of some sort, had apparently misplaced the pages while in the midst of preparing a travel guide to the current Bangkok sex scene.

Composed on a manual typewriter, much of the work was simply listings of whorehouses, bars and escort services, with clinical descriptions of services offered and prices, augmented with clipped commentary like "frequent visitors report varying degrees of cleanliness and STD surveillance." The grim story of the AIDS epidemic, which has infected "upwards of 25% of Bangkok's ladies (and men) of the night" was duly noted. Every so often, however, the author would break into a kind of reverie, offering descriptions of the various women he'd been with during his early days as a sex prospector in the Bangkok side streets. Many of these girls were "now certainly dead, or so diseased that they can no longer participate in the pleasure industry, which can make Bangkok a place of bittersweet memories," the author wrote.

Of course it was disgusting and exploitative; we were well aware of the awful stories of young girls, some as young as Rosie, being sold by hill tribe leaders to rapacious sex traders. Yet there was an oddly affecting quality to the author's quaintly rendered accounts of long ago liaisons (e.g., "the shrouded veils of her dainties offered only a hint of the treasures below"). One passage, seemingly part of the summation, stood out. In it the writer is walking through an especially crowded section of modern Bangkok, marveling at the crush. "So many people in the land of sex, so much reproduction," he writes. "Who would have guessed it? In the sex industry, reproduction is bad for business. No one wants anyone to get pregnant. So many babies have been prevented here, by the pill, latex, sponges, and far more primitive methods. Yet the place is still terribly overcrowded, traffic stalled, with more people all the time. Humanity is a weed, fecund, always spreading."

A couple of days later, we decided to take the bus down to the beach at Ko Samet. We would rather have gone to Ko Samui, the erstwhile island paradise two hundred kilometers to the south, where my wife and I stopped for a few weeks two decades ago. Once upon an underdeveloped time, the indolent traveler could take the overnight ferry from the hideous industrial town of Surat Thani, bunk down in an A-frame on Ko Samui, smoke a mountain of Thai stick, and eat freshly caught fish every meal for about $25 a week. At night, they had the Thai boxing matches. You walked through the forest in the moonlight to where the ring was strung between four palm trees and watched two sexy sweat-slicked boys, shocks of black hair flying, spring from the mantis position to beat on each other with purple gloves as big as soccer balls. But now they had an international airport down at Samui, giant hotels and package deals up the wazoo.

Still, Samet, with its genteel foot-high waves and snow-white sand that squeaked when walked on, had its attractions. It was only four hours from Bangkok, which made it the choice of what was called "the local trade"—that is, harried Thai week-enders who went there to party. This meant a lot of disco, drinking, and many hotheaded screaming matches. It is a well-worn sonic schism of the global vacation: if Bob Marley's *Legend* album is playing, look for neatly arrayed backpacks stitched with Canadian flags. If they're playing this god-awful disco with way too much bass, excess treble, or if the speakers sound like they're about to blow out altogether, it's local. We like local. Ko Samet, full of fruggers and Mekong whiskey sluggers, a short boat ride across the Gulf of Thailand from the industrial town of Rayong, home to the world's largest fish sauce factory, fit the bill.

The idea was to hang out, catch some rays, get relaxed without going Club Med—not that there was much chance of that at our two-dollar-a-night abode, Tok's Little Huts, a series of eight-foot-square bungalows set on a steeply angled, erosion-prone seaside hill. Notable among Tok's eccentricities was the electrical wiring system. The tiny sheds were connected by a series of orange extension cords that ran to a large, loud, generator. Should the lights fail in the middle of the night, guests were expected to follow their cord and reconnect it to the mother extension. As we attempted to do this one rainy evening, Bill, who retained a dim memory of biting through an electric cord at age two (one of his many visits to the emergency room), wondered if it might be safer to be wearing rubber-soled shoes. It was a reasonable concern, seeing as our cord had not merely been dislodged but rather had apparently been eaten through by a chompy representative of the Samet fauna. Right then, as if to demonstrate the range of Tok's full-service hospitality, a man in a shocking- pink slicker and bedroom slippers soon slogged through the downpour with a roll of electrician's tape, fixing the problem.

In leisure mode, we broke out the books at Samet. In our family, we read lots of books, even if it is mostly to get out of reading the books we're supposed to be reading. Rae, who says she knows a book is for her by the feel of the cover against her hand, was already through more than half of Nabokov by the tenth grade. Rosie is the same, doggedly marching through *The Mists of Avalon* on the bus down to Samet. Bill doesn't exactly read as much as reread, as in rereading the same five or six magazines about video games and sneakers over and over again. We deplore this blinkered activity, even as we buy him one more Max Payne shoot-'em-up manual. Bill is aware of our ambivalence on this topic. A couple of weeks before leaving, in a remarkable gesture of sacrifice, he declared he was leaving his Game Boy at home.

"I'd play it all the time. I'd miss everything," he accurately self-diagnosed, adding, also correctly, "that would make you mad." Instead he had a new crop of video game and sneaker magazines that he put into heavy rotation.

All this reading might help explain why our kids always score in the ninety-ninth percentile in the verbal part of the standardized tests, to go along with their usual twentieth percentile in the math. My wife and I also got the same numbers, so I guess that makes it kind of a family tradition, having your right brain hooked up wrong.

Books would be important on the trip, we told them, sending them to Barnes and Noble to stock up before we left. Nothing matched the joy of a bit of Faulkner (*The Wild Palms* would be a good choice) or even a brace of John D. MacDonald mysteries while chugging across the plains of India, soot from the steam engines flying in the windows and settling on every page. The hope was that the kids might pick masterworks set in far-off locales, perhaps a bit of Malraux, Conrad, or even Jack Kerouac. The road, man, we were *on the road*.

They returned with further additions to their already extensive collection of gothic wrist-slit lit, including yet another copy of *Girl, Interrupted* (in the movie tie-in edition featuring the tubby-lipped, bad role model Angelina Jolie on the cover). What was it with this teen mordancy thing, anyway? When we were in New Orleans we had to drive over to Anne Rice's house so the kids could pay homage to their treacle-weaving heroine and the stuffed dog statues that adorned the balcony of the vampire writer's Garden District mansion.

I must admit, I find this whole adolescent death trope unsettling. All that gloom, Wicca, and candle wax drippings around the house. Any day I expect to come home to a séance or a Salem witch trial in the kitchen. Of course, I wasn't all that different when I was younger, screaming Bo Diddley lyrics like "I'm just twenty-two and I don't mind dying!" as the A train rumbled through the tunnel, even if I was only seventeen and, on further review, I did very much mind dying. Still, I can see the attraction. For the ritually depressed teenager, what could be more "other" than escape from here? In the age of irony, it seems an open and shut case that living a short time is only the opening act to being dead a long time. Death: it is bigger than life.

All of which is almost enough to forbid the kids from listening to the Nirvana records they've stolen from me over the years. If Kurt Cobain, a rich genius, could actually kill himself, put his money where his mouth was concerning the supposed bleakness of modern life, the seductive legitimacy of his decision scares me. So, my jerk parenting style being what it is, I do as I usually do when threatened; I mock the children's cherished predilections. Seeing *The Bell Jar* in Rae's pile, I inquired if she'd also picked up the companion piece, *The Sylvia Plath Cookbook*, a lively culinary Baedeker in which every recipe ended with the final instruction: "Turn on gas, stick head in oven." This "joke" was met with the usual pained scorn.

As it was, at Ko Samet we would find a book that would become the must-read thematic tome of our trip, true words to live by. The book in question was a dog-eared language primer entitled *How To Learn Farsi in 29 Days?* by one Professor H. Hozhabr Nejad of Tehran University, which my wife acquired at the book exchange maintained by the Naga Hotel, the modest accommodation down the beachfront. The puzzling, possibly self-effacing conditionality of the question mark in the title of *How To Learn Farsi in 29 Days?* (especially when contrasted with the specificity of "29 days") was intriguing enough. Beyond that, since the Naga library operated on a "take-one-leave-one" trade policy, this gave us the opportunity to rid ourselves of *Reviving Ophelia*, the then best-selling parental guide to the raising of daughters that had been weighing down our backpacks since we left New York.

This isn't to quibble unduly with the no-brainer main theme of books like *Reviving Ophelia—Saving the Selves of Adolescent Girls*, which indicts the "girl-poisoning" aspect of the current culture as the main determiner in bad teen self-image and subsequent destructive behavior. Prepared, we also carried the equally best-selling *Raising Cain—Protecting the Emotional Life of Boys*, which dealt with the male version of the same issues. But I am wary of books so obviously concocted to prey on parental uncertainty. The shrinks who write them, like beat cops, seem a little too anxious to tell their most awful war stories, these fear-inducing sagas of dope use, bad sex, and the loom of doom among first-name-only patients, usually called Tammy or Craig. And they claim that if we, the hopelessly naive but overbearing parents, want to avoid a life of endless codependency in the theater of our children's pain, we'd better sign up these losers for several hundred thousand dollars of psychotherapy *before it's too late*.

Who knows if these confidence-undermining blackmailers are right? Are the people at the Steiner schools right, thinking children shouldn't learn to read before their big teeth come in? Dentition before literature—is this some strange Teutonic physiologic solution to the mind-body problem? Who really knows? Large portions of the country used to think John B. Watson knew what he was talking about. Watson, one of the truly undersung (and underblamed) architects of the twentieth-century self-image nightmare, was the founder of operant behaviorism and author of the first popular parenting books of the modern era, the 1928 *Psychological Care of the Infant and Child*. His "scientific," ultraplatonic theory of child-rearing, which included advice against the dangers of caressing or kissing kids before bed (a "firm handclasp" would do), and toilet training at six weeks old, was one of the main reasons Dr. Spock felt compelled to write his own, more user-friendly tome.

Watson is something of a legend in our household, mostly owing to the legacy of Little Albert, centerpiece of his most famous experiment. Anxious to prove the efficacy of behaviorist techniques, Watson, the first head of the psychology department at Johns Hopkins, "adopted" the eleven-month-old Albert from a local foundling home. Using a negative reenforcement regimen of loud noises and bright lights, Watson "conditioned" Albert to be afraid of white mice and eventually everything white (there is a small snippet of Albert recoiling in terror at the sight of Watson wearing a Santa Claus beard). After Watson's dismissal from the university following the discovery of an affair with his assistant, the experiment was discontinued, and Albert, fears intact, was sent back to the orphanage, never to be heard from again.

We often tell our kids we are planning on using Watson's techniques on them, to the usual derision. But truth be told, they have already spent their lives serving as the psychologist's guinea pigs. This owes to Watson's second career, as a vice president of the J. Walter Thompson advertising agency, where he employed his behaviorial techniques in several ad campaigns, including pioneering work on deodorant accounts, convincing people that they smelled a lot worse than they thought they did and they better do something about it fast. Needless to say, this application of fear conditioning to the marketplace was a watershed moment in American capitalism. Once acclaimed as America's answer to Freud, Watson continued to produce Little Alberts, a whole race of them: you, me and our children, Manchurian Candidate/consumers walking around really nervous, really afraid, except none of us can exactly remember why.

We were glad to be rid of *Reviving Ophelia* and embrace the more liberating vision of *How To Learn Farsi in 29 Days?* Ostensibly a straightforward presentation of grammar, nouns and tenses, the book largely eschewed such mundanities as "where is the bus station?" in favor of a trove of recondite phraseology, conveying mysterious messages both political and spiritual. Published in revolutionary Iran, it seemed bravely subversive that Professor Nejad chose to illustrate his "slang and colloquial" phrase section with terms such as "the day of judgment" (*ruz mabada*), "You are not free to make such a statement" (*exteyar darid*), or "Do not do anything that you will be sorry for" (*cera aqel konad kari ke baz arad pafirmani*). His choices for "everyday speech items" likewise revealed a potentially fearsome critique through the use of phrases like "By the time they bring the antidote from Iraq the person bitten by the snake will have died" (*ta taryaq az eraq arand mar gazide xahad mord*), "I saw a certain tyrant asleep" (*zalemi ra xofte didam*), "Meanwhile give me the end of the rope" (*sare tanab ra beman bedahid*), and "Below the truck there are legs" (*saqe pa zire tane qarar darad*).

Sitting beside a Thai sea, listening to Jamaican music, watching Will Smith in *Independence Day* in a small restaurant where they served curry chips from Gujarat, we pondered the semiologic import of Professor Nejad's post-Persian text. Across what impenetrable cultural divide might lie the true meaning of such sample sentences as "A hundred moths will be burnt by the time a candle burns out" (*ta bepayan rasa yek fam sadha parvane misuzad*) or "Saying if I escape the hand of this archer, I will be content with a corner of the old woman's ruined hut" (*ke gar jastam az daste in tir zan man o konje veiraneye pirzan*)?

Yet, even as we were saddened by Professor Nejad's lexiconic lament, "I, the unfortunate one" (*mane badbaxt*—found under "greetings"), we never failed to be buoyed by a singular phrase found under the heading of "semantic features of the imperative." There it was, the marvelous serendipity of "esteem the chance booty" (*forsat ra qanimat fomarid*).

Esteem the chance booty! What could better express the traveler's mandate? Here, in a phrase, was the freedom to come, to look, *to dig.* That's what we were after. The booty. The will to discover, seemingly by chance, the true treasure of the world, not only a diamond to see or hold in the hand, but also the one within. For this clarifying sense of purpose, we thanked Professor Nejad.

Here is a moment I think of when I think of esteeming the chance booty.

This was back in the spring of 1986, when my wife and I were in the Yucatán, in a rented car, driving along the highway outside of Merida. Rae had just turned three and we'd gone with my wife's parents for a vacation at Cancun, the recently manufactured resort on the Mexican Caribbean coastline.

I'd been in the area fifteen years before, when Quintana Roo, not yet a Mexican state, was still a "territory," a term that conjured wild and open images of Lewis and Clark and the exploration of a Louisiana bigger than Bourbon Street. You slung your hammock between trees on the beach by oceanfront Mayan ruins of Tulum and felt immortal, a victor over history and time. Four hundred years before, Cortez, the killer, sailed by these shores, looking for things to plunder. Thinking Tulum to be a great and unassailable fortress, he kept on going. In fact, the city had been abandoned long before and no Mayans remained to be conquered. Yet sleeping on the beach there, it was possible to dream a perfectly heroic hippie dream: that Cortez had made a different decision and sent his soldiers to shore, blood in their rheumy European eyes. And we, our hippie army, pot-addled brains suddenly fierce and free, met him and his ironclad pirates on the strand. Fighting side by side with noble Mayans, we pushed those clanking conquistadors back into the sea, thereby negating centuries of colonial hegemony and strife.

It was possible to dream of vanquishing Cortez, but outside of a giant hurricane, no scenario suggested a way to stop Cancun. The resort presented a far more nuanced adversary. Months before the first cinderblock was set in place, long lines of young men and women snaked through the wilderness, waiting in the broiling sun in front of Quonset huts. Some had come as far as five hundred miles or more, from Chiapas and Veracruz. Asked what they were waiting for, they said, *trabajar*. And work they would, first putting up the hotels, and then working inside them, as maids and busboys, and tending the vast golf course lawns no Mayan or Toltec king had ever seen. Soon enough, Liberty Travel was selling six-day, five-night packages.

In 1986, we were in one of those hotels. Why don't you stay a while, my wife's parents said, offering to take Rae home with them. Then we'd have a little time "to ourselves." Rae said it was okay with her.

Watching her walk down the jetway to the plane, blithely waving as she went, it seemed impossible. It was the first time we'd ever been apart from her. Back in the earliest days, we used to huddle over the cradle my father built for her, watching her tiny chest for hours, just in case she missed a breath. We imagined she might disappear if we weren't there to see her every move, as if she was somehow a phantom, a made-up thing only our constant attention kept alive.

So there we were, as we once were, my wife and I, just us two, lovers so entwined. In a way it was like the first days, when I'd visit her in her studio apartment on Bank Street, across the street from the old Women's House of Detention where once a wizened-looking prisoner had shouted out the window to me, "Hey, prince charming! I'm Rapunzel, I'm going to let down my hair," and threw an unraveling roll of toilet paper out the window. "Climb up, baby, I'm yours," she yelled.

How fantastic it would be to return, if only for a couple of days, to those amazing times, when it was only us. It is something we've done many times over the ensuing years, getting away for a night here and there, checking into a hotel. It never fails: even if you're a hundred, once you hand the credit card to the desk clerk, everything is sexy all over again. But back then, in Mexico, something was on my wife's mind, I knew, as we strolled through the zocalos and markets, eating oranges dredged in hot chilies and buying shoes with bottoms made from recapped tires.

It came to a head in Rio Lagartos, a spot of beach on the Gulf side of the Yucatán known as the nesting area for some of the last flocks of wild flamingos. It was a fabulous sight, driving down the dirt road, hundreds of the birds up ahead, a twitchy pink smear, rising up through the haze.

It was there my wife and I sat, arguing about having a baby.

I was against it. You know, here we were, after who could count how many nights of sleep deprivation, finally footloose in another place, not our ratty Lower East Side apartment. I mean: *check it out*—we're surrounded by *flamingos*! Look at those hinge-strung dudes, balancing on one spindly leg, like an art deco army of Amityville lawn ornaments. Couldn't we let the kid thing rest, for a minute or two?

No, my wife said. She wanted to talk about it, now.

Until then the debate over the final architecture of our family-in-progress had been low-key, a topic of vague priority. Neither one of us had ever been much of a planner, family or otherwise. Certainly, if we were in a tradition of big families, the issue would have been moot. After six or seven you start to lose count and it becomes a simple matter of enough shared bunk beds and a big enough washing machine. But we were us, young(ish) postmoderns, with things to do, places to go.

Like I said, I was against it. I was busy, I explained. Very busy. Didn't she appreciate that I was an artist, a writer of *promise*? Potentiality wasn't going to last forever. What about all those other writers, my supposed beloved colleagues but actually my untrusted competitors, how was I to keep pace with these childless careerists, not to mention the ones with full-time nannies.

How many kids did she think we needed, anyway? Love, like time, wasn't necessarily an unlimited commodity. Who was to say there would be enough to accommodate this new individual? This was a giant problem in the world today—not enough love to go around. So many people suffered from a shortage of love, walking around underpowered, low-amped and withering, like unwatered plants. Just because it sounded selfish didn't make it untrue. In this world you had to look out for number one, and number two, and number three. By number five and six, the hedging sets in. This was my argument, the statement of my fears. But my wife, she wasn't buying it.

Thinking of this incident now, a decade and a half later, invokes a strange duality. On one hand, everything I said then (and repeated so many times since)—the paranoia over work, the gnawing sense of insufficient love, and so on—continues to make sense, as true today as back then. Still hassled, still ambivalent, my fatherly heart is a besieged fortress, its walls breached more times than Troy.

On the other hand, there is the product of that Mexican negotiation.

Rosalie . . . I can hear her voice right now, in our Brooklyn home, downstairs from where I type these words. She's got a friend staying over, a girl she met at summer camp. Mostly they hang around and talk about bands, which ones are great and which ones suck, but now they're watching *Vertigo*, because even if there are other videos available—*Coyote Ugly, Mallrats,* and *The Breakfast Club* (their special totem)—Rosalie, the Hitchcock fan, has enticed her buddy to take a gander at the obsessed Jimmy Stewart fantasizing about Kim Novak.

Daddy's girl, watching *Vertigo*, reading *Clockwork Orange*, keeping that strangely small nose, by far the daintiest schnozzle in the family, firmly in the air. When you're from Brooklyn, a little haughtiness never hurt anyone.

"I'm so cultured, ain't I?" Rosie says, that sly, coquettish smile creasing her cheeks which are often flushed, a feature that, as people often comment, so well fits her name. Just the other day I saw her looking in the mirror, striking one dramatically attitudinal pose after another. "Dad," she asked, "is this how an existentialist stands?"

When we left for The World, Rosie was the only one who actually had her backpack ready more than an hour before the cab came. No surprise, since we've been saying for years that she's the lone person in the family who knows where her shoes are. Everyone else's, too. She notices things, remembers. She has from the beginning, lying in her cradle, saying very, very little, hardly ever crying, wondering how she wound up with this bunch of idiots and thinking how she'd decorate the living room once the rest of us were back in the SRO hotel from whence we came and the place was hers, finally all hers.

Yet, it was only Kukulkan, also known as Quetzalcoatl, the plumed serpent, puissant god of creation, who convinced me that my wife was right and Rosalie should be born.

This occurred at the ancient Mayan and Toltec city of Chichen Itza, which makes perfect sense. Chichen was like so many of the places we would visit in The World. It didn't matter that the tourist buses from Cancun arrived every hour. Or that they ran the Sound and Light show every night. Like the pyramids, like Machu Picchu, in this place the ancients scanned heaven and earth, arbitrated life and death. Here, people reached into the beyond. The vibe remained, a low, inextinguishable thrum in direct counterpoint to the whir of cameras, the groan of air brakes, the idle chitchat of bored day-trippers. Chichen Itza was, a hundred university-sponsored renovations and a million T-shirts later, still a sacred place.

We'd arrived at an auspicious time. Primal forces were stirring. Only the night before, Halley's Comet had made its way through blackness over the jungle. The comet only comes on its milk run once every eighty-six years, which meant we were a mere dozen trips or so removed from the Mayans, who built the great observatory a millennium ago. It was the vernal equinox, too, the first day of what we call spring. Religion needs magic and it was on this day that long-dead Mayans and their Toltec conquerors turned their best trick: they summoned Kukulkan's ghost.

What a stunt it was, a modern-day performance of an ancient merge of myth, astronomy and architecture. Each year, on this day, and only this day, due to the positioning of the late-afternoon sun shining on the step-like sides of the massive seventy-eight-foot-tall Castillo, a shadow of the feathered serpent's body undulated down the staircase of the adjacent pyramid. At the pyramid's bottom, the shadow aligned perfectly with the massive carved limestone head of Kukulkan, which served as the base of the staircase. Shadow and stone, it was a fabulous fusion of the material and the spectral, the solid and the mythic.

Except it was raining. There was no sun, no shadow, only a leaden sky that never brightened. Well into the afternoon most of the crowd that had assembled for the show had gotten back into the tour buses and left. It was disappointing, a missed opportunity. As the crowd thinned, the presence of the Mayans became more pronounced. The rain was not sending them home. All around were tiny ladies in their immaculate dresses, followed by kids with flat, open faces, their noses smacked down like bantamweight fighters. The continuing presence of Mayans only deepened the mystery. If these people, forty generations down the line from the great builders, retained the foggiest grasp of the secrets of their race, they weren't about to tell us. It was like that everywhere. You couldn't expect a bushy-browed Greek waiter to recite Aristotle simply because he worked at the Aristotle Coffee Shoppe on Lexington Avenue. Could any of these present-day Mayans explain to us why their ancestors decided to make their calendar 18,980 days long? Sans the sharp slice of the scimitar or the Crusader's lance, cosmology rarely travels over time or space. The genius of a human strain took hold of a people, blazed bright, then flitted away. Someday, and chances are the process is already well underway, descendants of our crowd will stand, blitzed and puzzle-struck, looking up at the Empire State Building, wondering what dimly recalled stroke of boldness moved people to thrust such a shaft up into Yahweh's sky, so He might notice us and praise our industry.

The rain kept coming down. The last of the disgruntled tourists had slung their daypacks over their shoulders and exited across the muddy grass. It was only our argument that kept us there, the heated back and forth about whether we would have another baby. There was no rush to return to the shabby plaster-board ephemera of Cancun. Here in the ruins, we debated our own version of eternity.

"No," I said.

"Yes," my wife said.

"I won't."

"Then, I will."

"What?"

"You heard me."

Who hears these conversations? Who pulls what string? The Mayan lady standing across the field was the first to look up. The sun, unseen for days, was breaking through, first in thin shafts, then pouring down, a hole burned through the clouds. Suddenly, the entire ancient city was ablaze in late afternoon Technicolor.

And then, there it was—the plumed serpent, undulating down the staircase. We stopped and stared, watching until the snake's body fused with its head, the spirit electric once again, according to the plan.

Signs . . . Wonders. A half hour later, we were back at the hotel, the old Mayaland, fresh flowers on the table at the end of our canopy bed. All reluctance on my part about the enlargement of our family had disappeared. There are forces in the Universe you simply cannot argue with, or ignore.

Rosie was a born traveling girl. She took her first step on the deck of the *Santa Anita*, a trim little cruising boat off the coast of Florence, one of the Galapagos Islands, as good a place as any for a member of the fittest species to assume the primacy of bipedalism. The *Santa Anita* wasn't the swankiest craft plying those waters, but at least it didn't hit a rock in the middle of the night and sink to the bottom of the blue Pacific like the fancier *Tip Top*, the boat we were originally scheduled to sail on. Each day, led by our guide, Roberto, whose bedroom eyes were all the rage with the trio of Ecuadorian grandmothers with whom we shared the ship's comfortable accommodations, we would visit one more island temple of natural selection, strolling among Darwin's finches and four hundred-pound, honking sea lions before returning to the strains of "People Are Strange" and pieces of Spanish sausage drenched in lime juice artfully arranged on a silver plate by the ship's cook, the smiling Alberto.

Rosie's breakthrough didn't come until the last morning of the trip. The ocean was rough, rolling all around. Everyone was seasick, moaning and ready to chunder. It was then, with the boat pitching at increasingly acute angles, that Rosie let go of the chair she'd been holding onto and took her first steps. Heads in hands, stomachs swirling, we didn't notice this maiden ambulatory voyage until she was halfway across the cabin.

"She's walking," my wife managed.

Even now I can see the giant smile on Rosie's face. Perhaps she was simply pleased at her own achievement, that first step. But knowing her, I'd have to say she was extra tickled to be walking without trouble as the ship's constant lurching caused her parents, splayed out on the cabin floor, to desperately grab hold of whatever support they could. Either way, she did not walk again for at least a month, eschewing the mundanities of dry, unmoving land.

These days you can fly directly from Bangkok to the great temples at Angkor, do your two-day tourist deal, zip back, and never set foot in the rest of Cambodia. But this would miss the point altogether. Home of the Killing Fields, land where Pol Pot's Khmer Rouge attempted to reset the clocks back to Year Zero, Cambodia is a heartbreak, a place of nightmares, an opportunity not to be missed.

In the long roster of the world's sad spots, Cambodia had already caught the kids' attention. Both Rosie and Rae had done school reports on the country and its unfortunate recent history. They knew about the great Khmer Empire that ruled here until the fifteenth century, and how the country, often invaded by the neighboring Thai and Vietnamese, had become part of French Indochina. They knew about the vain, flamboyant King Norodom Sihanouk, noted clarinetist and badminton player who had managed, through guile, charm and lies, to retain his small, beleaguered nation's neutrality in the early years of the Vietnam War. They also knew about the U.S. carpet bombing of Cambodia, and how people were shot dead at Kent State protesting it. That much was in the Neil Young song, "Ohio."

Mostly, though, they knew about the Khmer Rouge. In the three and a half years following the American defeat in 1975, the

Red Khmers, rulers of the Democratic Republic of Kampuchea, as they renamed the country, presided over the elimination of nearly two million Cambodians, as much as one quarter of the entire population, according to some counts. Pushing a theory of agrarian apocalypse, Pol Pot and his army of hillbilly teenagers emptied the capital city Phnom Penh, banishing the city-dwelling "new people" to the countryside to be worked to death on huge, pointless projects alongside peasant "base people." Intellectuals and artists were among the first to go, a fact Rae noted in her school report, one of the few assignments she actually completed during her tenure at La Guardia High.

"Everyone who wears glasses, stand up," Rae announced, delivering her report to her Global History class. "Everyone who doesn't have calluses on their hands, stand up . . . dance majors stand up, vocal majors stand up . . . everyone who can read, stand up. . . . " When she had all her classmates and teachers out of their seats, Rae leveled her gaze and said, "You're all dead." The drama of the presentation got her a rare A, plus a moment of revenge against the achievers of the so-called *Fame* school.

Now, in the courtyard of the former Tuol Sleng prison in Phnom Penh, a one-time secondary school that had been transformed into the regime's dreaded S-21 torture center, Rae was weeping. To be here, where twenty thousand dancers, singers and readers had actually been killed by madmen, was overwhelming.

Renamed the Tuol Sleng Genocide Museum, it was hard to imagine a more effective exhibit. The old torture chamber had been left much as it was back in 1977. Metal bed frames hooked to electric wires filled rooms on the ground floor. Upstairs were dozens of tiny brick enclosures, holding cells for doomed prisoners. A list of ten "security regulations," translated from the Khmer, hung on a wall.

The first was: "You Must Answer Accordingly To My Questions. Don't Turn Them Away." #3 said: "Don't Be A Fool For You Are A Chap Who Dare To Thwart The Revolution." #4 was: "You Must Immediately Answer My Questions Without Wasting Time To Reflect." #6: "While Getting Lashes Or Electrification You Must Not Cry At All." #9: "If You Don't Follow All The Above Rules, You Shall Get Many Lashes Of Electric Wire."

Even more horrific was the photo gallery. Like the Nazis before them, the Khmer Rouge kept scrupulous records, taking stark, black-and-white, three-by-five-inch mug shots of each prisoner to enter S-21. After Pol Pot's fall in 1979, the pictures were preserved and now filled the walls of several rooms of Tuol Sleng, from floor to ceiling. Row after row, they look out at you. Some of the faces seem disinterested, even blasé. Others, eyes blazing, show outright fear, or anger. They all had one thing in common: they knew they were about to die. Very few who entered S-21 ever came out alive.

The girls could not hack it. "I can't be here, not a second more," Rae said, walking into the next room. There, there was a fifteen-foot-high map of Indochina. Cambodian territory was denoted by a cluster of human skulls nailed to the wall. Outside, in the courtyard where schoolchildren once took recess, the nightmare of the place was only exaggerated by the fact that Tuol Sleng (unlike the Choeung Ek Killing Fields, several miles to the north, where mass graves are marked by signs saying "108 bodies with no head") is right in the middle of a bustling Phnom Penh neighborhood. Auschwitz's arched entryway is situated at the end of a rail line, deep in the wintry Polish countryside, but here everything is sunny, palm trees swaying in the breeze like in Santa Monica. On the other side of the fence cars speed by, people push carts full of merchandise, sit on balconies of apartment houses. The presence of so much death, all those tormented ghosts, amid the normality of the everyday, seemed the most terrifying thing about the place.

Evil lurked here, close and palpable. It had been two decades since Vietnamese forces had stormed across the border to overthrow the Khmer Rouge, but horror remained. Not a single Khmer Rouge higher up, several of whom continue to live in Phnom Penh, has ever been tried for their crimes. Pol Pot himself had survived until a year and a half before our arrival. After waging hopeless, ruinous guerrilla warfare against the current government, Brother Number One, as he was called, passed away of natural causes at the age of seventy-three, nearly twenty years beyond the usual Cambodian life expectancy. In contrast to those who died at Tuol Sleng, Pol Pot's deathbed was surrounded by vases of freshly cut purple bougainvillea and the shortwave radio on which he listened, religiously, to the voice of America.

Returning from Tuol Sleng, the rest of the day was spent in a kind of sorrowful stupor, the not inconsiderable charm of Phnom Penh taken in with numbed silence. The elephant blocking traffic on the road fronting the Mekong River was barely noticed. A trip to the National Museum, with its hundreds of tiny Buddhas and silver-plated floor, elicited only sobs. The kids seemed spaced out, saying odd, non-sequitorous things. "My science teacher doesn't like octopuses," Rosie remarked, out of nowhere, apropos of nothing. A minute later, looking up at the sky, she mused, "This is the longest time I haven't worn my boots in two-and-a-half years." Billy stuck his head deeper into his video mags and didn't come out, reading the same game reviews one more time.

That was the key—keeping your head down, averting your eyes. Several years earlier we'd driven to the impoverished Pine Ridge Reservation, to the burial ground at Wounded Knee, and peered at the mass grave there. In 1890, the Oglala Sioux, heeding the vision of the Paiute shaman Wovoka, performed the

Ghost Dance, which the prophet imagined would bring back murdered ancestors and banish the encroaching whites, thereby returning the world to sanity. The prophecy failed. In the climactic battle with the United States government at Wounded Knee, hundreds of Sioux were killed. We expected a solemn memorial, but the site, more of an open pit than a hallowed cemetery, was covered with a layer of beer cans and candy wrappers. A whole way of life had ended here, and all that remained was this sullen indifference. Yet, somehow, it seemed fitting. As one Pine Ridge resident told us, he didn't feel like maintaining a tourist site "so people could come here in their rental cars and feel better about themselves."

Cambodia was a more recent look at doom. Even with new genocides being reported on a regular basis, these killing fields were still relatively new, the dirt freshly turned. This was a place in flux, where fortune could change quickly, unpredictably, probably for the worse. It could happen right in front of you, the way a motorcycle driver came around the corner balancing a ten- foot-long roll of foam rubber on his handlebars and smashed into the 100cc motorcycle taxi carrying Rosalie. Being seventy-five feet behind on the back of another "moto," there wasn't much I could do but shout in horror, not that any fruitless cry would be heard over the whine of the two-stroke engines. I was her father, her protector, and I was helpless to intervene. What would happen, would happen.

The bike skidded, but the driver, whom I would give a large tip, managed to keep it upright. Cambodia was a place where the space between life and death had been whittled very thin. Close calls were to be expected. It was something to fear, especially in a country with only one functioning hospital and not one single accredited neurosurgeon in residence. Indeed, this was the reason Billy, who you'd figure would love a moto ride, refused to get on the putt-putts. "Not in a country with no brain doctors," he said.

It made you jumpy. Holed up inside our less-than-deluxe accommodations at the optimistically named Sunshine Hotel, the girls sought solace in a fuzzy transmission of their chief fitness guru, Gilad, a buff and bossy Israeli, and his Bodies in Motion team. Then, right in the middle of a fat-burning segment, one of the lightbulbs in the spider-infested bathroom exploded, apparently what Cambodian lightbulbs do when they feel like it. Everyone screamed. Then, catching her breath, Rae said, "Well, at least I'll always be able to say I've been a lot of places no one I know would ever want to go to."

Prior to our departure, my wife and I discussed this trip as partly a mnemonic exercise, to implant in the kids' tender minds a better class of memories than total recall of *Buffy* episodes. It was important to us that forty years from now they might recall the whoosh of an airplane propeller as they walked across the tarmac in a hot and far-off place. Call it a kind of managed nostalgia, but at least it was a nostalgia of action, *good* nostalgia. Now, in the wake of Tuol Sleng, we wondered about this strategy. Wasn't it the job of parents to steer their children clear of potential bad memories? Was it really right to puncture the however deplorable media cocoon with this "reality"?

The kids were mopey, and it was time for Dad to step up, to change the mood, do something truly spectacular, something that would be talked about for years, whenever spectacular Dad gestures were mentioned.

At the Central Market, a brilliant bustle of primitive capitalism beneath a vaulted Art Deco–styled roof, I had my chance. Here, along with every manner of entrails, multihued textiles and stacks of "Danger! Mines!" T-shirts (the Ur-khmer collectible, with a large skull on the front and line drawings of various Soviet and Chinese-made mines on the reverse side), local merchants peddled deep-fried tarantulas. There were large wicker baskets of the frizzy-legged critters, each inches across. We stood spellbound as locals picked through the arachnids, tossing them into brown paper bags with spreading grease stains at the bottom. The challenge came when a tall white man, possibly a businessman or perhaps one of the many NGO workers, stooped beside the basket, picked out a tarantula and bit into it, his teeth piercing the shiny black body with an audible snap.

"Eccch," the kids exclaimed in astonished disgust. It was one thing for Cambodians to eat tarantulas—they even ate durians, the only fruit that smelled like a busted sump pump. But a white guy eating a tarantula? This raised the stakes.

All eyes were on me. The dare was there. Would I come through like the time I jumped into the surf at Coney Island one frigid New Year's Day? Would I eat one of the giant spiders, swallow the whole hairy body in a single gulp and spit a leg, just for effect? The answer was no. You know, I told the kids, tarantulas live twenty-five years. How could I eat something that lived twenty-five years? It would be like eating a cat. It was inhuman. Yeah, right, the kids scoffed, shaking their heads: big talker.

Luckily there was Happy Herb's. The first and still one of the only pizza parlors in Phnom Penh, Herb's pies really are happy, especially the sauce, which contains a secret ingredient that Herb, being happy, sometimes reaches for instead of the oregano. We were at Happy Herb's with Hurley Scroggins III, who should be a Dickens character with that name but is really an American expatriate from Santa Barbara. Pleased that we had remembered to bring him four bottles of Walker's Wood Olde Style Jamaican Jerk Chicken Mix, an item plentiful on Utica Avenue in Brooklyn but in short supply in Phnom Penh's marketplaces, Hurley had suggested Herb's, which is where he usually spends his evenings, drinking himself into proper expat oblivion.

After a couple of slices of the Khmer version of pepperoni, a general giddiness was coming on. Of course, it could have been the weekly dose of Larium. Before taking the malaria prophylaxis we had been alarmed by the many Internet reports of the drug's side effects, which reportedly included severe psychological reactions. People said a single Larium pill had induced panic attacks, depressions, even full-scale schizophrenia. For us, apparently somewhat more loosely strung in the neocortexial region than other families, Larium ingestion resulted primarily in a series of exceedingly vibrant dreams. We took our Larium on Wednesday mornings. On Thursdays, like a Jungian theater group, we spent the mornings discussing grand sagas of animal morphing, jaunts through hollow earth catacombs, and Billy's now weekly installments of the drama of the wicked clowns. At first the clowns, with their ever-changing hair color and bowties that were really coiled snakes, had Bill on edge. Once he woke up shaken. However, hearing that it was merely the effects of the drug, that he wasn't going crazy, Bill began to look forward to Larium nights, as if the chemical had been invented primarily for his amusement. Whether or not I was supposed to be concerned about this, I could not decide.

But it was Saturday, so it couldn't have been the Larium. Probably it was just that the pizza tasted so good. Really good. In fact, the kids agreed, this was *by far* the best pizza they had ever eaten, and we were from New York, which is famous for pizza, especially Joe's at the corner of Bleecker and Carmine Streets.

Happy Herb's left Joe's in the dust. We were well into the second pie when one of Hurley's acquaintances, Pauk of Phnom Kulen, happened by. Barely five feet tall, yet broad in the manner of a Samoan, his large head covered with a red-checked traditional Khmer scarf, the gap-toothed Pauk was a tree rustler. After his family had almost starved to death in the famines of the 1980s, he joined with one of the ad-hoc lumber gangs operating in the minefield-strewn landscape, cutting down large swaths of Cambodia's once-abundant forests. Careful to avoid competing Khmer Rouge loggers, Pauk and his crew made a good living selling teak to Thai and Vietnamese entrepreneurs. But now, with the hardwood forests largely gone and the environmentalist elements of the World Bank demanding the government stop the logging in exchange for the restoration of international loans, Pauk claimed he had retired from tree cutting. This was good, he said, because, when it came down to it, he loved trees more than the money he made chopping them down. He had grown up in the forest before the Pol Pot time and was happy that there was an effort to save it, even if he did not trust the government people, who, despite putting up banners saying "Love and protect forests" and "Trees, our future," Pauk swore maintained their own very active logging gangs.

As it was, the children were most interested in the ornate amulets Pauk wore on a thick string around his neck. Pauk explained in Khmer that each had a magical property, which was in turn translated by Herb, the happy pie maker.

"What's that one?" Billy asked, pointing to a bluish piece of what looked to be lapis.

"That is for tigers," Pauk related. It warded off tigers in the jungle.

"How about this?"

"Snakes!" Pauk said, rubbing a piece of green jade in his ruddy fingers. It kept away snakes.

There were others for disease, including three for malaria, none of which bore the slightest resemblance to a Larium pill.

"What about that one?" we asked, indicating a reddish stone.

"Oh, this one," Pauk said. "This is a special one. This one is for . . . you know . . . have you ever put something down, like a key, and then you cannot find it? This helps you."

Somehow, after two of Happy Herb's happy pizzas the idea of a toothless Cambodian tree rustler having an amulet to help him find his keys struck us as funny. So we laughed, which was a very good thing, especially here.

The roads in Cambodia, where they exist, are bumpy, prone to flooding and not so safe due to lurking bandits, which leaves two ways to get to Siem Reap, site of the great Angkor temples. There's the "speedboat," a six-hour-plus sojourn up the Mekong via the Tonle Sap, the nation's sacred lake; but these boats cannot be trusted, often sinking or running out of petrol, which makes them sitting ducks for lurking pirates. The better, and quicker way is Royal Air Cambodge which, like any other respectable national carrier, no longer flies rickety Fokker-28s or has the flight attendants collect creased and torn paper boarding passes to be reused. Still, things happen. Only a few months before our arrival a well-known local businessman (and rumored Golden Triangle dope smuggler), angered that the airline had lost his luggage, shot out the tires of his plane with a submachine gun. But we encountered no such difficulties.

As with many of the world's great ancient structures—the Mayan temples, the Pyramids, the Borobudur in Java, and many Indian palaces—Angkor is the product of multiple generations. A worker could be born with Angkor unfinished, spend an entire lifetime hauling stones through the jungle and die with the complex still unfinished. The fact that none of the project's planners lived to see the final product spoke to a kind of collective design that exceeded the solitary vision of any individual artist. These were God's buildings. They were supposed to last till the end of the world, and in the sense that they outlasted the cultures that invented them, they had.

Of course, we understood, as Rosalie, the activist, never failed to point out, that almost all these monuments had attained their eternalness through the labor of slaves, hundreds of thousands of captives who had no choice but to set one sacred stone on top of another. It was a harsh irony that many of the greatest works of man were nothing more than giant hard labor and death camps.

This way of thinking brought up a debate that would continue through the trip, and to a large extent onward until today. Did the fact that so much blood and toil of subjugated peoples—their bones often crushed right into the foundations—had gone into the creation of classic structures take away the awe we felt when viewing them? What human cost was acceptable in the creation of both beauty and utility?

It made us think of the great buildings of our own city.

I remember when Rae, probably four at the time, realized that the Zeckendorf Towers, one more cheesy yuppie pueblo cluttering up the New York skyline, would block the view of the Empire State Building we had always enjoyed while walking across Astor Place. Rarely had I seen her so angry. As symbols of the hometown went, we loved the Brooklyn Bridge, but nothing matched the Empire State Building. It was the most perfect of modern structures, rising to hitherto unreached heights in just two years of construction time, a record alacrity more in keeping with the lickety-split moral/spiritual time frame of the jazz age than the wide generational arc taken to put up earlier wonders of the world. We loved to go to the observation deck, especially on windy days. We walked out into the howl and spread our arms, waiting to be swept up into the sky. How wonderful would that be, flying over the city, especially since we were properly dressed in our down jackets. The Empire State Building belonged to us as much as it did to King Kong or the building's owner, Harry Helmsley, who was married to that awful woman, Leona, who once said, "taxes? Only little people pay taxes." Now our view of Empire was being blocked.

"Stupid, ugly buildings," Rae snarled, shaking her little fist at the still uncompleted Zeckendorf apartment houses. "I'm going to go up there and unbrick all its bricks and unhammer all its nails."

Years later, Rae's reaction would inform how Billy felt about the destruction of the World Trade Center. We were all shaken up, of course, but he took it the hardest. For him it was more than the outrage, more than the horror that several of the guys from the Engine 122 firehouse up the street—he played ball daily in their driveway—were now buried under all that steel.

The fact was, he loved the World Trade Center, as much as Rae and I ever loved the Empire State Building. This was a minority position, especially since, despite what people say now, the Twin Towers never were embraced by most New Yorkers. They were tall, yeah, but they had flat roofs. They didn't challenge the sky with mighty spires like the Empire State or Chrysler buildings, churches of capital but churches nonetheless. The World Trade Center, skulking about the edge of the skyline like kids too tall for their age, were just places to work. It figured that when they remade *Kong*, they had him climb these mundane shafts; it was a remake, after all.

For one reason or another, I never took Bill to the top of the Empire State Building, the way I did Rae and Rosie. Instead, he went to the top of the World Trade Center with his school. So, when Billy came to stand out overlooking the great city that was his home, the gusts of wind urging him to flap his arms and fly off into the sky, it was the drab, functionary World Trade Center that enabled his feeling of ultimate freedom. For that, he pledged undying devotion to the WTC. So on that day, when he stood on the roof of our Brooklyn house, staring into the smoke welling up across the river, Bill was stunned. How could an eleven-year-old boy have known the Twin Towers, unlike the Mayan temples and Egyptian pyramids, were not eternal? That they would not always be there?

Angkor, however, had survived Year Zero and a hundred other nightmares. The Angkor Wat, the central building of the vast complex, was the largest religious building in the world when it was built by King Suryavarman II in the twelfth century and it remains the world's largest religious building today.

Mr. Long, a thin, somber, soft-spoken man in his mid-thirties, was our guide. Until the relative political calm, the guiding services at Angkor tended to be ad hoc, usually consisting of a gaggle of eight-year-old boys tugging at your arm, screaming "Guide! Guide!" Asked what exactly they planned on showing you in the grand temple, or over at the Bayon with its massive smiling Buddha faces, these boys could only stare blankly. They knew little, if any, English. Establishing this, you would walk away, upon which they started tugging again, screaming, "Guide! Guide! Guide!"

Mr. Long was "a symbol of the New Cambodia . . . the Cambodia to be." Graduate of a year's study in the government's "tourist school," well versed in the study of Khmer antiquities, speaking a somewhat marble-mouthed but wholly serviceable English, Mr. Long was attired in a mountie hat and neatly ironed green uniform shirt bearing an official laminated badge. He looked as if he would have been at home behind the information desk at Yellowstone, or Carlsbad Caverns, a resemblance Mr. Long seemed well aware of, asking us the name of "the bear who says no forest fires."

"You mean Smokey?" the kids inquired.

"Yes, Smokey," Mr. Long said with a sly smile. "I am Smokey! The Khmer Smokey Bear."

Standing on the grand esplanade that spans the moat surrounding the temple, Mr. Long pointed toward the building's central tower. This was a representation of Mount Meru, which Mr. Long called "the temple mountain . . . the metaphor at the middle of the world." The kids should take a deep breath, look toward the great pinecone-shaped towers, and contemplate "the universe navel," said Mr. Long with a straight face. In this way, he said, they might come to understand "the great drama of the Khmer people."

There were particulars to be known about Angkor, Mr. Long said, leading us past the beggars and amputees who lined the imposing entryway. It was useful to appreciate the fact that the complex was 1.5 kilometers around and that the central tower stood 213 feet tall. But the "true heart" of the building, Mr. Long said, was in the sandstone bas-reliefs, scenes from the Hindu epic narrative the Ramayana, adapted by Khmer artists and spectacularly carved into the long, dank corridors of the huge temple.

"*The Churning Ocean of Milk,* it is very famous. Very famous," Mr. Long explained in his best tour guide–ese, pointing out the fifty-foot-long phantasmagoric scene on the wall in the eastern gallery.

"It is a story of redemption of the stinking world, to make the world new again . . . You see here: ninety-two demons and eighty-eight gods, all have hands on the giant serpent. Very long serpent. They pull on it, like a great tug-of-war rope. Back, forth. Back, forth. This stirs up the sea of milk, brings up the fresh milk. Otherwise, the milk turns sour. Poison. The fresh milk is the sweet taste. It is a battle which always goes on. Never stops, forever and ever. Sometimes the result is good, sometimes bad. We hope always for the good result."

Mr. Long addressed our attention to a segment of the incredible tableau. "Look, here, a best part. You see, the *apsaras,*

the celestial dancers . . . very beautiful dancers . . . springing
from the good milk, dancing in the air. This is a good result.
See how the rocks shine? That is because so many people have
touched here, for good luck. Look . . . you can see your face, a
reflection. People want to see themselves in the good result."

The Ocean of Milk showed the hopeful side of life, Mr. Long
said, but mostly the walls of the Angkor Wat were filled with
scenes of carnage. In the west gallery we saw the great victory of
Vishnu over the demons. An army of devils, riding in monster-
drawn chariots, marched toward the center of the panel. There
waited Vishnu, four arms flying, sitting atop the head of Garuda.
In the next panel, like in a colossal comic book, Vishnu's peacock-
feathered army was in the midst of dismembering their enemies,
chopping off their garish heads, casting them down to hell. In the
north gallery it was more of the same: Vishnu, reincarnated in the
guise of the thousand-headed Krishna, smashing the Demon King
Bana. The southern gallery depicted the plundering Skanda, god
of war, accompanied by his consort, Kubera, the many-armed god
of riches, advancing upon the huddled mass of hideous creatures.

Though these scenes were from myth, Mr. Long noted that
it would be wise not to consider the images on the Angkor walls
to be "dead, like in a museum." To him these pictures were alive,
"like a great pageant which does not stop."

To Mr. Long, this brutal pageant mirrored Cambodia's recent history. Indeed, it was only twenty-five years ago, in the
final days of the civil war, that Lon Nol's embattled troops, their
American backers long gone, had taken refuge inside the stone
walls of the Angkor Wat. Khmer Rouge forces surrounded the
temple and lobbed mortars over the walls. Eventually the Khmer
Rouge stormed the place, charging past the great reliefs, *The
Ocean of Milk* and the rest, with their AK-47s, red-checked scarves
around their heads. The fighting went on for some time, much
of it hand-to-hand combat.

"Right here, these demons fighting," Mr. Long said, pointing out a bullet hole in the wall. Outside you could see where Pol Pot's tanks had gouged Angkor's walls, but the tourist department had filled those up.

Back at our hotel, we invited Mr. Long in for a cold drink. We were staying at the Angkor Suites, on what used to be the outskirts of the rapidly growing town of Siem Reap. The Suites, or "the Sweets," as the menu in the restaurant had it, was a brand-new place. You could still smell the paint. A bullet-headed American expat from Omaha who'd arrived in Cambodia as "one of those NGO do-gooders" and stayed to form what he called "one of the biggest private security firms in Southeast Asia" had told us about the Sweets back in Phnom Penh. He'd organized the private army that had guarded the construction of the hotel, and rated a "serious discount," which he was happy to pass on to us.

Plus, the Sweets had a pool. "Best pool in Siem Reap," the security guy said. He'd overseen the concrete pouring himself. It was by the pool, drinking lemon sodas, that Mr. Long told us what it had been like to grow up in the former Democratic Republic of Kampuchea.

Born in Phnom Penh, Mr. Long said he thought he was thirty-three or thirty-four. His father was an engineer, his mother a teacher. It was a "good life" as a child, Mr. Long said, although he remembers little of it. What he did recall was the coming of the Khmer Rouge and "walking, walking, out of the city, into the countryside. My father was gone then. I didn't find out that he had been killed until later. My mother told me nothing." Later he said, "They would not let my mother eat. Working all the time and no food. She starved to death. My two brothers were killed. One shot. Other from disease. There were no doctors."

Things improved little after the 1979 Vietnamese invasion, which supposedly liberated the country. "My sister was still alive.

We went to a refugee camp near the Thai border. It was a very bad place. The KR rebels came there, to try to make us join with them and fight the Vietnamese. One time we escaped to Thailand, but the Thais did not want us. Police shot at us and made us go back. My sister and I had to walk through minefields to go back to Cambodia to be with the Khmer Rouge. There were bandits everywhere. Raping, stealing. . . ."

It was nothing to talk about, Mr. Long said, indicating the kids. "To grow up without knowing of these things is much better. They will make a bad memory."

Besides, it was over now. Pol Pot was dead. Ta Mok, Ieng Sary, and Khieu Samphan, all KR higher-ups, would soon be dead, whether they were tried for their crimes or not. Cambodia was becoming "another place." It was easy to see, especially in Siem Reap. After the 1997 coup during which Hun Sen ousted Prince Ranarith, son of King Sihanouk, there were no tourists. The hotels were empty, the airport deserted. Now everything was crowded. It was no big deal to eat lunch at the Bayon Restaurant and see a vacationing party of Japanese company men in identical straw hats with the word "Braintop" logoed on the crown drunkenly sing an a cappella version of "You Are My Sunshine." Although he was too old to realize his goal of becoming an engineer like his father, at least now Mr. Long could make a living as a tour guide. He was the father of two; this would keep his family going. To Mr. Long, this was the great miracle, that he had survived to have children.

Then Mr. Long said a strange thing. Asked if there were any KR people still around, he said he knew a lot of them. They were everywhere. Hun Sen, the president of the country, used to be KR. There were ex-KR people sitting in the lobby of the hotel right now. Some were his good friends.

"But they killed your parents," Rae blurted out, stunned, as we all were.

"That's true," Mr. Long replied, solemnly. "I will always suffer from that. I will always hate them for that . . . but those times, it was difficult to know what to do. People were swept up."

To hear him tell it, for Mr. Long the horror of the Khmer Rouge years, especially the evacuation of Phnom Penh, was not unlike the tumultuous scenes on the walls of the Angkor Wat. For him, the Ramayana myth world and his appalling childhood had merged together into an endless spectacle of approaching armies, heat and doom. Constant war left images of war. It was the same all over, Mr. Long said, referring to the scenarios of opposing alien fighters in the stack of video game magazines Billy had left on the table. The Ramayana was not all that different than Nintendo, Mr. Long noted, thumbing through the cartoons of virtualized Armageddon. Once what Mr. Long called "great forces" started up, they were very difficult to stop.

This was why he could tolerate, if not forgive, the KR, Mr. Long conveyed. It sounded as if he believed that many of the KR people, even the leaders, were in some kind of state of possession during those years. "It was more like they became the demons, but they weren't the demon. They acted in the role of the demon. Understand?"

Well, yes and no. It was a dense issue. Back in New York, after Rae delivered her Khmer Rouge paper, we'd talked about Cambodian genocide, and that is why both of us were so interested in it, reading all these books with titles like *How Pol Pot Came To Power*, watching the movie *The Killing Fields*. It came up that perhaps our interest might arise as a kind of avoidance of our own however marginal brush with genocide, the Nazi Holocaust. The numerous stories about survivors in the *New York Times Magazine* had always struck me, and now my daughter, as ultimately frustrating. Our reaction puzzled us. We certainly weren't inured to the nightmare of six million dead. We mourned the dead, and hated the Nazis. But perhaps we didn't hate them enough. We saw ourselves as citizens of the world. If we mourned the Jews who might have been our relatives more than fifty dead Tutsis or Armenians, what did that say about the limits of our humanity? In so many ways it was just easier to care about slaughtered Cambodians than our "own kind."

Now Mr. Long was throwing in another intractable problem: the nature of evil. Were people truly evil, or was evil freefloating, a virus in the atmosphere, which flared up in certain groups and situations, sweeping up individuals in its contagious pestilence? To hear Mr. Long describe the events of his youth, it was as if the entire population was thrust into a vast morality play from which there was no escape. Pol Pot and his crew were simply cast as the heavies.

The subject seemed to be exploding inside Rae's head. "But the Khmer Rouge were horrible!" she exclaimed. "Worse than the demons on the wall."

Mr. Long sighed. Who knew why people like Pol Pot were brought into the world? Cambodia had been very unlucky in the distribution of nightmares. Students of Khmer history would tell you the KR weren't the first apocalyptic clique to cause havoc in the country. Questions of collective karma came up; after all, what had such a small nation done to deserve such terror? It was confusing, Mr. Long said. It was difficult to seek revenge when you felt somehow inextricably part of the drama that produced the crime.

This was Mr. Long's attitude: the KR failed because they were cruel and selfish. But also because their thinking was flawed.

"They said Year Zero, they want to start over, from Year Zero. This is a wrong idea, to think the past can disappear. The beginning is not the beginning. Something is there before the start." This was something Mr. Long, who had lived through catastrophe, told his children, and now he told my children. What really mattered, Mr. Long said, was survival, that the "world was still here. After the end, no matter what happens, something is always left. So there can never be anything like Year Zero."

Mr. Long was not a millennialist. As he did not accept the Year Zero theory, he certainly, had the topic come up, would have eschewed Y2K. Sandwich-board shouters proclaiming the end of days caused him no alarm. He'd persevered through the apocalypse and had had children, a statement of faith about the future. Mr. Long was a firm believer in a round earth, a world where, if you kept going, the sun would come up again. This seemed a very good thing to believe in, especially for someone who had lived through the "flat earth" theory of Year Zero.

We were lucky to meet Mr. Long, we agreed. He inspired us. Indeed, as Rosalie would point out, quoting Professor H. Hozhabr Nejad and his *How To Learn Farsi in 29 Days?*, it was an excellent opportunity to "esteem the chance booty."

And so, that's what we were doing the very next day, our last in Cambodia, as we went over to the Ta Prohm temple for a second time. Built by King Jayavarman VII in the middle of the twelfth century, Ta Prohm was our favorite of the Angkor buildings. We liked it for the same reason everyone did: it hadn't been restored in the manner of Angkor Wat and the other temples. Several massive, sinuous banyan and fig trees had grown up around the structure, twisting amid the stone pillars and walls.

A couple of days earlier, during our first visit to Ta Prohm, Mr. Long had dutifully supplied his usual surfeit of facts and figures. "There are two hundred sixty statues of gods. Thirty-nine towers with pinnacles," Mr. Long intoned. In the temple's heyday "it was maintained by eighteen great priests, 2,740 officials, 2,202 assistants and 615 dancers. Property of the temple included golden dishes weighing more than five hundred kilograms, thirty-five diamonds, 40,620 pearls, 4,540 precious stones, 876 veils from China, 512 silk beds and 523 parasols." All this was verifiable on a twelfth-century plaque written in Sanskrit, which was still visible on one of the Ta Prohm walls.

But, of course, these numbers, however tremendous, did not represent "the true story" of Ta Prohm. "What do you suppose that is?" Mr. Long asked.

Billy knew. "If the trees weren't there, the temple would fall down and if the temple wasn't there, the trees would fall down."

This was an excellent answer, Mr. Long allowed. "They are together."

This was one more thing to remember from the land of Year Zero, we thought, climbing around Ta Prohm. We'd gone by ourselves this time. "You don't need me anymore, I told you everything I know," Mr. Long had said the night before. Besides, a planeload of tourists was coming in from Bangkok; he was booked. There was no lack of potential guides, however. The usual crowd of boys stood around, offering their services. One, a boy who walked with a limp, was particularly insistent.

"Here," the boy said, calling to us from a pitch-dark passageway deep inside the eight-hundred-year-old temple. Motioning us to be quiet, he assembled us in a small, claustrophobic chamber. One of the great banyan trees had pushed through this segment of the building, warping the laterite walls and opening a hole in the roof. A thin shaft of light filtered down from above.

The boy began to pound his fist into his chest. Perhaps it was a unique confluence of the occasionally concurrent geniuses of man and nature that produced the chamber's singular acoustics, but the sound of the boy's fist was much louder than could ever be expected. A deep thump filled the space. At our new guide's behest, we joined in, also beating our chests. A near-deafening polyrhythm echoed off the chamber walls.

"Your heart . . . a drum," the boy said, continuing to thump his chest. "You hear?"

"We hear," we screamed in unison, esteeming the chance booty all along.

Talkback/Backtalk # 2

by Rae Jacobson

So we went. Good days found us staring in touristical amazement at one fascinating world wonder or another, enjoying the company of newness and beauty with attitudes of adventure and discovery. Bad days found me lying on the bed in whatever given hotel howling a fractured rendition of "Sloop John B.," which goes, "I wanna go home . . . why won't you let me go home?" And then *with feeling, "This is the worst trip I've ever been on!"* This was particularly upsetting to my mother, who is a devoted Beach Boys fan.

I had been avoiding my family for a good two years now. I liked the vast amount of space and independence afforded me by my beloved New York City subway system, and took full advantage of it. The city held intense possibility and I'd just recently been given total freedom to enjoy it. New York was my heartbeat; the lights, noise, and people made me feel at home, and now I was very far away from there, very far away indeed. I was off on an alien planet, the only other inhabitants of which were my family. But horrifying as that thought was, it also held comfort. Not only was the idea of letting someone else plan for me relaxing (even if that someone was my father) but, when it came down to it, I'd missed them.

There, I admitted it. As much as I'd been hiding out, there are things only they know, inside jokes only they get. These people changed my diapers, for chrissakes.

Also we were travelers, people of movement. I have always entertained the thought that we are the single greatest troupe of trippers, if only because we have all been branded with the same sense of kitsch. I mean, who else would return not twice, but three times to Mitchell Corn Palace, which is a castle-like building in South Dakota constructed entirely from multicolored ears of corn, and still find it just as fab as the first time? We really loved that schmaltzy stuff. And somehow it only seemed right seeing it together. No one else exactly enjoyed it the way we did. We did these things, like throw a New York City subway token into a giant rock canyon in Arizona and sincerely expect that someone would one day find it and put it to good use.

I have always just accepted that the trips I've taken with my family have been the best possible. But they were always by car, in America, filled with such things as hour-long games of "A my name is Alice and I'm bringing applesauce . . ." and counting out-of-state license plates (still haven't seen an Alaska, after all these years). This was completely different. This wasn't comparing the food from roadside diners or mercilessly tormenting my father for his Elvis obsession (he once threatened to leave me by the highway in Montana if ever again I spoke ill of the King). This was more serious, more final. We were going to places unknown, beyond the comforts of the American borders, and I felt as if I was in too deep, drowning in the ubiquity of *them*.

My journal is punctuated with little notes such as *"Memo to self—Kill parents."*

My journal . . . that book was very important to me. I used it as an outlet for my feelings and after a while it became my only real release. I kept a list of things to do when I got home, ranging from things like "eat lots of cereal," "learn to walk in heels," "get another fake I.D.," to the more thoughtful "catch fireflies," and the just ridiculous, such as "clean my room." I counted the days we'd been away and the days until we returned.

Here are some excerpts:

Day 3, Thailand. *"I won't lie, I'm not extremely happy to be here. I kind of wish I were at home in the Village drinking coffee soda with my friends, not in Thailand with my family drinking pineapple juice, dressed like a giant grape in my purple clothes. My brother just walked in, turned off the air conditioner, threw an Oreo at me, said nothing, and left. My family is really odd. This is how it plays out to me; I'm a sixteen-year-old girl on the other side of the world from everything I know, armed only with Pepto-Bismol, lip gloss, a guidebook and a really bad cold. Help me, I'm going to die."*

Day 5, Thailand. *"We're on a boat-taxi passing all these really beautiful buildings, and I'm finding that it's really hard to accept that this is NEW. I mean new in the weirdest possible way. In New York everything always looks somewhat familiar even if you've never been there before. But this is new. Too new. I love exploring, but only when I know where I'm going. Strange, I know."*

I wrote about everything I saw. I was hoping to bring it back filled with descriptions that would evoke mental pictures of the places we went, but nothing could describe Tuol Sleng. Usually I vehemently avoid such things; I've never been the kind to stop and stare at a car crash or watch *Schindler's List*. The year before I wrote a paper on the Khmer Rouge for history class, and found out no one in my class even knew it had happened. It was not in our textbook; in short, as far as the Board of Ed. knew or cared, it had never happened. I've always thought that one of the points of learning history is to keep it from repeating itself, and how could a holocaust that had happened only twenty years prior be ignored? I wrote more papers, did presentations, forced teachers to rent *The Killing Fields* and then cut the class when they watched it, because I can't take the violence. So when we were finally in Cambodia and there was the option of going to see a part of the history I'd been fascinated by, I had to go. Sometimes, descriptions are pointless. My journal entry from that day is the best explanation I have.

Day 14, Cambodia. *"Oh god. Today we went to Tuol Sleng. I have never seen anything like that before and I will never see anything like that again if I can help it. Ten minutes in that place was enough to reduce me to tears, and I rarely cry. I HATE people. I really do. How could someone do this? There are pictures on the walls of people holding numbers like mug shots in one room and then the next room has just case after case of skulls. I was almost sick. Words cannot describe this place; pictures won't take you there and make you feel it. I'm still nauseous. I wonder if things will ever seem the same after this."*

So it went. Every morning I woke half expecting to be home, and every morning I was in another strange place I never imagined I'd ever be. At one point I made a list of pros and cons, trying to organize myself somehow. They were as such:

Day 23 . . . *"Thinking about the good parts and bad parts of this trip.*

PRO: It will help me get into college.
CON: I feel like crap.

PRO: I should be really happy.
CON: I'm really sad.

PRO: We eat out every night.
CON: Most of the time I don't know what I'm eating.

PRO: I get to see my family.
CON: I have to see my family.

PRO: It will probably get better.
CON: It better get better.

PRO: No chance of getting my heart broken this summer.
CON: No chance of having a boyfriend this summer.

PRO: I'm trying new things.
CON: I crave familiarity.

PRO: I have a lot of time to think.
CON: I have no one to talk to."

Roof of the World

I t is another twenty-year-old story, time of another time, eleven thousand feet up in the Nepali Himalayas near Tatopani, which means "hot water," on account of the thermal springs that bubble out of the ground there. This is opposed to Ghorepani, "cold water," the desolate settlement where we'd spent the previous night huddled around a potbellied stove along with a bunch of smelly, raggedy-haired hippies. My wife and I were walking the Jomson trail, a three-week stroll that took us past Machupuchare, Nepal's sacred fishtail-shaped peak, through to Muktinath, north of Annapurna.

Nowadays, two decades deeper into the Nepali tourist trade, the Jomson, never all that taxing, is kind of a Himalayan Appalachian Trail, complete with interstate-style pull-overs every few kilometers so everyone can show off their sleek new equipment. However, in the days before North Face became Snoop Dogg's winter wear of choice, the Jomson was funkier. You could get by with a Sears sleeping bag, a couple of space blankets and some itchy local knit socks. For harder climbs, there was pharmaceutical-grade Dexedrine available over the counter in most of Nepal's finer apothecaries. It was enough to get you over the next ridge before dark. If not, you could always sleep with the yaks.

Tatopani was the R&R capital of the trail. Climbers checked into one of the tiny, beat-up lodges and quickly lost the will to go higher, sometimes staying for weeks at a stretch. At Tatopani, a pair of less motivated hikers could spend hours making love in earth-heated pools as locals engaged in slash-and-burn farming on the other side of the river, flames spreading out across the rolling hillside in the shape of a gigantic V. Back at the lodge, stern-faced university agronomists warned of the environmental backwardness of this agricultural technique, the way it led to terrible erosion, flooding and potential famine. But cuddling in those pools, ashes pelting down like black leaves, sizzling when they touched the surface of the water, was a fun kind of love among the ruins.

This was how it was, above the tree line. The consequence of acts, the future itself, seemed very far away. Things were too sexy to be burdened with the weighty freight of procreation. Besides, we already had a son, of sorts.

Humbador was his name and we'd met him in the village of Naudanda, about a week down the trail from Tatopani. We were making our way up the hundreds of stone stairs, so much steeper than our St. Marks Place walkup, when he appeared from the mist, offering to carry our packs. Exhausted, we accepted. Humbador put both bags on his head and ran off, disappearing over the ridge.

"Shit," we noted, almost too tired to care. "That kid just stole our stuff."

It wasn't until we reached the village that we saw him again, in front of a tumbledown guest house, which happened to be owned by his uncle. He'd already taken the liberty of checking us in, placing our packs on the hard wooden pallets that passed for beds.

No more than five feet tall, with a Beatles-cut bowl of black hair and dark, shining eyes, he said he was sixteen but was probably closer to twelve. If we were planning on trekking the

Annapurnas, we'd need a porter, Humbador told us. It was two weeks more to the top, plus it was easy to get lost. He'd been up there dozens of times and knew the way, he claimed, brashly chewing on a four-inch-long cheroot. Five dollars a day and food was the going rate. There was no better porter in all Nepal, he said.

Well, sure, we said, but hadn't we better talk to his parents first? Wouldn't they miss him?

"No," Humbador said. He was "a Chetri man," a member of a high caste. He was born in the mountains; he didn't need his mother's permission to walk among them.

In any event, Humbador added, his parents were not in Naudanda. He lived with his uncle, the innkeeper. We could ask him, the boy said, for all the good it might do. Expecting to die at any moment, the old man did nothing but sit in a corner and chant, in the hopes that these last-minute entreaties might improve his future positioning in the next life. We'd have to take his word for it, Humbador said.

So, Humbador became our guide, leading us into the semi-wild, through Berethani, Ghasa, Marfa and the rest. With his nonstop punkish swagger and strutting good humor, we loved him, especially while trekking through the desolate mile-wide Kali Gandaki valley, where he donned the headphones of our Walkman and sang along with Elvis Costello, his hoarse Nepali elocution of "What's So Funny 'bout Peace, Love and Understanding" melding with the wind shear and clattering bells of approaching donkey caravans.

Humbador's discourse lives on in our family lexicon even now, especially as it pertained to plumbing. In Ghasa, one of the gamier stops along the trail, Humbador returned from the outhouse and, finding the sanitary conditions lacking even by his relaxed standard, said, "The toilet . . . is . . . no."

This shorthand continues to work for us, and not simply in roadside gas stations. Whole thought constructs, entire groups of people can be dismissed with a simple "is . . . no," as in "That dude is . . . no." We also retain Humbador's commentary on drinking, uttered upon consuming too much *raksi*, the Nepali homebrew. "My mind," he said, dark eyes spinning in deep-set sockets, "is going out."

The original plan was to get to Muktinath, then decide whether or not to try to make it to the Chinese border where the Mustangi people were. Some hippies claimed to have gotten up there, flaunting Mustangi jackets with swastika-embossed buttons as proof. However, after four days holed up in a mud hut in Marfa with the runs, long enough to track through large swaths of Frank Herbert's endless *Dune* trilogy, these plans were scrapped. Suddenly the battered Royal Nepali DC-3 sitting on the tarmac at Jomson, due to depart for Pokhara the next morning, looked mighty tempting. The question was, what to do about Humbador? He was supposed to guide us back down the mountain.

No problem, said Humbador. He would walk back alone. All the real porters walked back alone. Just give him his five bucks a day and extra for food.

It wasn't until that evening that we realized Humbador's true feelings concerning our imminent departure. Tears in his eyes, he confessed that he wasn't quite telling the truth when he said he'd been to Muktinath "many times." Actually, this was the first time he'd ever been past Tatopani. He'd been strutting around with his cigars like a pint-sized straw boss, lording his Chetri pedigree over grown-up men and women. But now, faced with the idea of having to walk home alone, he looked, for the first time, like a little boy.

"I am thinking to Naudanda," he said, mournfully. "But it is far. And I've heard there are tigers in the forest."

He put his head on my wife's shoulder and cried. "My uncle is old," moaned Humbador, mentioning the man for the first time since we left. "He worries and wonders if he will ever see me again."

There was no other choice. We couldn't leave Humbador up there by himself. We forked over the extra forty dollars, and took him back with us on the Royal Nepali flight.

It was, of course, the first time Humbador had ever flown in a plane. Outside of the occasional droning speck in the sky, he hadn't even ever seen a plane. Face glued to the window so as not to miss Naudanda as we passed over it, Humbador shared his seat with a pair of goats, which for him was the only normal part of the experience. We got the pigs. The trip was quick: it took two and a half weeks to walk up and twenty minutes to fly down.

Back in Pokhara, a mere day's walk from Naudanda, Humbador's self-assurance returned. He shook our hands formally and took a few steps toward home before turning around and giving us giant hugs. That out of the way, he started up the mountain again, a "Chetri man" once more.

Twenty years later, we wondered if that jaunt in the sky had shifted the course of Humbador's life, possibly even leading him into a career in aviation. Who knew, maybe that was him, with the golden epaulets, at the controls of the Royal Nepali 757 that flew us from Bangkok to the Kathmandu airport.

Then again, he could be dead. He'd be in his mid-thirties by now and people in the Himalayan foothills didn't live all that much past forty. He could be dead and reborn by now. In Nepal everyone who was someone used to be someone else, once upon a time. This was the way it was in places where they believed in reincarnation. You never knew who'd been whom.

As a parent, this brought up issues. The intellectually alluring concept of reincarnation seemed to be a contradiction to the general rules of evolution. If, as many Buddhist and Hindu beliefs have it, souls are subject to the eternal ordering and reordering of karma, with an individual's fate depending on the "imprint" of good and bad deeds, didn't this undercut the notion that a person's heredity is determined by the supposedly disinterested genetics of their forebears? If the human offspring primarily consisted of a reshuffling of existing traits with a few wildcard mutations thrown in, how could one guage the mysterious effect of karma on family trees and the viscous sap of DNA that ran through them?

It is an unsettling thought, especially when confronting the question of *whose* karma energizes the soul of a child. As presented in the *Tibetan Book of the Dead,* a main text of reincarnate philosophy, *bardo,* the forty-nine-day-long state of "in between" during which the soul leaves a dead body and enters another "womb door," appears to be a fluid zone, abiding by no earthly determined confines as to nuclear family lines or even the perimeter of an extended clan. That means, as far as I understand it, that you never exactly know which soul is about to come knocking on that womb door, flinging itself over the threshold, which is a whole new way of looking at your children, or the people you thought were your children.

They could be anyone! Mexicans. Uzbeks. People from China. Illegal aliens. There could even be invaders from other species, hairy primates and those hailing from even lower orders and genera, who, through uncounted generations of karmic permutation, landed a seat in the back of your car, a place at your dinner table. The weird part is: they still look like you. Rae has my mother's eyes, Rosie my wife's coloring, and Billy my general bone structure. But this could all be a trick, a series of masks. Who knew the true identity of these room noncleaners, these showerless interlopers, these backtalking ghosts in the machine. Who were they really, down deep, and where had they come from?

Vexed by these issues, I explained my concerns to no less than His Holiness the Dalai Lama, whom, I imagined, might know something about the topic, being widely regarded as the four-teenth reincarnation of the Tibetan head of state. It was on an-other trip, at another time, a thirty-two-hour car ride from Delhi to McLeod Ganj in Dharmasala, where the exiled leader has lived since fleeing the Chinese in 1959. I was supposed to interview him. But you can't go to see the Dalai Lama without bringing him a present, or at least I'd been told it wasn't polite. Before leaving Brooklyn I was stumped, because what could I bring the D. L. that his movie star admirers like Richard Gere and Harrison Ford hadn't already given him? Then it came to me, standing in front of a sporting goods store a block from my house.

A Brooklyn Dodgers hat—the storied lid of Jackie Robin-son, Duke Snider, Campy and Pee Wee, a snow-white *B* set against a sky of blue: it seized me like a line drive of an epiphany. So many memories were conjured up: Happy Felton's knothole gang, the lone series victory, but mostly walking to Ebbets Field with my grandfather, the baseball fan, who lived with my grand-mother on Franklin Avenue and Eastern Parkway, only six blocks from the stadium.

At first the Tibetan leader seemed not to recognize the ob-ject, regarding it with wary curiosity from behind thick bifocals, fingering the brim with large hands and polished nails. His Ho-liness listened carefully as I explained, detailing the rudiments of the game of baseball ("a man with a stick hits a ball thrown by another man . . ."). More to the point was the fate of the Dodgers, wearers of the B. Just as his own Galupa sect were known as the yellow hats when they ruled from the Potala in Lhasa, this was the emblematic headwear of a group of individuals who were driven from their rightful place by the evil one, in this manifesta-tion, a man named Walter O'Malley, the Dodger's owner, who moved the team from Brooklyn to Los Angeles. I explained how New Yorkers considered him the fourth worst man of the twenti-eth century, close behind Hitler, Stalin and, of course, Mao.

"Ah-ha!" the Dalai Lama said, smiling widely as he took the hat from my hand and slapped it onto his head. "B for Buddhist!" he said, another wide smile crossing his face. "These men, these Dodgers, they are exiles from their rightful place, like Tibetans!"

"Yes!" I shouted. "You got it, exactly right!" I guess that is why he is the Dalai Lama and the rest of us are not.

Unfortunately, the D. L. did not appear so intuitive pertaining to the apparent conflict between reincarnation and genetic reproduction. For instance: were souls produced at the same rate as bodies? Over the past several decades the world population had exploded. The birth rate exceeded the death rate. Did this mean that many people were born without a soul ready to enter their mother's womb door? Did this mean that many people were literally soulless? Did this account for the spiritual crisis of modern man?

These were all good questions, the Dalai Lama said. But, as his assistant made clear, my interview was over. It was time for His Holiness's nap. Grabbing my hand, the Dalai Lama thanked me once more for the hat, and told me to go to the institute of Buddhist Dialectics, just down the road, and put my questions to them. Unfortunately the institute was closed. I wrote out my questions, slipped them under the thick wooden door, but have yet to receive a reply.

I was thinking of these things and Humbador, too, as I watched Billy smash a few hundred spaceships to smithereens. Blam! Those gnarly space invaders had no chance once the B-man and his itchy trigger finger drew a bead on them.

We'd been in Kathmandu only twenty-four hours, and had already found the only video parlor in town. The game was pre-Edison by New York standards, an antediluvian "alien versus predator" gizmo with dim graphics on a pixel-scarred display and only one working blaster/controller. But Bill was hot. Sweat-stained New York Knicks Eastern Conference Champions hat perched at a rakish ghetto angle on his head, he'd already racked up the fifth highest score ever recorded on the battered machine, with the top number, set in 1998 by someone named "Mad Raj 2," well in sight.

Bill had drawn a crowd. With each exploded space invader, the dozen or so scruffy children, some teenagers but others no older than seven or eight, sent up a cheer. Kathmandu was full of street kids these days, and judging from the pile of blankets shoved beneath the unfunctioning Streetfighter machine, the video parlor, located on the third floor of a vertical mall filled with auto parts stores, photography studios and chapati bakers, was currently serving as a resting place for several of the youths.

This had been the case since we got to Asia. Everywhere we went, there were homeless children. In Phnom Penh they were everywhere, roving bands, some without arms or legs. In Bangkok they lived behind buildings, cooking over campfires, like little hobos.

Having grown up on St. Marks Place, the kids were used to street people. They knew all the neighborhood fixtures, like the guy who stood outside the Gem Spa candy store screaming he was "the human radio, operating on station W-I-N-O." And the strange, skinny woman who was only seen in public wearing a football helmet and a scarf wrapped around her face, a most idiosyncratic *burka*.

There was also the Tree Man, our favorite, who never went anywhere without adorning himself with several large branches, arranged so it appeared that they were growing out of his head. Once, when the TV weathermen were going on about a summer drought, the children became concerned about the Tree Man. Seeing him coming down the street from our fourth-story window, they grabbed a bottle of Poland Spring and ran outside.

It was so hot and dry, did the Tree Man need watering, they wondered. No, the Tree Man replied, with his usual gentle smile, a giant ailanthus branch protruding from the back of his jacket. "The Tree is cool. The Tree is green and growing! But thanks anyway, kids."

Still, no matter how marginalized, how crazy, how stoned, these street people were grown-ups. When things got really rough, they could fend for themselves, get food, go to the shelter. But here, in The World, it was different, these were kids in the street, and there were no shelters, no choice.

"It is like they are waiting to have their picture taken and put on the wall at another Tuol Sleng," Rae said with pained gloom. To her the genocide was continuing. One of her Larium dreams depicted an army of children, walking toward her, their bodies literally dissolving as they came closer, until there was nothing but a pile of dust at her feet. Rosie felt the same way. Those were the days they didn't want to come out of the hotel.

Billy's reaction was not unlike his sisters'. In Phnom Penh he asked one of the kids, no more than seven, why he had a rusty screwdriver stuck in his pants. After much language misconnection, it turned out that the kid used the screwdriver to corner and kill rats. The implication was that these kids cooked and ate the rodents. Bill couldn't believe it. Eating rats to stay alive! There were plenty of rats in New York, but most of the ones we saw were in the subway stations, running alongside the tracks. Maybe they were deaf from the train clatter but no one ate them, that we knew of. Yet these kids, these potential rat-eaters, were barely ten, twelve at the most. Billy wondered what he'd do if the roles were somehow reversed; would he be able to ram that screwdriver between a rat's shoulder blades, keep pushing until it was dead? Back home, kids were bragging about their sneakers, making a big deal out of getting three or more inches off the ground on their skateboards, like this was supposed to prove something. Here seemed to be a tougher, truer hip-hop nation, unrestrained, and way, way over the edge.

So it felt good, Billy said, to have the street kids of the video parlor crowd cheering. He felt like he was playing for them, these poor souls who would never march in the Park Slope Halloween parade, or play in the Seventy-Eighth Precinct basketball league.

Billy would probably have surpassed Mad Raj 2's record if it hadn't been for those sadhus. Three of them, seemingly also sleeping at the video parlor, joined Bill's peanut gallery. The B didn't like it. The sadhus' proximity adversely affected his game. A number of alien invaders, previously stopped cold, were getting through.

Back home we had spoken of sadhus, the Hindu religious ascetics who roam the Indian subcontinent, often dressed in saffron-colored robes, with long beards, face paint and walking sticks. Nothing if not eccentric in devotional behaviors, these holy men were known to anchor themselves to trees on hillsides and not speak for a dozen years. They would lie down on hot coals, stick great metal rods through their skin and perform all manner of self-flagellating hijinks. One particular subset was known for dragging along hundred-pound rocks that they lashed to their penises. We'd seen these guys, Bill and I, on the Internet, before leaving New York.

"Gross," Billy said, barely able to look at the screen. "Why would you do that?"

"They do it to show their faith," I replied, none too authoritatively.

"Faith in what?"

"Well . . . you know . . . what they'll go through to show how much their devotion to their idea of God. . . . You know, people going to churches and synagogues . . . they have some pretty strange rituals, too."

Billy gave me that dismissive sneer he's been working on. He'd been to several houses of worship and never once seen a guy with a boulder tied to his nuts.

"Doesn't that stuff hurt?"

"That's the idea, to build up enough mental willpower to ignore the pain."

"I thought pain was the body's warning system that something was wrong. That's what they taught us in health."

"Yeah . . . that's right," I agreed. "But sadhus are kind of extreme. Most people in India and Nepal are not like that. Most of them are pretty much like us."

"I guess," Billy said, unconvinced. Long before fundamentalism would impinge dramatically on his life, the notion of God and the lengths humans go to to demonstrate Oneness with Him was a difficult concept for Bill. As opposed to his sister Rae and several of his Dungeons and Dragons–centric friends, he was not a dreamy kid. He didn't believe in things he couldn't see. People who did made him nervous.

Luckily, these particular video parlor sadhus, apparently part of a more urbanized, modernist sect, came equipped with no burning coals, no rocks hanging from their penises. Ratty dreadlocks hanging over wraparound bubble shades, they could be seen around town riding their 120cc Honda bikes, looking more like a subcontinental version of the Jamaican bobsled team than living simulacra of Vishnu.

"Your son, he is an excellent player," said one sadhu, offering me a sliver of *papadum*. "Has he learned this from you?"

Actually no, I had to admit. I'd wasted the better part of a few college semesters playing pinball, but did not make the transition to electronic games. I couldn't even rack up a decent Pac-Man score. It was a generational thing; I wasn't hooked up for video.

"Still, you must be very proud," the sadhu said—to have raised such a consummate joystick manipulator.

"Oh, yes," I replied, like an eager ninny. Parents are such suckers when someone, anyone, compliments their kids, for anything.

Eventually, though, enough aliens got through. He went down fighting, but Bill's game was over.

"Those sadhu guys were bothering me. They threw off my concentration," he groused, declining to play again.

The girls were upstairs at Chitra's Beautiful Serene Stop getting their legs waxed as part of the one-hundred-rupee, full-treatment special. Who knew how long that would take, so Bill and I went for a stroll about old Kathmandu, walking the Dharmapath, past the flute and sweater sellers, the dung piles and the massive slope-roofed temples.

We were looking for the dentist. It was Billy's idea. I'd told him the dentist story, and now he wanted to find the guy. This tale dated back to when my wife and I were here. I had a toothache. It was a molar, the filling was cracked and I figured I'd have to have it fixed sooner or later, preferably later, like back in New York. Except it was killing me.

It seemed a grim joke, going to a dentist in Nepal. Their offices, were almost always in medieval, trash-strewn back alleys, with cartoonish paintings of bucky beaver-like choppers on swinging saloon-style overhead signs. What a bad idea, opening wide for one of these croakers. Why not simply tie a rope to the offending tooth and slam the door? But a friend of ours, a mossy-toothed Brit (should have been the tip-off), said this particular guy, Dr. Ramesh, was all right. He'd been trained in Bombay, as if that was supposed be a recommendation, and kept a handy canister of laughing gas, the contents of which he was not shy about dispensing.

A stocky man in a pale blue smock, exuding a thick smell of eucalyptus, Dr. Ramesh was sitting in his basement office, which was just big enough for a dental chair, a table for his instruments, and a drill dangling from what appeared to be a homemade pully system. Of course, he would see me, he said. He had plenty of time. "It is not such good business to be a dentist in a country of so many totally toothless individuals," he said, lamenting his homeland's poor dental hygiene.

Yes, Dr. Ramesh said, my filling was very definitely cracked and should be fixed immediately, lest I need a "rut canal." Preparing to operate, he told me I might feel more vibration than I was used to. High-speed drills had not yet come to Nepal at the time.

As a drill-bit the size of an unsharpened number-two pencil point ground into my enamel, the electricity went off. The room was thrown into pitch darkness. This was not a particularly unusual occurrence in Kathmandu in 1980. The power functioned only on alternate days, but not always the same alternate days, depending on what section of town you happened to be in. Dr. Ramesh was prepared, however. He lit a candle and asked me to open wide. No reason to stop now; the tooth needed attention.

Looking up from the chair into the chiaroscuro, Dr. Ramesh appeared to me as a massive, goggled frog, the gleam from the single flame glinting off his metal dental probe. But it wasn't until a drop of hot candle wax fell on my lower lip that I bolted. The promise of laughing gas notwithstanding, I told the doctor that perhaps the tooth wasn't bothering me so much after all.

This became my Third World dental story, one I've told to periodontists and endodonists alike over the years, mostly to delay whatever nightmare procedure they had planned for me. I take it as a testament to the mobility of travel tales that only last year I encountered a dentist at a social function who told me my same story back to me, saying he'd heard it from a friend. The recitation was very close, almost word for word, except transported to Xi'an, in China.

As it turned out, Billy and I could not locate Dr. Ramesh's office. That was too bad; I would have been interested to see how business was going, whether he'd acquired a Mr. Thirsty and what kind of insurance he took. But no matter. The fact is Bill and I just like to walk around. We don't need a particular place to go.

Back when he was two and three, we'd stock up on Reese's Peanut Butter Cups, get on the subway and spend hours looking out the window of the front car. Or we'd drive over to Coney Island, our promised land, to the beach and the derelict amusement park, happy to be strolling along the deserted boardwalk in winter with bags of steaming french fries in our hands. Sometimes, on the way back, we'd stop under the massive span of the Verrazano Bridge, where the Bensonhurst boys, preteens of the type once called "hitters," collected horseshoe crabs which they flung through the frigid air like prehistoric Frisbees, smashing open the shells of the ancient animals just to see their iron-free blood.

"It's fucking *blue*," they marveled, in their early Travolta way.

We went anywhere. We walked through Queens, all the way uptown in Manhattan, into Inwood Park where the last of New York City's virgin forests (a couple of trees, really) grow and the bums live in caves watching rabbit-eared TVs powered by stolen electricity. We walked outside the city, too, along the Louisiana back roads of the Bayou Teche where moss hangs down from cypress trees, and through the jutting geology of Monument Valley, where John Ford shot Westerns that told a man how to be a man. Monument Valley was cool. At the hotel store they sold rolls of toilet paper with John Wayne's face on every sheet, along with the legend, "The Duke don't take crap off just any butty." This is one of the reasons we like to walk alone, Bill and I, because, when it comes down to it, girls just don't think poop jokes are funny.

*   *   *

Some fathers I've known went crazy if they didn't have any boys. Someone to toss the old football around with, to carry on the family name, the family jewels.

Years ago, in a sketchy section of Oakland, California, I lived upstairs from a guy named Richard who had five daughters. He loved them, but it was driving him nuts, all those girls. "Zero for five, what's up with that?" he wanted to know. At the suggestion of a pipe-fitter friend of his who lived across the street, he went to a "love doctor," a voodoo roots woman with a crystal ball in her living room over in Emeryville, across the street from a manhole cover manufacturer.

"'When you screwing, day or night?'—that's what she asked me," Richard reported. "I told her I was screwing in the night. "'*The night!*' she screamed, throwing up her hands, 'Well, there's your problem! You ain't gonna get no boys screwing in the night! Don't you know the night is luna-time? When the women rule. The manchild is conceived in the sunlight! You want a boy you got to put a boy in there. You got to screw in the day!'"

Actually, Richard confided, he did not like to screw in the day. To him, the nighttime was the right time. But he followed the advice of his love advisor, rushing home every lunch hour from his job as a maintenance man at Oakland City Hall. "I'm doing it," he said, "screwing in the day." Nine months later his first son was born. Pointing to the squalling boy, Richard smiled proudly and handed me a cigar. "High noon," he said, with a thumbs up.

Throughout my wife's pregnancy with Billy, the old ladies in our building, assuming I was desperate for a male heir, said I should relax, because it was definitely going to be a boy. "Because she is carrying high. High is always boy," said Mrs. Showty, the Ukrainian lady with the two tubby kielbasa-fed dogs. The next apartment, Mrs. Benante, born in Sicily, agreed. "Boy! Definitely boy," Mrs. Benante said, leading with yet another bowl of (fabulous) meatballs. "She is carrying low. I know what I'm talking about. Low is a boy, every time."

As for myself, my line was I didn't care. Ying, yang, it was all one big swirling mesmerist mandala to me. I held no brief with the red-meat prejudices of the faux-Hemingway contingent and their semenological obsessions.

Girls were cool. Girls were great. Girls were true. Little girls always loved their dads. It was hardwired. They imprinted themselves on Dad pheromones and later on in life sought men whose aromatic aura reminded them of their fathers. I'd often heard that. It was no small responsibility, being the first man in their lives, the template for their interaction with the sexual Other. But it was a responsibility I was prepared to bear. To have another girl with two already in hand did not strike me as zero for three, but rather as a hat trick.

Besides, my wife, who had a sister and no brothers, was leery of boys. It was her stated fear that snips and snails and puppy dog tails inevitably mutated to beers and leers and hairy bellies yowling about being ready for some football. Down deep, she said, she didn't think herself capable of creating a boy, as if there was a chip missing in her male-making machinery.

Early on the day Billy was born, before my wife went to the hospital, my daughters and I took a walk around the neighborhood, down to Houston Street and then back around to Tompkins Square Park. The often volatile park, home to 101 varieties of temperate zone trees, all of which have been pissed on more or less constantly by mangy neighborhood dogs for the past 150 years, was a pivotal piece of real estate in our family's American procession.

In 1902, a now long-ago demolished tenement on East Seventh Street on the park's southern edge served as the first safe haven in the New World for my father's mother, my beloved grandma Sue, whom my sister and I always called Grandma Sugar. She was born in a small village in Bassarabia, near the border between Russia and Romania. The Romanians had forced her father, Alfred, from whom I'd received my long-hated middle name, to fight in their army. After being gone for three years, he managed to get out. Soon the Russians arrived, claiming that the border had changed, and now, as a proud citizen of Mother Russia, he would have to fight in their army. If he didn't like it, they said, the Cossacks knew where to find him.

"That was it," my grandmother told me, explaining how her parents stuffed the children into potato sacks so the Cossacks wouldn't see them, put them on a wagon and headed for Constantsa on the Black Sea. "I was four years old but I remember it like it was today. My father said to stay inside that sack and keep my mouth shut. It seemed like weeks that I was in there, bouncing up and down in that cart. To get out of Romania I had to pretend to be a potato!"

It was months in steerage, through the Dardanelles, the Mediterranean, and finally across the Atlantic, but it worked, my grandmother said. She loved to tell me of those first days in America, the sights and smells on the teeming streets of the Lower East Side. First they lived on Rutgers Street, farther downtown, but the building burned down in the middle of the night. So they moved to Seventh Street, not too far from her father's favorite Yiddish theaters on Second Avenue.

Grandma was about six when what she would call "the incident" occurred. She was playing in Tompkins Square when she was approached by a man she always referred to as "olive-skinned, with a thick moustache and hair on the back of his hands."

"He had a big black cloth bag," my grandmother recalled, always with a shiver. "He chased me. If he'd caught me, I don't know what would have happened. There were many stories of

girls being kidnapped back then, and shipped off to be slaves in
foreign countries. So I kept running, for blocks, until the man
disappeared. I remember thinking, I came to this country in a
bag, but I am *not* leaving in one."

From then on, my grandmother said, she avoided Tompkins
Square Park, refusing to play there, a fact she never failed to bring
up whenever she came to visit me on St. Marks Place. After more
than three quarters of a century in America, Grandma Sugar said
with dismay, she would have hoped that our family had come
farther than living a block and a half from her 1902 cold-water
flat. What was wrong with Cedarhurst? Woodmere had a very
strong temple, too, plus everyone drove new station wagons. Was
I too good for the Five Towns? Great Neck had very good schools,
too, she had heard.

"Beatnik, shmeatnik," Grandma Sugar said, whenever we
said we liked living on the Lower East Side because that was
where the artists were. "Forget these dirty painters already,"
she'd reply with a sigh, because even if she spent twenty-five
years selling baby clothes at the Kameo Children's Shoppe in
Crown Heights, she was also a painter in the Impressionist style.
Her Eastern Parkway apartment was full of the canvases she'd
never show to anyone, because "this is not anything serious to
be done with a life."

Nowadays, I think of my grandmother and her generation
of my relatives as the Titans of our family. These were the people
who emerged from the chaos of the old, other world. Traveling
on a one-way ticket, grimy stevedores shoveling coal into furnaces
not ten feet from their bedrolls, they arrived in the Olympus of
America and never looked back.

The Old Country cast shadows—and how could it not?—
but I never heard much talk about it. As far as my tender ears
were allowed, the world began for these people the day they
got to New York. The city was their own personal cut-rate

Emersonian Acadia, the perfect place for people like us. It was here that the great characters of the family played out their particular dramas, made their marks.

My favorite was always Uncle Larry, one of my grandfather's many brothers. The day my grandfather brought my grandmother to meet his family, Uncle Larry gave them a ride in his new Pierce-Arrow, reaching speeds of forty miles per hour on the narrow Lower East Side streets, knocking over many pushcarts as he went, just to hear the screams. My grandmother thought Larry was a bully and a fool, but my grandfather looked up to his older brother as a real operator. Once he won a Cadillac in a crap game. The next day, a uniformed chauffeur brought the car around to Larry's tenement home.

"Well, thanks," Larry said, handing the chauffeur a tip and waving good-bye. "Oh, you don't understand," the chauffeur said, "I comes with the car."

There was another time, Larry threw seven and won a Chinese restaurant, Joy Gardens on Mott Street. He lost it back a couple of weeks later, but for decades after, whenever anyone in the family wanted a bowl of Yat Gaw Mein, we went to Joy Gardens. The place is still there, even if the name has been changed half a dozen times. A few years ago there was a big shootout in the doorway of the restaurant. The *New York Post* ran a picture of a sixteen-year-old gangster named Joseph "Applehead" Wang dead on the staircase. "Look," my mother said, "right there in Uncle Larry's."

So it made sense for the girls and me to go by Tompkins Square on the night Billy, one more Jacobson, would be born. We had had our own little chapter in the family history here, hanging out in the park, watching the bums rise and shine in their lean-to city over by Avenue B, listening to anarchist squatters scream at the police. Once Rosie, five at the time, found a loaded gun, a cute

.38 snubnose special, in the bushes over by the basketball courts. Unruffled, she casually handed over the pistol to her teacher at the Tenth Street Tots Preschool, who just as casually called the cops, barely missing a single chorus of "Wheels on the Bus."

It was freezing as we made our way to the hospital the night Billy was born. It was always that way. Things must get extra happy for my wife and me around mid-May because all three of our children were born within a week and a half stretch in late January and early February. For a while there, if the AFC team was getting blown out in the Super Bowl, we were having another kid. The proximity could cause problems. Rosie was born on the day of Rae's fourth birthday party. I'd barely cut the cord before fetching a cab across town, a slightly battered cake under my arm as I ran up the tenement stairs, just in time to play pin-the-tail-on-the-donkey with twelve little girls in pink dresses.

The night Billy was born, I sat with Rosie and Rae in the hospital discussing how the new arrival would change the life of our little household.

The baby would be sleeping in the kitchen of the back apartment. I say "back" because we had two apartments in the building at the time, both on the same floor but not contiguous. We ate in the street-facing, five-hundred-square-foot "front forty," and slept in the back. Both cost $300 a month, neither had a sink in the bathroom, and if you wanted to run from one to the other without any clothes on, this was possible, but you had to look both ways first lest Mrs. Panasiuk across the hall see you and have a heart attack.

The crib had remained in the back apartment kitchen following Rosalie's occupancy, between the filing cabinet and the now doddering mini Sanyo washer-dryer complex we received from my parents when Rae was born. The girls would move in together and sleep on the red metal bunk bed in my old office. We'd just replaced the security gate on the window. The window had previously been covered with a thick wooden shutter held in place by a braced horizontal two-by-four. It had been put up by the previous tenant, a young woman, who had been attacked in the room. The guy had come in from the fire escape. We didn't like it, setting the girls up in the very room where such things had gone on, but the cramped bohemian lifestyle sometimes dictates creepy choices. The gate was strong, though. The locksmith, not quite your sensitive *feng shui* consultant, said it would "keep out King Kong, even if he had an axe, no problem."

Having just turned seven and three respectively, the girls said they had discussed the matter and while their preference was for a girl, for my sake, they had decided to hope for a boy.

"Because you are so outnumbered. Boys like to do boy things. With other boys," said Rae, ever the sage, patting me on the shoulder.

"That's right, we won't mind if it's a boy," Rosalie agreed, sharp in her tiger-striped boots, her hair still in the blonde ringlets that brought her so much unwanted attention that she eventually demanded, "Who is this stupid Shirley Temple?"

This was very nice of them, I replied. But I was not going to be unhappy if it was a girl. If all the girls were as nice as the two of them, then we could have one hundred girls.

"Sure, Dad, sure," Rae said, not falling for this soggy claptrap.

The labor took all night, into the morning. By dawn I could see the midwife getting that look on her face, that C-section look. It was strange, labors are supposed to get easier, not harder with each successive baby. My wife looked so weary. But then, I saw her smile.

"Okay," she said. Later she said it was like someone whispered in her ear, told her he was sorry he'd kept her waiting. Who knew how long it took to get from wherever he was, or if he had to wait for whomever is in charge of these things to open the gateway, which our sad friend Mr. Sen would later call "a *tirtha*." But there he was.

I never would have guessed, once he finally slithered out, that little wanger visible, that I would jump up and down.

"It's a boy," I yelled into the phone, talking to the girls, home with a baby-sitter, the first to know.

"See, Dad," Rae said, sleepily. "We told you you'd be happy."

One of the dimmer credos of New Age child-rearing claims is that there is very little difference between boy babies and girl babies. To be sure, *all* babies are different. Rae kept us up all night when she was very little but became as sweet as can be soon after. This put the lie to the so-called "terrible twos," we thought. Then came Rosalie, the dream baby, sleeping through the night from the first, cute as a button until she hit twenty months, when, if she wasn't shouting, stamping her feet and screaming "no," she was hiding under the bed refusing to come out "ever!"

Kids—they get you sooner or later. Years ago I used to see screaming children on a bus, their parents either screaming back or ignoring them. Poor kid, I thought. Now, knowing what I know, I see a child grinding its tender little face into the sidewalk, yelling at the top of his or her lungs, and think: poor parent.

I analyze the early behavior patterns of my two daughters as reactions to abrupt separation from the womb. Rae, dreamy and never good at transitions, was upset at being cast out, interrupted in the middle of whatever diffuse activity she was pur-

suing in the uterine world. Once outside, however, after a period of adjustment, she was happy to be here. As for Rosalie,
she's the light traveler, aloof in her attachments. She was happy
to be born, with all the new sights to take in. It was only when
she began to understand the slackness of the crowd she'd fallen
in with that she began to complain with increasing bitterness.

Billy was another thing altogether, cut from a different
swatch of the genetic fabric. When he was about three months
old, I slipped and dropped him. The descent seemed to take
several distended moments, the thud shook the apartment
building to its funky core. I expected wails, tears. But as soon
as I picked him up, I saw a wide-eyed, exhilarated look with
which I would become well acquainted. "Again!" the look said.

Again . . . *and again.*

So it went. Through the headlong leaps into walls, arms
crashed through plate glass windows, near electrocuting chomps
into extension cords, buckets of blood which would keep us on a
first-name basis with ER triage nurses throughout the city, one
word held constant: *again!*

It was Billy who finally moved us out of the Lower East Side.

He pushed Mr. Tortorelli over the edge. Poor guy, he'd
been born in the building, spent his whole life in that third-
floor apartment, right below us. You almost never saw him.
People came and went, their nametags changing beside their
bell, but his yellowed sticker remained, untouched: the classic
invisible New Yorker. During the first two baby sieges, replete
with midnight crying jags and requisite crawling marathons, we
never heard a peep from him, outside of the occasional faint
strains of Fred Astaire singing "I'll be seeing you in all the familiar places."

It was only after Billy first learned to walk, then run, that
the thumps of a broom handle slammed against the ceiling of
the apartment below were heard. Then came the shouting,

relatively gentle at first, an entreaty. "Please stop that running," came the voice, mildly. This became a more guttural "Stop that running," which quickly escalated to a guttural "Stop that damn running" and, eventually, "Stop that *f-ing* running!"

We did everything we could: put down rugs, wore slippers, carried Billy from room to room. But the building was old, rickety. It had been built in the 1870s, slum housing even then—two women living there had died in the famous 1911 Triangle Sweatshop fire. The foundation was set on a series of tree stumps, which vibrated like tuning forks every time the M-13 bus went by.

Mr. Tortorelli kept screaming. "Stop that *mother f-ing* running!"

"Don't curse! It is not nice to curse! There are children up here!" we shouted down the airshaft. Who was this jerk anyway, to use such foul language within earshot of our tender children? The old man had taken to screaming about Billy's running when he wasn't even running. Once the shouts woke Billy up from a nap, which started him running.

I went downstairs to have it out with the old guy. "Open up!" But no one answered. I knocked again, hard. From within I heard a familiar voice: "Stop that running . . . stop that f-ing running. . . ." He kept saying it, over and over.

"Sorry," I said, quietly. "Sorry for everything." The next day we started looking for a new place to live.

The madman who beat out the other madmen for the privilege of driving us into town from the Kathmandu airport said we were crazy to want to stay on Freak Street.

"Freaka Street no family place!" he implored, hurtling his Toyota van past a slow-moving bullock cart. "Freaka Street not

for children! Freaka Street is for dirty people. No one stays on
Freaka Street anymore!"

He said we should stay in Thamel. All the tourists stayed
in Thamel. "Americans are in Thamel, exclusive," he shouted,
appealing to our sense of nationalism.

Once, Thamel was considered a backwater. The Kathmandu
Guest House—home of the weekly hot shower and the ten-rupee-
per-day space heater rental (no refund for no-electricity days) was
pretty much the whole ballgame. Nowadays, the KGH was a
sprawling Hilton-like entity perimetered by a wrought-iron fence
straight out of Kane's Xanadu and a front yard tended by turbaned
landscapers. The area was filled with dozens of swankish hotels
and even more restaurants, and not just the usual banana pancake
traveler dreck. These places had become a package tour destination, with altitude sickness thrown in for free.

Our driver was a tout, working on commission, trying to
steer customers to the Roof of the World Lodge, which, according to the card was "Thamel's newest—tiptop quality, own bathroom, best mountain views."

"See! Mount Everest!" the tout said, pulling out a photo
album from beneath the seat and flipping through the plastic-
covered pages until he found several roof garden shots. The
pictures appeared to have been taken during the hotel's construction phase. Large squares of Sheetrock and piles of bricks
surrounded a lonely potted rhododendron.

The children examined the pictures a moment. "I don't see
Mount Everest in these pictures," Rosalie said.

"Not these. But from the Roof of the World, it is very visible." This seemed highly unlikely; the world's tallest peak is
several hundred kilometers away.

"Definite! The best view," the driver declared.

"I can't see any mountains in these pictures," Rosie said.

"No, the mountains cannot be seen," the driver replied. "The hotel is new. Just opened. You will be among the first guests. This picture is from before it was finished."

"But you still should be able to see the mountains," Rae insisted. "Even if the hotel is unfinished, the mountains are still there."

"No," the driver begged to differ, slamming on the brakes to avoid hitting several schoolchildren. "If the hotel is not finished, the mountains cannot be seen. They are not in the picture."

"I know they're not in the picture," Rae persisted. "I don't see them. But they're there. They're the biggest mountains in the world. They've been there for millions of years. They're *old.*"

"Millions of years? No. The hotel is not finished, completely. Only the lobby needs work. The rest, perfect. It is okay for you to stay, but until it is finished, there are no mountains."

Was this some elaborate kind of Nepali cabbie Abbot and Costello routine or was the guy simply dense? It was true that we had arrived in the middle of summer, when the Kathmandu Valley is often subject to low-lying clouds, which often lingered for weeks at a time. Few came here to trek at this time of year for that very reason: you couldn't see anything, plus the trails were often filled with foot-deep mud and leeches.

"You mean you can't see the mountains because of the clouds, right?" Rae said, giving the driver the perceptual benefit of the doubt.

"If you come to stay, you will see. I will speak to the owner." The driver flipped open his cell phone and pulled out the antenna with his betel-nut-stained teeth. He would be happy to call ahead and make a reservation for us.

"I beg you," he said. "Do not stay on Freaka Street. It is cold and dark like a basement. It is no good picture of Nepal, no good place for children. Only freaks on Freaka Street. I beg of you, do not go to Freaka Street."

Sorry, we told him. We didn't want to stay in Thamel. Freak Street might be dirty and cavelike, but it was right around the corner from Durbar Square, with its fourteenth-century temples, brick alleyways, millions of pigeons and living goddesses. Besides, that was where the history was.

Back in the day of the late to middle part of the twentieth century, Freak Street, or Jhonchen as it is known to Nepalis, with its cafes serving gooey chocolate cakes and playing Big Brother and the Holding Company, was the grail, the last stop on the Hippie Trail.

The route was well known, a ritual passage like the Oregon Trail or Ulysses' way home, a path that was beat but not beaten down. The starting line was the Pudding Shoppe, with its twin spinning lamb gyro towers, a little dive across from Sultan Ahmet, the Blue Mosque, in Istanbul. From there, the path went east through Anatolia, Cappadocia and Kars, alleged birthplace of the trickster Gurdjieff, he of Beelzebub and Ouspensky. This was the realm of whirling Sufi dervishes and Mount Ararat, where Noah's Ark came to rest, or so said the man in the lambskin hat who claimed to have the original wooden planks for sale, just for you, cheap.

Iran was next, the erstwhile Persia, an easy shot across the sand when the Shah sat upon the Peacock Throne, ruling the rotting roost, along with SAVAK, his secret police, their Uzis and CIA walkie-talkies at the ready. Days and nights were spent in Mashad and Tehran, where teenage boys clawed at the windowpanes of cheap hotels, trying to sell themselves. When asked how come there weren't any girls for sale, they were outraged, screaming of honor-crushing infidels, and threatening to return with shotgun-wielding brothers.

Then came Afghanistan, wonder of wonders, dusty jewel of the journey, land of black kohl eyeliner, musk and chypre. Herat was beautiful and so was Kandahar. Chicken Street in Kabul was the strip, the hash-bound ghetto. Days were spent on the balcony of Ziggy's Hotel, checking out King Zahir's dented Fleetwood Cadillac and the mangy bear in the market, rope tied around his balls. At dawn the buses left to go over the Khyber Pass, in the carriage tracks of Marco Polo, to Pakistan. Inside were hippies gone native in their embroidered wolfskin vests, bodies full of dysentery and parasites, picked up from being too stupid to wear shoes in the bazaars. Soon enough everyone was at the dollar-a-night Red Shield Hotel in Bombay, and on the steamer down to Goa, where they lay on the famous beach, tanned and blotto. When the season changed, the magic bus, a Green Tortoise or Gray Rabbit, wound its way through Delhi and Lumbini, birthplace of the Buddha, and on to Kathmandu, where the keeper of the fifty-cent-a-night sub-Dickensian hovel of a Freak Street lodge was waiting with another lump of hash and scratchy sheets.

Was there ever a better time to be nineteen?

By the time I came to Freak Street with my wife, the Trail was already truncated, choked with roadblocks. The Soviets were in Afghanistan. The Ayatollah had Iran. An American passport was the mark of the Beast, something to keep well hidden. The overland continuity of the great utopian trek had turned into a patchwork of no-go zones, spaces to jump over like the bad squares in Monopoly. Once the relative conformity of the pressurized 727 cabin became unavoidable, the great game was finished.

It is a basic canard of the baby boomer generation that a lot of the really good youth got used up back then, with a guitar across your shoulder like a 30.06 (some even wrote Woody Guthrie's dictum, "This machine kills fascists," on the body of their $600 Martin GLs) with the Vietnam War and the Civil Rights movement to supply the necessary poetic gravitas. But this is a dumb, self-serving idea. There is no way to gauge the quality, or quantity, of fun. People find their own way to the party.

The lines of the generational divide are blurrier these days. Once the pathways of rebellion were as wide and well-marked as a super highway. For me, the most obvious way to piss off my parents was grow my hair long, and drop out of college to become a porter at the Port Authority Bus Terminal in New York. This was a career move that did not compute with my mother and father's GI Bill orientation of upward mobility. What sort of disinformational dybbuk, they wondered, had stowed away from the Old Country to possess their only son that he should come ot think it was "cool" to carry the bags of scruffy Greyhound bus travelers? They could only stand speechless as I propounded a class analysis to explain my action. Working at the bus station was not a move down, but rather a celebration of the endless opportunity we had attained since our arrival in this new land. To be a porter was actually one of most upward things a young man could do, demonstrating as it did, freedom from the yoke of endless striving. This was the real genius of America, I told the parents, that in the space of two generations, we Jacobsons could move from the Romanian potato sack to someone like me, so hip I can barely stand myself. Needless to say, often times conversation between my parents and myself might as well have been between two different species.

Our house is not like that. We're close, tight. Culturally speaking our family is very *familiar*. I mean, the kids are always stealing my Nirvana records (I mean CD's, of course), playing them to death, trying (with no small success) to make them theirs. This drives me crazy, but I've never been mystified by the process. The canonized template of teendom, if not the current specifics, is known to me. I'm onto them, more than I'd really like to be, if you want to know. The other day Rosie was talking about how her post-punk friends gave her "scene points" for growing up on St. Marks Place and liking early Blondie records. She felt pretty good about it, like she was clued in. "You liked Blondie, didn't you?" she asked me. To be perverse, I said, "Who? . . . You mean the comic strip?" I just didn't feel like saying, Yeah, I knew Blondie. One time I went over to the loft where she lived with her boyfriend Chris Stein and her underwear was all over the place. Is this a parental thing to brag about, seeing Debbie Harry's drawers? Rather than a Grand Canyon of generational abyss, I fear we're suffering from a lack thereof, a paucity of attitudinal discrepancy, an excess of proximity.

It is something to think about when you have kids, especially teenagers or those on the cusp of that thrilling, bone-chilling transit point of life. (Early on, I did the math: we would miss, by a hair, having three teenagers at the same time, Rae turning twenty two weeks before Billy hits thirteen.) Not long ago I was on the subway, going uptown. A stylishly dressed woman sitting across from me was reading a book called *Get Out of My Life, But First Could You Drive Me and Cheryl to the Mall* by Dr. Anthony Wolf, the standard, if suburbanized, tome about how to deal with the teenage Frankenstein in your midst. Our eyes met and we sighed. Nothing needed to be said.

Everyday, it seems, we go through the usual byplay, the full litany of parental crud coming from my mouth. The phraseology spews out involuntarily, the "we'll see," the "maybe," the ever popular "because I said so"—all the loathsome, seemingly unavoidable elocutions my parents threw at me, recycled again. Slipping into a current vernacular does no good. Just yesterday Rosalie and I were locked in a knockdown drag-out about her curfew. She wanted to go out, I didn't want her to. In the midst of battle, I found myself shouting, "You're just not going, *dig it?*"

"*Dig it?*" Rosalie repeated, cracking up in peals of laughter. "Dig it?" For her it was a moment of sitcom victory, as if she'd turned her father, who was trying to be *the Dad* for once, into a ridiculous figure from the Ozzie Osbourne school of discipline. Still chortling, she went back upstairs, suddenly happy enough to stay home.

If many of the conflicts are the same, the rules of engagement are vague. It wasn't all that long ago that Rae came home with a ring in her nose. It was the culmination of a long-running throwdown. You know, why couldn't she get pierced? All her friends were doing strange stuff to their epidermis—jabbing hoops through their eyebrows, hardware store-sized grommets in their cheeks, bling-bling caps on their teeth, clack-clack silver buttons in their tongues. Opposition was hypocrisy, her argument went. Hadn't we always mouthed a prejudice against judging people by their appearances, made the tired case for not telling a book by its cover, railed against the fascism of the surface?

She had a point, of course. Fashion was nothing but fashion. Skin deep. Besides, I silently reasoned to myself, a statement was being made in the way the younger generations had taken control of the canvas of their own bodies. Kids walked by with shaved heads, chainsaws tattooed on the sides of their skulls. When they wiggle their ears, the saw moves. This was art, this was politics. In a world where most people thought little of wearing T-shirts covered with corporate logos, the body was the last sacred space, the final surface of true self-expression. Piercing was a kind of collective, heroic antidepersonalization gesture, like South Bronx kids, doomed to the faceless sudden death of the housing project, spray painting subway trains, because, as one artist said, "I want to see my name go by."

"It is my nose," she said.

"Yeah, but who's got to look at it?"

"*My* nose! In the middle of *my* face!"

It was about then my wife started sobbing. It was a dense moment. As a prop in the ongoing theater of youth, a nose ring might serve the same purpose as carrying bags in a bus station, or a seven-day visa to Burma. Being young manifests itself differently now. In our Big City neck of the woods the category of youth cuts across many class and race lines. Our kids hang around with way more people of other colors than I ever did while walking protest lines, shouting slogans of equality. They don't even really think about it anymore. This is their slacker utopia. A nose ring, worn as a symbol of youthful crossover, was a small price to pay for enviable progress.

Still, caught at a tender time, my wife was crying. No longer would Rae's nose be exactly as it was that memorably bright day at St. Luke's Hospital all those years ago. That was something to mourn. Immediately, Rae, sensitive to such things, also became choked up. The confrontation became a reunion. Maybe it wasn't totally her nose, Rae said tearfully. In a way, it was "a family nose," a kind of common property between all of us. If we really wanted her to take it out, she would.

No, we said, she was right the first time. It *was* her nose. She could do what she wanted with her nose. She could stick a Hula Hoop through it if she wanted. Which was how it went on, the limp footsie of alternately drawing and erasing lines in the sand: our kind of generational battle.

This said, we still felt sorry for them, having to come to Freak Street with their parents. For, even in its current decrepit state, places like Freak Street are about the feralness of youth. Even amidst the dirt and cow leavings, Durbar Square remains a realm of randy, gloriously aimless minds, taut flesh. The kids recognized this right away. Everywhere else they stayed close, huddled up against us, as if we were actually necessary, for advice, even protection. Freak Street was different. Familiar in its bizarreness (when you're born on St. Marks Place, Freak Street *is* your street), it was about hanging out, wondering what was on the mind of that kid over there, and that one over there.

It was like that time in New Orleans, when the girls, so desperate to drench themselves in magic, not reality, insisted on walking around the quarter by themselves. NOLA, the most dangerous big city in the country, so inviting in its slatternliness wasn't a place to be with parents. The seven-hundred-year-old towers of Durbar Square, where statues of the goddess Kali, with her bloodstained necklace of skulls, were lit by a thousand candles, had a similar kind of hoodoo to it. An aftervibe of the hippie trail roiled up with its crystal spin of expectation, amped by the sultry presence of the Nepali boys, lean and shirtless.

It was unlikely that someone in their set would see them here, with their mom and dad. But why take the chance? Word could get around. Next time they walked into the Waverley Coffee Shop in Greenwich Village or thumbed through the anarchist zines at SeeHear on Seventh Street, there'd be smirks, little knowing glances.

This is the magic of the place, of Kathmandu, and Nepal in general. Things had changed, true. The city was full of cars, Thamel was a drag, and the NCP, the agrarian Nepali Communist Party, whose revolutionary rhetoric sounded a tad too close to Year Zero for comfort, was waging a "Maoist people's war" against the monarchy they said was full of "kinsmen, yes men, maladministrators and misdeeders." Only two weeks before, they had shot up a bus traveling along the Prithvi Highway to Pokhara, killing half a dozen people. Madness was afoot, no doubt. Not long after we left, the lovesick, egomaniacal Crown Prince Dipendra, barred from marrying the princess of his choice, would murder King Birenda, Queen Ashwarya and ten others, in the single largest act of violence against royalty since the Bolsheviks iced the Czar and Czarina in 1917.

But much had stayed as it was. The same as, say, seven hundred years ago. Every morning the traders came into Basantapur Square where the great pagodas etched against the dawn sky.

They came with their goods balanced on their heads and set up blankets on which they laid out brassware, textiles, a hundred different calendars. At night they cooked their evening meals, lanterns blazing across the ancient square. Then they put their unsold goods back on their heads and left. Watching from the second story of the Cosmopolitan Restaurant, there was a voyeuristic, almost erotic allure to the procession. Even though many of the customers were tourists, the feeling was that very little of this was being done for our benefit. This was life here, the everyday; it had gone on for a long time and would continue to go on.

Over at Swayambhunath, the great temple with the coquettish plucked-eyebrow Shakayamuni Buddha face, it was the same. More than one thousand stairs up the hill, the only ones who seem aware of your presence are the monkeys, who sneak up from behind and try to pick your pocket. Inside, fifty monks sang deep in their throats, blew long horns and banged on drums. We watched them through a window, huge fat old men and young thin ones, some no more than teens in their yellow and red robes. On and on they played, burrowing deeper into their trance. Every once in a while one would get up and another player would take his place. We knew we weren't supposed to clap, but we liked this particular monk, weathered and pudgy with a face like a bulldog. We didn't clap loud, just a small cheer. We expected no acknowledgement, but he tapped on our window and smiled.

It was like that everywhere. Little sagas with happy endings. In the Snowman, one of Freak Street's more impressively dirty banana pancake and yak butter emporiums, hung a note on the wall. "Emergency!" it said on tattered paper. "In jail! Dope charge! Totally unfair! Set up! Need help! Need board games to keep mind alert and keep from going crazy! Cards okay." We were about to donate our travel Scrabble set when we realized the note was dated "2/95." This was sad. Given the likely condition of Nepali jails, this poor guy was toast long ago. But then we noticed a second, much more recent posting in the same handwriting. "Out! Got Out! Charge Unproved! Thanks for games! Saved my life! Thanks! Thanks!"

What fun it was, watching the kids take this in. Even with the Maoists at the city gates, Starbucks on the corner and electricity twenty-four hours a day (mostly), Nepal offered its special scent of romance. Like several millennia of travelers before them, the hippies too, our children took a whiff and pronounced it good.

Besides, they weren't the only kids to have come to Freak Street with their parents, as we would soon find while eating breakfast at the Himalaya Guest House, our four-dollar-a-night hotel. With so many Freak Street dives to choose from, we actually had another place in mind, but couldn't get past the giant, mottle-hided bull blocking the alleyway in front of the hotel. He took up the entire trash-strewn alleyway. So we figured, what the hell, it's a sign.

It was at the Himalaya that our host Lobsang Dorje told us of his arrival on Freak Street, along with his mother and father, in the late 1960s.

"I was six, when we got here, from Tibet," said Lobsang, a genial man in his forties with soulful, doleful eyes and a drooping moustache covering the lips of his otherwise nearly hairless, leathery face. "It was my father's idea to go. He was a religious man, a lama. The Chinese hated him. They were killing monks. So we left and came here. My father got sick in the mountains. He died only a few days after our arrival. It was a very hard trip. It took us more than a year to get here from the border. I lost my toes, one on each foot. They were frostbitten, but since I was so young I do not remember these toes, so I think of myself as a naturally four-toed Tibetan man."

This was such an odd thing, Lobsang said, pointing to his sixteen-year-old son, Kalseng, who was outside the hotel, sweeping up around the unmovable bull. "When he was born, he had only four toes on one foot. This is strange, isn't it? Somehow, it was passed on, from me to him." Lobsang laughed.

Lobsang said he didn't know what to make of Nepal when he first arrived, which was during the hippie influx. "I saw these people, I thought, these are the Nepalis. What a strange country! Pale-skinned people speaking so many languages lying on the ground covered with scarves and smoking hashish."

He started working at age ten, digging trenches, working in a rug-making factory, and eventually in a shipping warehouse in Thamel, where he learned some English. Hotel management was better. Indeed, just a few days ago he had seen a hopeful sign in the *Kathmandu Post*. A giant shark tooth had been found in the Annapurna range. Judging by the size of the tooth, local paleontologists were estimating that the shark from which it had come would have been as much as one hundred feet long, perhaps even bigger. This was good news, since by Lobsang's reckoning, any Abominable Snowman story had to be good for business.

"The Yeti is a good travel agent for us," Lobsang said. "But who would have guessed the Yeti is a fish?"

Even though most Tibetan refugees go to India these days, Lobsang tries to help the ones who turn up in Kathmandu, many of whom have taken the same route he did over the Nanpa La Pass. Most of them tell similar stories, how they were kept from working by the Chinese, the rigors of their journey, and especially the brutal treatment from the Nepali police at the border. "When I hear this, I think of Tibet, the home I do not remember," Lobsang says. But over the years he has come to think of himself less as a Tibetan and more of a Nepali. Now Nepal, Freak Street in particular, is his home.

"Yes," Lobsang said again, liking the sound of it. "Freak Street is my home. . . . It is here where my children have been born and grown up."

When it came up in the conversation that our family had come from other places, albeit not so recently, to America, Lobsang declared the bunch of us "immigrants" and thought this reason enough for us to eat lunch together at the wooden table in the modest hotel lobby.

Eating with other families, or in public under any circumstances, is often a challenging experience for us. The manners of *der kinder* are not quite up to finishing-school level. They'd actually been looking forward to East Asia because we'd told them people ate with their hands. Too bad you couldn't eat with *all* your hand. Much to the children's dismay, there were rules here, too. Curry stains above the first knuckle were severely frowned on by subcontinental Emily Posts.

Still, it was important to make a good first impression. First impressions were of paramount importance when it came to eating habits, we stressed, addressing the children's attention to a sequence in the novel *Rabbit Boss* by Thomas Sanchez, which describes the Washoe tribe's first encounter with the white man in the American northwest. The Indians look through the trees, spying on the newcomers, who turn out to be the Donner party. Amazed and horrified, the Washoes said, "They eat of each other. . . ."

As it was, however, lunch went well enough. Nima, Lobsang's wife, made curry. Rinzen, fourteen, their shy, studious daughter allowed, after some prodding, that she was at the top of her class and hoped to become a doctor someday. If the Nepali schools were not sufficient, she planned to go to India to study. Kalseng, seventeen, he of the four toes and brilliant smile, was somewhat more outgoing, especially in his purple print rayon shirt and neopompadour. Earlier that day, entrusted to keep most of the electronic equipment at the hotel running, he'd come to our room to see what he could do with the ancient TV set, eventually securing a blurry transmission of baseball's all-star game. They were wheeling Ted Williams down the third base line in a golf cart. One by one the current all-stars came over to shake the Splendid Splinter's hand.

"A great master," I said, perhaps a bit too flippantly, as Cal Ripkin, Derek Jeter and the others came over to pay homage to the game's most scientific hitter.

"Oh, an American guru," Kalseng replied, his English more than adequate to provide an unmistakable layer of sarcasm. "Parents," he seemed to say, flashing his marvelous smile at Rosalie and Rae.

Now, sitting around the lunch table, Kalseng was saying he would like to be a hot dog skier because it was stupid for Nepalis to live in a place with so much snow and never have any entries in the Olympics, especially in the extreme sports. An alternate plan was to move to Hawaii and become a surfer. Of course he'd never tried it. Nepal was a landlocked country, thousands of miles from any ocean. Kalseng had rarely ever been outside the Kathmandu Valley. But he'd seen surfers on television and was certain he was a natural. As if to prove this, he got up from the table and proceeded to execute a nearly perfect Michael Jackson moonwalk, especially for someone with nine toes.

This was about enough for Lobsang, who told his son to sit down and finish his food. Kalseng immediately obeyed, but you could see the two of them had gotten into it before, and they would again. Rinzen, for her part, gave her brother a sidelong glance, like, what a jerk, you had to go get him mad.

It was one of those moments of knowingness. We'd all been there before.

In our earlier conversation, speaking in a dad-to-dad tone, Lobsang had told me he hoped Kalseng would graduate from school and become a hydraulic engineer—Nepal having great potential for generating hydroelectric power, which the nation

might be able to sell to the Indians. It would be an excellent
field. But he feared the boy wasn't a great student. He didn't
apply himself, choosing instead to run around with his friends.
But children were like that, Lobsang said. Eventually they
found themselves. Perhaps Kalseng would want to take over
the hotel someday.

"This is why I do everything. For them," Lobsang said,
sounding for the moment like any immigrant parent anywhere.
"They are what comes next." This, Lobsang explained, was his
view of karma, as it related to reincarnation. After his father died
escaping Tibet, he hadn't paid very much attention to Buddhism
or its teachings. But he still believed in reincarnation, after a
fashion. It was just that he believed his reincarnations already
walked the earth, present in the bodies of his children. For him,
this was the true escape from eternal suffering.

"They are my heaven," Lobsang said.

This answer was at least as good as anything the Dalai Lama
had come up with. But, as Lobsang quickly added, his particular heaven was not perfect, not some flawless nirvana. Families
rarely worked like that.

After lunch, Rae related her strange conversation with our
airport taxi driver about whether or not the Himalayas could be
seen from the hotel roofs of the Kathmandu Valley. "He said you
could only see the mountains when the hotel was finished, isn't
that strange?"

Lobsang thought about it a moment. Perhaps the guy meant
that the hotel wouldn't be finished until fall, when the visibility
improved. But even on a good day it wasn't easy to see the high
peaks from a Kathmandu rooftop. Of course, that didn't mean you
couldn't try. The cloud cover wasn't too bad today. You never
knew. Lobsang had some old binoculars he could lend the kids.
Why not take some up to the roof and see what could be seen?

So we went up on the roof and peered out over Durbar Square. The usual sprawling Bosch painting unfurled below. The daily flea market, hundreds of sellers with their metal bowls, wooden rolling pins and auto parts laid out on multicolored blankets was in full swing. Rickshaws crisscrossed the old bricks, dodging a procession of pilgrims heading for the temple of Kali. Kids ran up and down the fourteenth-century temple steps. These were the details, but as for the feel of the place, it wasn't all that different than the urban phantasm we used to behold from the roof of our ratty tenement tar beach back on St. Marks Place—life and life only.

But there were no mountains. Not a single mountain could be seen.

That seemed right. The mountains were the real magic of Nepal, a mystic invitation to danger and freedom. And so, it was good that they withheld themselves from view. Nepal was a world in which to travel young; it was a place that understood Youth. It knew that when you come to Freak Street, with your parents, you have to have an out, a reason to come back again, the right way—fine, feral and on your own.

Night Train

I remember the moment my father and I realized our interaction would forever be limited. We were as close as we would ever get to each other. Any attempt to diminish the distance between us was not only likely to fail but also entailed more effort than either one of us were willing to put forth.

We were sailing across the sullen blue waters of Long Island Sound, halfway between the giant spans of the Whitestone Bridge and the then-uncompleted Throgs Neck Bridge, tacking against the wind on my father's boat, *L'Chiyam*, which is Yiddish for "to life."

My father built *L'Chiyam* inside our garage in Fresh Meadows, which is what real estate interests called our section of Queens, even though everyone knew it was just more Flushing. He bought the vessel, or what was left of it, for $150 after it was wrecked during Hurricane Donna in 1960. Hurricanes hardly ever reach New York but Donna had, the storm's hundred-mile-an-hour winds breaking the nineteen-foot skiff from its mooring near LaGuardia Airport. The mast was snapped and a piling punched through the hull, but that only whetted my father's appetite. The realm between broken and fixed was where he operated.

Until then my father's boat building had been confined to making models of eighteenth-century sailing ships that he managed to stuff into glass bottles, a trick he steadfastly refused to explain to me. It took Dad two years of weekends and nights to repair the future *L'Chiyam*, which had formerly been called *Bright Mary O'Hare*—Irish civil servants getting to own boats before Jews, most of whom had no desire to commune with the sea beyond the nickel fare on the Staten Island Ferry.

Some boys might have found grand opportunity sanding down the hull of the *L'Chiyam*, but I was not one of those boys. This was something of a break with tradition, and a small sort of tragedy. Several Jacobsons had been carpenters, but it is safe to say my father was the most sublime of these woodworkers. He made the occasional animal carving, but mostly he worked in the realm of the functional, the everyday of chairs, tables and cabinets, hundreds of cabinets. He did most of these things fast, to make a little extra money, but as many remarked, he did it with style. Even the most routine Formica-covered cabinet installed in the most ordinary Queens kitchen could be identified by his signature precision.

For reasons that are both self-evident and eternally confusing to me, I willed myself to utter incompetence in my father's realm of expertise, steadfastly resisting the urge to join him in his sawdust flecked basement lair, where he spent the majority of his time surrounded by his imposing array of power tools—the jig saw, the band saw, the giant lathe. In his presence, the simple act of driving a nail straight through a board became a physical, geometric impossibility for me. Nor could I, due to either incompetence, rebellion, or both, fully adhere to his unwavering fealty to the inviolateness of a right angle.

"Ninety degrees," he said. "Not eighty-nine degrees, not ninety-one ... only ninety, no negotiation, no maybe, ninety or nothing." In a world of cheap compromise, there were certain absolutes he would not surrender.

I tell people he could have/should have been an artist. This is my vision for him, my version of his life narrative. If you are a storyteller, there are stories you tell about your children, stories you tell about your parents, not quite lies, but little alterations of reality, the way things might have gone—stories that eventually wind up being about yourself, cadges for attention and sympathy. But calling my father an artist is not a stretch, because he was. Many basements of our Queens borderlands were fertile grounds for the production of marginalized, eccentric art. Few days went by that my friends and I did not unknowingly pedal our bicycles past the home of Joseph Cornell, the hermetic builder of little mystery boxes who lived with his Mary Baker Eddy–revering mother a few blocks to the west on the extravagantly misnomered Utopia Parkway.

As for my father's art career, he never had a chance. He came on the scene at a time in the Jacobson dynasty—the first post-Titan, American-born generation—when the golden exotica of the new land had transmuted, through the adverse alchemy of history, to leaden responsibility. No longer a landscape of unglimpsed sights, sounds and smells, my father's New York was not a place where a man might work for a variety of government agencies, eat tuna fish every day, live for fifty years in the same small apartment in Williamsburg and then die with $112,000 stuffed in his mattress like my uncle Benny. The Depression, and the New Deal to follow, was not without prospects, however. What was offered was limited but sure mobility. Civil service precluded the option to invent oneself, but if you played the cards as dealt, for once the odds were with you. Even a Jew, the last ones allowed onboard before the race ladder was pulled up, could sink roots and be like everyone else.

Fitzgerald wrote with derisive fear about the ash pits that once swirled not far from our house, but he was a snob and a fop who didn't know the anvil clang of workaday opportunity when he heard it. Out here, near the city line, there was a pioneer spirit about having to take the Q-17 bus to the subway train. I remember one time someone ran over a raccoon in the Bohack supermarket parking lot. As the animal twitched its last, everyone stood around congratulating each other about how the area was "still the country, in parts," not totally tamed. On our block everyone's dad worked for the city. The Italians were sanitation men; the Irish, cops and firemen; the Jews, teachers. My friends were named Citelli, Pelligrini, Coonan and Longenecker. This was diversity, circa 1959.

My father taught industrial arts, which everyone called "shop." This meant he got to watch wave after wave of recalcitrant, all-thumbed teenage boys make the same crummy ashtray in his ceramics classroom for thirty years. Who cared about "shop"? It didn't even go on your permanent record. The steady parade of mediocrity wore my father down, made him withdraw; or at least, this is how I tell his story.

This didn't mean there weren't spates of rebellion, flashes of flamboyance. Like the time he invented the electric fork.

Seems as though my mother had one day brought home an "electric knife," one of those ersatz slicers usually advertised on late-night TV, although Mom likely got her version during her extensive dealings with the Green Stamp people. My father took this amiss. Even if his kitchen duties in the scheme of my parents' division of labor were largely confined to the making of pancakes and the occasional scrambled egg, the man did the carving. Like spreading insecticide on the lawn, washing the car and going out for the paper on Sunday morning, carving was a substitution for the sacred masculine roles lost since the hunter/gatherer times. Dad was peeved about the electric knife, not that he said anything about it.

Instead he stayed downstairs, in his workshop, appearing at dinner one evening with a fork embedded in a plastic handle. A long electric cord protruded from the end.

"My new invention," Dad announced, as dinner, cooked to his overdone specifications, came to the table. As always, the vegetable, tonight a pile of gray-green canned peas, occupied the upper-lefthand quadrant of the dinner plates. My father reached over toward my sister's setting, nestling several peas onto the tongs of his strange fork.

"Let's give it a test run," Dad said, plugging the fork cord into the wall. The fork started vibrating and immediately the peas flew about the dining room, splattering the walls, hitting the ceiling, rolling like roulette balls around the bowl of the light fixture above the table.

"And that is what I think of your electric knife," my father said, putting his napkin into his lap.

The electric fork inspired one of my first (and very few) entrepreneurial ideas. It seemed the perfect April Fools' gift. Mass-produced, it could be as big as hand buzzers, plastic vomit or the gum that turned your teeth black, I proposed. My father saw no merit in this idea. The electric fork was a one-of-a-kind item, he said. The only reason the device existed in the first place was to display its own inanity. So why make more of them? One was more than enough.

It has often occurred to me that my father regarded me as just one more talentless laggard passing through the classroom of his life, another bozo who couldn't join two boards at a sacred right angle if his life depended on it. Not that he ever quite came out and said it. Still, I avoided his workshop, rarely venturing down there. Which was a good thing, I realize now. Because the longer I live, the longer I am a father, the more I understand why he stayed down in the basement, amid the sawdust and blinking fluorescent lights.

I can picture him down there, with the saws and hammers, thinking, "This is my world, my *real* world. Everything outside of here—my life with your mother, with you and your sister, with everyone I know and my crappy job, my every interaction with the so-called world—is a flawed negotiation, an eighty-nine-degree angle. Only down here, where I make my things, am I wholly free."

The *L'Chiyam* was Dad's big gesture, his last, best attempt to meet me on neutral ground.

I can follow his thinking. Perhaps I didn't like machines and wood the way he did, perhaps I didn't care about how the boat was put together. But the sailing part, the sun and sea and bounding main deal, that should be different. Clearly, I liked the outdoors. My friends and I played baseball so deep into the evenings we couldn't even see the electric tape–covered ball. In the winter our hands had to freeze before we'd put away the basketball.

The things I liked, my father didn't. From the start, I could tell, he couldn't catch a ball. He just didn't have the right approach. One of my earlier memories is throwing him a softball and watching it go right through his outstretched arms and knock off his glasses. Sports weren't his thing. His father, my grandfather Sugar, who once dreamed of playing for John McGraw, told me how nice it was to have someone around, finally, to take to the games. It was my grandfather who took me to Ebbets Field on May 12, 1956, my eighth birthday, to see the Dodgers play the Giants, the game in which Carl Erskine, my favorite pitcher next to Don Newcombe, pitched a no-hitter. You could look it up. When I got home, my father was downstairs, working.

"Some game," he yelled up, "no hits."

L'Chiyam was about, I suppose, the two of us skimming along the surface, the breeze and foam against our faces, just father and son, out there in all that blue, even if it was just Long Island Sound and the Queens coastline never disappeared from view. Saturday mornings we drove over to the mooring on Flushing Bay near College Point and took the ship out, my father teaching me the rudiments of sailing, how to come about, how to set out the modest spinnaker.

But as seaworthy as *L'Chiyam* might have been, with its wooden hull, it was never light across the water. Flags would be out stiff as we cast off, but, invariably there we would be, the sun beating down, tacking back and forth at about a knot or two. Edging toward seasickness, not wishing to admit it, I fixated on the unfinished Throgs Neck Bridge. One of Robert Moses's last grand projects, the construction had gone slower than expected. The two towers were in place, but the roadways, like two foreshortened gangplanks, hadn't yet met in the middle. Separating them was open air, a gap, a space between.

I kept looking at those two unconnecting roads, the empty air separating them. How can it be explained, to be so close to someone, to be father and son, to truly love one another (because I can think of no other way to describe the way we felt) and still have next to nothing to say? We sat on the becalmed *L'Chiyam* and knew: it wasn't going to get any easier than this. We could go out a hundred times, and we would never get any closer. There would always be that space between.

I remember that day in the middle of Long Island Sound, how the sun started to go down, and finally the wind began to whip, filling the sails. That would have been the time to let it rip, cut through the channel, make time. But, as I said, we were already done for the day, for the days to come as well. We had made an honest try, and that seemed enough. The overriding feeling was relief, and it was mutual.

I was thinking of Dad and the space between us as my current family rolled along in the tight confines of the Shatabdi Express, the midnight flyer out of the holy city of Varanasi, bound across the dusty plains of Uttar Pradesh toward the likewise holy city of Haridwar.

The plan was to get a first-class sleeper, nonair-con, which beats first class, air-conditioned by a mile. In India, an air-con compartment is just asking for trouble. If the air-con is actually working, the temperature often plunges to arctic levels. You lurch past the parched, sweltering countryside inside a meat freezer, tracing the contrails of your breath. If the air-con doesn't work— a distinct possibility—the windows will not open, turning your compartment into a sweat lodge. A nonair-con sleeper is the same size as the air-conditioned compartment and one-fifth the cost. The windows open (thereby gaining access to the myriad sights, sounds and odors of the so-called real India). The windows also close, thereby muffling the aforementioned sensory onslaught, including the boys with their buckets and terra-cotta teacups who come banging on the side of the coaches at four in the morning, shouting "Chai!"

Too bad the first-class, nonair-con sleepers were sold out for a week. With the kiddies anxious to leave Varanasi and its burning funeral pyres way behind, we opted for the second-class sleeper, a whole other scene, India-invasive-wise.

A second-class sleeper comes with no closed compartment, no private bathroom, no buffer zone from the tumult. Rather, it is a six-person nook off the main passage of the train, with three fold-down "beds" on either side. The bottom-most of these bunks doubles as a seat in the daylight hours, the middle tier folds down from the wall on chains, with the luggage rack serving as the upper level, which means the top sleeper gets to share his ironing board berth with his fellow travelers' parcels, including the de rigueur hundred-pound bag of basmati rice and ripped cardboard boxes full of greasy auto parts. Berth poaching is endemic. Screams of "full," "six" or "no room" have little effect, these terms being open to highly elastic interpretation.

Nonetheless, as we told the children, an overnight trip on an Indian train is a must. Developed primarily during the British raj—the English taking up the racial challenge of bringing stiff-lip decorum to their crazy-quilt colony while plundering the heck out of it—the vast crosshatch of tracks and trains was an unending, Sisiphysian struggle between expressionist Order and Chaos, a siege of well-made design against the entropy of man and machine.

To catch a train in a major Indian city, especially in the middle of the night, is no walk in the park. First the would-be passenger passes through the several hundred people sleeping beneath loose-woven blankets on various station platforms, taking care to avoid the usual cowherds and turds. From there the task is to determine which one of the many smoke-belching super chiefs—heading for such locales as Calcutta, Madras, Hyderabad, Puri, Gorakapur—is yours.

We had reserved tickets, secured from the "tourist allotment" window between the doorways of the "veg" and "nonveg" restaurants. But these sweaty scraps of tissue paper covered with the tourist officer's blotty chicken scratch notations seemed to be nothing more than snippets of Hindustani black humor. Right in front of us a rubber-tired bullock cart had found its way onto the tracks, blocking the path of a freight train. The engineer was blasting his ear-splitting horn, but the cart's driver had fallen fast asleep and could not be stirred. Local residents appeared and disappeared like wraiths amid the fifteen-watt gloom, several of them brushing their teeth with long reedy sticks, the choreography of their quick and choppy dental strokes falling in and out of unison.

Asking directions brought little more than shrugs. How were we to find our train in this bedlam? Yet there it was. After a couple of false starts and a hasty exit from a departing mail train bound for Orissa, we soon came upon a piece of neat railway stationery pasted to the side of the Shatabdi Express headed to

Haridwar and other points west. In block letters were our names, and beside that, our compartment number.

These were the lessons of the Indian railways, I pointed out to the children, drawing their attention to the following morning's breakfast. When buying the tickets, we were asked to order breakfast. Little boxes were provided to tick off "cereal choice," "eggs choice," "bread choice," and so on. The selection process seemed an exercise in local hubris and/or extreme optimism. Yet along with the rising of a pallid sun over Lucknow came scrambled eggs, nan, orange juice, exactly as we had asked for them.

This struck me as a grand feat of bureaucratic magic, a miracle of travel and life itself, a triumph of organization over pandemonium. The children, however, were shockingly, depressingly unimpressed. To them, it was only one more meal in India, like so many other meals in India: an overmoist pile on a metal plate, with a faint undertone of curry, and bad, really bad. Besides, what was the big deal about ordering something and then having it brought to you? Wasn't this the way things were supposed to work?

For the hundredth time since we'd arrived in The World, I raged against their lack of wonder. Ask, get, ask again, get more: this was their receptor/consumer interface with the world beyond their blunted, self-possessed needs. They had no zeal to peek behind the Wizard's curtain, to see what was *really* up. Spoiled brats. Primitive dimbulbs. Ingrate bloodsuckers. Incurious losers. It was all our fault. How had we managed to bring up such morons?

What a drag they could be. Back in Varanasi, I went over to Sarnath, a few miles south, to the Deer Park, where the Buddha had preached his first sermon. The kids were too busy to come. After five nights at the Vishnu Guest House, our sweet hellhole by the Ganges, where the bill came to $98 for two rooms, all meals, a total of fifty-seven lemon sodas, thirty-four Cokes and nineteen bottles of water, we thought the kids might enjoy a break. So we checked in to Clarke's, the old British colonial place where one room for one night was $120 and every soft drink from the minibar cost another $3. But Clarke's also had cable TV, with actual real color reception, which in kidland made the price way worth it, especially since *Rumble in the Bronx* with Jackie Chan was on.

No doubt the Buddha, a consummately compassionate bo-dhisattva, would make sense of why my idiot children preferred a dubbed version of Jackie Chan to him. Since the Buddha, like Jesus, never had any children, that gave him plenty of time to get to the heart of matters. In the middle of the Deer Park (which really does have deer, as well as peacocks, ducks and enough bea-vers to build a ten-foot-high dam) is a large bodhi tree, which, it is claimed, grew from a cutting of the original tree of enlighten-ment in Bodh Gaya. Standing under the impressive spread of greenery, I faced a small conundrum. If you want a souvenir of a sacred bodhi tree, from the place where the Four Noble Truths and Eightfold Path were first expounded, should you pull still-growing leaves off a branch, thereby possibly intruding on the natural cycle of existence, or is it more virtuous to humbly pick up some old, browning leaves already lying on the ground?

As luck would have it, at that moment, a most auspicious wind rose up, swaying the Deer Park's tall grass. Several bodhi leaves were blown free from their branches and fluttered down. One landed upon my outstretched palm. Two more I plucked from the air. Now I had three leaves, each one fresh from the magic of the plant's life force, yet unsullied by contact with the ground below. One leaf of enlightenment for each child.

Back at Clarke's, Jackie Chan was over. Now they were watching Harrison Ford, the president, punching the tar out of a brace of post-Soviet terrorists dumb enough to try to take over Air Force One.

"Check it out," I said, displaying the leaves. Like a psychic hunter returning to the lair, I had brought back symbolic sustenance of knowledge, the chlorophyll of wisdom.

"Hey, they have MTV here," was the muffled reply.

"Forget that junk. Look at these leaves."

No one looked up. This was the way it always was when we checked into a hotel with the familiar amenities of life in the U.S.A. Their intellectual curiosity decreased in proportion to the upscaleness of the accommodation.

"*Come on, guys,* snap out of it." But they did not.

As a parent, you never quite know which of the myriad snubs your children hand out should be taken seriously, or which one of their indifferences is going to hurt your feelings. I might as well have brought them a bottle of dirt, a rock. Grumpy, I put the leaves down on the hotel room night table beside a postcard Billy had written to his friend Luke, back in Brooklyn.

"Hey, Luke, big news!" the card said, in his nine-year-old's scrawl, "I will be getting Sega Dreamcast on September 12!!!" It was true, give or take a few days. I'd promised him the video system as a perk for being an extra good sport on the trip. In our family we are not shy about the use of bribery to serve the perceived overall Good. Yet it was appalling. We'd gone halfway around the world and this was his "big news!!!"

"This isn't going to work," I told him.

"What?"

On the card Bill had affixed three U.S. stamps, which he deemed sufficient postage. "We're in India. You need Indian stamps. Every country has its own stamps."

"That's dumb," Bill said, not looking up from the screen.

"What's dumb?"

"That India has to have its own stamps. Can't they use real stamps?"

*   *   *

On the Shatabdi Express, I studied the bodhi leaves, followed their spade-shaped, sawtoothed outlines. If only I could chop them up, put them in tea, make the children drink it, jam it down their throats like some castor oil of enlightenment. Maybe I should drink some of it myself.

After all, the Buddha always preached against unreasonable expectation. Maybe my wife was right, we were being too hard on them. Cognitive dissonance-wise, India was a lot to take in. Just the other day we'd turned a corner in old Varanasi City and seen two guys squatting in the middle of an alleyway, their drawers down, defecating while engaged in casual conversation. They just kept talking and dumping, dumping and talking, as if this was a totally normal manner of discourse. Billy stood there dumbfounded, until the girls pulled him away, saying it wasn't polite to stare.

Compared to most, our kids were troopers. How might my sister and I have reacted if we'd been drafted into a trip like this? About the only place we ever went with my parents was Ausable Chasm, and the occasional jaunt to the Revonah Pretzel factory in Hanover, Pennsylvania. We'd sit there with our father, the pretzel maven, watching the Amish ladies with their black dresses and parched white skin whip the dough into those familiar twist shapes, which they lovingly called "little prayer boys" as they shoved them into giant coal-fired ovens.

Maybe our kids weren't such bad sports after all, I thought, placing the bodhi leaves between the pages of our current favorite book, *The Inscrutable Americans* by Anurag Mathur. Being Americans, and largely inscrutable to ourselves, we had purchased Mr. Mathur's novel in an English-language bookstore near the Hindu University in Varanasi. The novel tells of one Gopal Kumar, son of the manager of the Indian National Hair Oil Company, who, having studied the lifestyles and mores of Americans in the *Penthouse* letters column, leaves his small-town home of Jajau, "the Paris of Madhya Pradesh," to come to Eversville, Oklahoma, where he plans to study marketing at a small college.

"Kindly assure mother," Gopal writes home soon after arriving stateside, "that I am strictly consuming vegetarian food only in restaurants though I am not knowing if the cooks are Brahmins." But the most surprising thing about America, Gopal declares, is that it is "full of Americans. . . . Everywhere Americans, Americans, big and white . . . it is a little frightening."

Finding India to be full of Indians, Indians, brown and forever in their faces, Rosie, Rae and Billy forged a bond with Gopal, the innocent abroad, stranger in a real strange land. They regarded the hair oil heir's maladaptations to the American experience with equal parts of gentle mockery and sympathy. It was, after all, pretty funny when Gopal's big and white student guide introduces himself by saying, "Hi, I'm Randy," and the startled Indian asks, "Why?" It was also funny when the guide returns the next day, saying, "Hi, remember me? I'm Randy," and Gopal, taken aback, replies, "Still?"

In line with *The Magic School Bus*, *Goodnight Moon* and who knew how many more, *The Inscrutable Americans* became our official bedtime reading. Night after night, curled up with *Pat the Bunny*, *Stuart Little* and a dozen adventures of *The Stupids* might not qualify someone as well read, but it has its compensations. Before the kids came on the scene I hated to read aloud. The tinny sound of my own voice clanged in my ear like a tone-deaf gong. They cured me of that. Nothing matched the hellbent channeling of Dr. Seuss's fractured iambuses, or reciting the tear-producing description of how parents never really understand how tightly children grab hold of the rope while swinging over the pond, from *Charlotte's Web*. Reading books before bed, attention so fully focused, stopped the splay of mundane time. We were rarely as close as then.

So it was that night on the Shatabdi Express, snug as bugs on our rock-hard pallets, packs and suitcases padlocked to the window grates, that we settled in for another chapter of *The Inscrutable Americans;* us and about twenty-five of our fellow travelers. Apparently bedtime stories are something of a novelty in the second-class sleeper section. Whole families, Harijans in dhotis, Sikhs in turbans, half a dozen soldiers, some from as far as three train cars down, crowded around our little compartment, hoping to get an earful. It was one heck of a slumber party.

Right up front, as expectant as any four-year-old, was our recent acquaintance, the constable. Grayish curls sprouting from his round head, belly hanging over the belt of his khaki uniform, when he first sat down in "our" compartment, the constable had been jovial enough, asking questions about our lives in "the great America." Was it true, as he had heard, that many Christian Americans had more than one wife? "One man, many wives?" he asked, with semiprurient wonder. Well, we said, polygamy had once been practiced by Mormons, but this was no longer the case, at least according to the church.

"Mormons? Where are these Mormons?" the constable inquired.

"Utah."

"U-tah . . . u-TAH," the constable said, playfully bouncing the syllables around with his tongue. However, as the train inched past the pilgrimage town of Ayodhya, the constable's mood turned darker. As we would soon find out, Ayodhya was the site of widespread religious rioting in December 1992. After years of bad feeling, Hindu nationalists destroyed a sixteenth-century mosque that they claimed had been built on the site of Lord Rama's birth. The incident set off a renewed spate of Hindu-Muslim tensions, leading to many deaths on both sides.

"People say the mosque was pulled down by a mob, but it was not a mob. It was honest people who could no longer stand the insult," said the constable, a strong supporter of the hard-line Hindu government currently in power in New Delhi.

It would always be like that with the Muslims, the constable said, because "they know no decency." The embattled situation in Kashmir was more of the same. The recent Indian victory over invading Pakistani forces (led by the current Pakistani President, General Pervez Musharraf) was extolled on wildly patriotic billboards throughout the countryside. "Next time . . . total victory!!!" said a massive placard along the train line, showing an Indian soldier with his foot on the neck of a Pakistani trooper. The rhetoric became only more alarming now that both India and Pakistan had the bomb.

In a test match between the Muslim bomb of the Pakistanis and the Hindu bomb of the Indians, the Indian bomb would prove far superior every time, the constable contended. Letting Muslims have an atomic bomb was "like giving matches to nasty boys." If the "Pakis" really did have the bomb, he said, there was no way they made it themselves. Every day the newspapers had stories about power blackouts in Karachi. Islamabad went without running water for weeks. So how could the "Pakis" make something as complicated as the bomb? They couldn't even use the pull chain on a lightbulb. They talked a lot about piety, but so few of them even knew their mother. Islam may have come to India more than thirteen hundred years ago, the Moghuls might have built many of the country's greatest buildings, but it would be better if all the Muslims got out now, the constable said.

With that, he asked the children, "What is the name of your God?"

For the traveler, this is a frequent query, and it is a potentially dangerous one. Just as street killers in Northern Ireland used to scream, "What leg do you kick with?"—which gave the addressee a 50 percent chance of being shot at from a speeding car—people all over are curious as to a stranger's religious affiliations. Having once made the potentially grievous error of telling a microbusfull of Indonesian Christian gynecologists we were Jewish (they slammed on the brakes at the mention of the word and engaged in a ten- minute-long conversation in the pouring rain before deciding that it would be "their honor" to give members of God's first chosen people a ride, but only as far as Surabaya), we informed the children that it is always better to play it noncommittally. "Just say, 'we believe in God,'" we said.

So, when the constable asked his question again, the children dutifully replied, "Um . . . we believe in God."

"Yes, but what is his *name?*" the Indian demanded, his voice gaining in ardor and volume. "What is the name of your God?"

"His name is . . . *God,*" Rae replied, nervously.

"God," Rosalie echoed uncertainly.

"God . . . his name is God," the constable said, apparently satisfied with this answer, at least for now.

Luckily, however, it was now time for bed, and the constable was curled on the compartment floor like a khaki rug, a boyishly expectant look on his ruddy face. Along with the other interlopers in our compartment, he wanted to hear of Gopal Kumar's escapades in the far-out land of the free.

As any parent knows, for all the marvelous intimacy of the bedtime story, there exists another, more practical goal, which is to get those buggers to nod off. The sandman can drive a hard bargain. How many times had it happened? To have read *The Very Best Home For Me* or *Color Kittens* yet again and think the coast is clear, only to see those beloved little peepers pop open another time. *Still open!* Open and ready to cry loud tears should you tiptoe away an instant too soon. *WAH.*

There was no such problem on this night. I was reading through an episode in which Randy, the guide, takes Gopal to a topless bar out along the Oklahoma Interstate when the sounds of snores rose in counterpoint to the clack of the train wheels. The kids were asleep, along with several others, the constable included. Beside him lay a Muslim lady, also asleep. Another bedtime story had achieved its objective.

My children are my teachers. This is one more thing I learned on the Lower East Side, on Sixth Street between First and Second Avenues, home to one of the oldest Orthodox Jewish temples in New York, as well as many Indian/Bangladeshi restaurants so similar in menu and quality that urban legend posited they were connected via pneumatic tubes to a single central kitchen. In the midst of this is a Buddhist meditation center where I'd signed up for a class. The leader of the group was a monk from Haiti. In the spirit of spiritualistic mix-and-match, he'd grown up believing in voodoo and zombies before discovering an Alan Watts book on Zen in the lobby of a tatty Port-au-Prince hotel where his mother worked as a washerwoman. Later he would escape his poverty-stricken homeland in a ten-foot boat.

"Think of your true teacher," the monk said, leading the meditation in his rollicking Creole English. "Think of the teacher as small, then growing bigger. Bigger and bigger. Think of your teacher as bright light streaming from the center of your forehead. See the face of your teacher. Your teacher is smiling at you. Your teacher is pleased, delighted at your progress . . . it is good to have made your teacher happy!"

This was followed by a moment of grand suspense. Because, as the monk always said, the character of the teacher was not fixed. Different situations, different meditations called for different teachers. As the world was fluid, so would be the identity of the teacher. "See your teacher," the monk said. "The face may surprise you."

Legs aching from my haphazardly configured lotus position, I waited for my teacher to make himself or herself known. It was a moment to pay homage to all the real teachers I'd had, the ones who actually succeeded in teaching me something, anything. There was Mom and Dad, of course. There was Billy Raphan, who taught me how to look cool throwing a baseball, Linda Porinno, who taught me how to kiss, Mr. Frederick, my eleventh-grade English teacher, who taught me how to write, a little.

But really, there were three, at least only three faces that ever projected from the center of my forehead like white light: Rae, Rosie and Billy, in rough rotation—each of them, their faces as big as moon-sized Cheshire cats, smiling down at me, so delighted at my progress.

Now, clattering through the Indian night on the Shatabdi Express, I paused to examine what my children, a trio of glowing gurus, had tried to teach me over the years, and what of it I had actually learned. Much of their teachings involved time, I understood—the way it goes by, eternal in its crossing, each moment distinct. I could trace their flow through my life, how each stage was sown with the seed of its own dissolution, a built-in short fuse.

Sometimes, riding on a train or bus, I'll idly remove their photos, outdated and dog-eared, from my wallet. Rae blowing a soap bubble at age five, Rosie still small enough to take a bath in the sink, Bill with his blond curls, long since grown crew-cut straight. The knowledge that this was what they once were, and now they had grown to something altogether different—the simple idea of them *growing*—would be enough to set me off.

How long does it take to get used to being a baby? To familiarize oneself with the vicissitudes of simply being alive? So much information passes to obsolescence the moment an individual stands upright. It is like this throughout childhood, data gathered, then filed away, or discarded. This is how it is: you get comfortable, they spring something else on you. The twelve-year-old kid, boy or girl, is a most perfect master, a king among kids, worldly in their world. They get so confident they forget to duck when blindsided by adolescence.

A sense of urgency entered the subcontinental night. An Indian train may go slow, it may stop. But sooner or later it gets to its destination, often quicker than the lulled, indifferent passenger might imagine. Time on the journey, seemingly unending, was actually fleeting.

They would not be children long. The three of them walked around with expiration dates on their heads. The girls were already, uh, women. I'm already looking at girls on the subway younger than Rae. Who knows, I'm probably looking at girls younger than Rosalie. Fashion has created an army of doggy Humberts. No doubt, the dads of those girls I'm looking at are probably looking at my girls, not that any man will ever be as intimate with their skin as I once was.

Pressure, man. I can feel the tick of the clock. Soon the hair will sprout from under Billy's arms. Stubble will sully his smooth face. Who he is now will be found only on photographs and in addled memory. There is nothing to be done about it. When he complains, about not wanting to grow up, about wanting to stay his perfect twelve forever and ever, it is my job to tell him it is only in Never-Never Land that boys never get old, and the boys in Never-Never Land aren't boys at all, but middle-aged women, Mary Martin and the rest, who pretend to fly but are really suspended by ropes that you can see if you look hard enough.

A man, that's what I want him to be—big, smart and sweet like he is now. It won't be long, either. Already he doesn't mind beating me one-on-one, employing that killer crossover dribble he practices every night, up in his room, until the house shakes.

Everything has its limit. Children are excellent teachers when it comes to limits. The limits of patience, the limits of forethought, the limits of empathy and ego. Like tracing the border of a leaf fallen from a bodhi tree, like sailing on the flat earth, if there is one lesson my guru children have taught me it is that there is an edge, a boundary to everything. Once it was impossible to imagine any of us without others, but those days have begun to fade. There is a place where I stop, a place where they begin.

It has become visible, the spaces between us.

Back home, we almost always eat dinner together. None of us thought this strange until the kids' friends said they hardly ever ate dinner with their families. As it turned out, many people we knew actually admired us, primarily because we were supposed to be so close. People were envious of our closeness, the kids said. But how close was that? Out here, pitched across the alien sea of the Indian plain, all the kids could talk about was how homesick they were. Every time Gopal longed for his homeland in *The Inscrutable Americans,* audible sighs of longing could be heard. I hate that. Homesickness is a useless sentimentality. I never get homesick. You should be happy to leave and then be happy to come home. Montaigne says that. So what if they hated India. We were together; that should be home enough.

We'd taken our Larium pills before boarding the Shatabdi Express—it was our day—so everyone was having strange dreams. Rosie saw fruit with legs. Rae was riding on white camels. Bill had another session with his killer clowns. Larium always amped up the detail.

It was vicariously exciting, a smack of the forbidden, having these little drug chats with the brood. Instead of going to the movies or to eat in a Chinese restaurant, we took the family outing at an opium den. People prepare for years to tell their children everything they know already about sex. The birds and the bees, it is a trope, from the Disney movies on. As for drugs, however, the discourse is pretty much limited to: *don't do it!* Even if I smoke pot, and have for many years, I know it is my duty to keep our children from doing the same. A seed is enough for permanent grounding. It is a tolerable hypocrisy, one I am intent on enforcing. This was the wonder of Larium. If you wanted to "just say no" to malaria, you had to take it.

Caveats notwithstanding, it was easy to see the potential therapeutic benefits of the family drug experience. The same drug, at the same time, taken by people with nearly the same DNA presented interesting bonding possibilities.

Once I drank some *ayahuasca*, a glutinous mash made from the hallucinogenic *Banisteriopsis caapi* vine. In the Amazon, shamans mix up vats of this incredibly foul-tasting stuff that is ingested by dozens, sometimes hundreds, of people who are reportedly transported en masse into a collective telepathic state in which they are said to make contact with their ancestors (*Banisteriopsis* is called "the vine of the soul"). The result—especially in cultures wounded by the often brutal ingress of modernity—is the restitution of past and present, the connection of individuals dead and alive back into one vast continuum of kinship.

The *ayahuasca* was research. I was writing a piece on the late Terence McKenna, a Northern California–based ethnobotanist and drug philosopher, a well-known advocate for the sacramental and societal benefits of what he called "natural plant hallucinogens." So it was in the spirit of hands-on journalism that I found myself in a friend's apartment on the Lower East Side, under the influence of the telepathic vine of the soul.

Ethnobotanists say the *Banisteriopsis* vine can grow to seventy-five feet long and is able to retain its psychotropic powers for up to one hundred years even after it has been cut from its source. It's got a kick to it. And under its influence, in between much throwing up and bouts of diarrhea, I found myself catapulted into the deepest Amazon. I'd been transformed into a loincloth-wearing Indian, stretched out on the banks of the mighty river. The air was thick in there, the tree canopy was so dense I could not recall if I had ever seen the sky. My feet, clammy and cold, had never been dry. All I knew was that it had rained yesterday, it was raining today, and it would rain tomorrow.

After stumbling home the next morning, my wife told me a startling story. Seems that Billy, not quite two at the time, had been sleeping in our bed. He woke up in the middle of the night, and noting my absence, had asked, "Where Daddy? *Jungle?*"

It was the first time he had ever used that word before, at least that anyone had heard.

"*Jungle?*" This is the sort of experience for which the old hippie locution "far out" was invented. My friend's place was only a couple of blocks from our St. Marks Place apartment, but still, that is a lot of concrete, a lot of wallboard, a lot of mucky air for a thought beam to pass through. But who is more likely to be tuned to your frequency than someone who loves you as unconditionally as a two-year-old boy? Then again, Bill and I, we've always been close.

My Larium dreams weren't like that. I kept dreaming we'd lost them, forgotten them in the last country, like left luggage. The scenarios were similar. My wife and I would awake in an unnamed hotel, in an unnamed city that could have been Bangkok, or Phnom Penh, or Chicago, and they were gone. The three of them vanished. It is something all parents worry about, not that it had happened much in real life. Once Rae got lost in the supermarket but we'd found her quickly enough after she started singing the Clash song "Lost in the Supermarket" at the top of her lungs. Rosie disappeared at the zoo in Connecticut, but typically enough, she just walked around with another family, trying them on for size no doubt, until my wife found her in the cow-petting pen. Once we couldn't find Billy in Bed Bath & Beyond. We had him paged on the loudspeaker, which caused him far more duress than being lost.

These dreams were worse than that. They were really gone. My wife and I spent the rest of our lives looking for them. In one dream we were beside a giant warehouse in a desolate part of town. But there was a heat, a presence. Something was alive, inside. We picked the lock with a credit card. The room was enormous, filled with glowing spheres, millions and millions of them, as big as basketballs, piled on top of each other. Immediately we knew: trapped inside these globes were the spirits of the missing people of the world, all the disappeared. Suddenly, the pile began to move, shake itself, like Ping-Pong balls at a lottery. Three spheres tumbled from the pile, rolled up at our feet.

It was them, our children, trapped inside those globes, rolling around our feet like hungry cats. Outside we heard a stirring. The townspeople were out there, banging on the walls. They'd kidnapped the missing of the world and were not about to give them back, not if they could help it. We grabbed the three spheres and started to run. If we could get away, we could liberate them from the spheres. They'd be back with us. But we couldn't hold on, the balls slipped from our grasp, floating upward into the blackness of the building's unseen ceiling.

Love—is there ever enough of it? I despaired, lying awake in our second-class sleeper.

Mostly I worried about Rae. Once she was my girl, the Princess of All, and now we couldn't have a conversation beyond a few grunts. Whose fault was it? Who knew? Years ago, my wife said something that has stayed with me. "Rae's like the first pancake," she said, which I took to mean that when you make a batch of pancakes, often time the first one comes out a little funny, not as round as the others, not as smooth. On the other hand, while the first pancake might not be perfect, it does soak up the most butter, which makes it taste the best. This was the dialectic of the first pancake. A shocking idea, really, because it connoted that we might have a "starter child," a first pour of batter on the platter with which we would make beginner's mistakes.

Who knew if this was true, but things hadn't really been the same between Rae and me since that time at the Minnesota campground when she first said I wasn't looking at her the same way (with absolute, total love). It was a terrible thing to hear then, and it would be terrible to hear now, not that I got to hear it anymore. There was nothing but sidelong looks and, mostly, avoidance.

It was hard to think about, for both of us, because we still loved each other, as much as ever. There was just so much stuff in between. A landslide of stuff, blocking our ways to each other. Thrumming across the Gangetic Plain, each of us lost in our separate Larium dreams, the idea of loving someone and having that love truncated by nothing you could put your finger on or explain struck me as a very sad thing, as desolate and lonesome as a train whistle in the black night.

I thought of that day, on the Long Island Sound, sailing with my father on *L'Chiyam*.

He was dead now, keeled over in the bathroom of the house where I grew up. It was sudden. For years he'd suffered from failing kidneys, hooked up to dialysis machines, sugar out of control, and then he comes out of the shower and has a heart attack. It was over in about twenty seconds, long enough for him to fall into bed, which is where he said he always wanted to die, although not quite like that. When I arrived at the house he was still lying there, except in the wrong place. He was on Mom's side of the bed. This was something that never varied. His mystery books, skull and crossbones on the spine, were stacked up on the right side of the headboard, her mystery books were on the left. In the end, they'd changed places.

The undertakers came with their black bag and zipped his body inside it. I knew one of them. We were on the track team together, thirty years before. A time or two we passed the baton to each other on the second and third leg of the mile relay. Now he was carrying my father's body away.

"Oh, hey," he said, his face brightening with recognition. "How you doing, man?" he said, clapping me on the back with his momentarily free hand. Maybe some other time, when he was "off work," we could get together, have a coffee, discuss old times.

What stays with me most about those days was the moment before the funeral, when they needed someone to identify the body one last time. It was to fend off lawsuits, I suppose, to make sure they put the right stiff in the right hole in the ground.

The man from the funeral parlor—black suit, black shirt, black tie, white shoes, a little American flag pin in his lapel—opened the coffin. We'd gone with the plain pine box. The rococo plastic and gold leaf jobs were out, of course. My father, rabbi of the right angle, might have enjoyed a perfect twenty-one in Atlantic City, but he wasn't about to be buried inside something that looked like a slot machine. Still, there was the temptation to get something better—mahogany, cherry or walnut, a wood with a finer grain, more subtle to the touch. An artist should be surrounded by his favorite medium. But this would have been a mistake. The Depression pragmatist in him had always kept the subversive artist in check; it would be presumptuous to change the formula now. Pine would be fine, especially at these prices.

The box looked two or three sizes too small, like they'd ordered the wrong one and then hunched up his shoulders to cram him inside. Didn't they bother to measure? If the roles were reversed, he would have measured. He could make any cabinet fit into any space, even in the crappiest of civil-servant kitchens, where he'd listen to housewives whine and husbands chat him

up, like they, too, "did a little woodworking, down in the basement, you know." For sure he would have made sure a coffin was
the right size.

"It is a standard size," the funeral parlor guy said defensively.
We could have ordered "an extra long," the way men go to the
"big and tall" shops for suits. But we hadn't checked that box.

Death is the ultimate claustrophobia. Creeping, closing in,
tight around the geography of the small place upon which we
stand, until the cover comes down. All that finality, so much left
unsaid, unresolved—that's the lament, isn't it, the enduring
refrain: so much I never said, so much I wanted him to know. . . .

Yet, what really was there to say? Not so long ago my mother
gave me an old, fraying album that said "Snap Shots" on the front.
They were pictures from my father's war days, one more thing
we rarely discussed beyond his stories about how he came upon
the German helmet he kept in the basement.

"He saw me, I saw him, and he fainted first," my father
recounted. That was good enough for me since he used to let
me wear the helmet outside, which, swastika notwithstanding,
made me a real star in the neighborhood war games. Of these
photos my mother gave me, most of them of bombed-out buildings and stalled tanks, one jumped out.

It is a shot of him, sitting on the ledge of a balcony in his
fatigues, helmet and long government-issue coat. Behind him is
a large expanse of countryside. With its rolling hills, the land looks
very pleasant, a grand view. My father, only twenty-five, sits there
on the balcony wall, smoking his pipe, as casual as if he were at
the dinner table in Queens reading the school page from the *World
Telegram and Sun.* It must be late afternoon because he's squinting a bit and the sun is glinting off his wedding ring.

On the back of the photo, in my father's distinctive angu-
lar handwriting, it says: *"6/45. Corner of Hitler's Balcony—me too—
The ring is shiny, huh?"*

Now, it couldn't have been easy street, getting to Hitler's balcony in Bergesgarten in "6/45." The war was over, but it had been a long trip in from France. The *wehrmacht* didn't fling open the doors for you just because you happened to be in the neighborhood. Along with the picture came a book called *XII Corps— Spearhead of Patton's Third Army.*

My father had underlined several passages. One of these is on page 316 where Pfc. Frank H. Albertson is quoted as saying: "We launched eight boats and started across but the current was so swift that the boats started heading downstream. . . . This was right where the Germans were but there wasn't anything we could do about it. The Jerries opened up, first with one rifle shot, which rang out clearly, then with burp guns and machine guns, and flares all let go. Several boats were hit with mortars and our men had to swim ashore. Most of us made it." My father put two lines under this. In the margin is written, "good old Frank."

But it was worth it, of course. Worth it for a Jew to come sit and smoke his pipe on Hitler's balcony in June of 1945. How could that *not* be worth it? But it is the wedding ring part that really slays me. My parents were married only a few months before my father went overseas in the beginning of 1944. They could have waited, I guess, to see if he was going to live through this, but my mother says it never occurred to them. She went with him to Granite City, Illinois, where he did some training before shipping out, and then she didn't see him until 1946, when he finally came home. It was a long time to be apart. Yet at this great moment of triumph, on the balcony where Hitler and Eva Braun once frolicked, when he peered off into the Bavarian sunset, my father wanted my mother to know that what stood out was their wedding ring, which was "shiny, huh?"

If this picture had turned up earlier, my father and I could have talked about what it was like when those pontoon boats started going the wrong way, into the German fire. We might have talked about it during one of those interminable tacking sessions under the uncompleted Throgs Neck Bridge. But I doubt it. Even if I'd been able to reach into his coffin, lay my hands upon his unmoving chest and bring him back to life, we probably wouldn't have talked about it. If he'd lived to be a hundred, we might not have mentioned it. This was how we were: we didn't talk much.

I couldn't remember the last time I'd ever kissed him. It had to have happened, but knowing him, knowing me, it couldn't have occurred much after my sixth or seventh birthday. Even now, with him in that cramped little box, the space between us seemed impossibly huge, the motion of my lips toward his face an endless journey through layered veils of stunted feelings. Were we lazy or were we afraid? Was it chemical, something between the two of us that didn't mix? Or were we simply too busy, preoccupied by our little secretive art gigs? Sometimes I thought, well, I turned out like him after all, sitting here in this room, this semi-remote figure working on these articles, these stories. My own little, however fudged, right angles.

His forehead was cold, like ice. They must have just wheeled him out of the deep freeze. Only the embalmer's makeup felt of this world, greasy like bad hair cream. Everything else—his grayish skin, his neatly combed hair, the part on the wrong side—had moved on. But even then, I couldn't shake the self-consciousness, the sense that I was trespassing, violating the boundaries of a long-held treaty. My lips withdrew quickly, back to safer ground.

"That's him all right," I told the funeral parlor man.

Twenty years ago, when my wife and I first saw the Taj Mahal we both immediately broke into tears. There was no other reasonable response. The ultimate of postcards, the great marble building looked the way it did in every tattered, ghee-streaked poster in every lousy Sixth Street restaurant. Yet here, even in the harsh morning sun, it transcended numbing representation. To be in the presence of the Taj, you had to weep, spontaneously and happily, for no other reason than the sheer exhilaration at being part of a species capable of creating something so beautiful.

The Taj was built by slaves, twenty thousand of them laboring out in the hot sun by the Jamuna River, for more than twenty years (we felt it was our political duty to know these things) but, as the locals whose ancestors had likely hauled the stones pointed out, the Taj was different. The Taj wasn't built for love of God, or love of empire. It was built for love itself. Shah Jahan, King of the World, son of the emperor Jahangir, grandson of the great Akbar, constructed the building as a tomb for his beloved second wife, Arjumand Banu Baygam (a.k.a. Mumtaz Mahal, Chosen One of the Palace), a memorial to the deepest romance, everlasting and unconquerable, even by death.

Twenty years ago, my wife and I stayed on a single five-foot-long charpoy bed on the roof of one of the forty-rupee hotels right outside the Taj gates. But we didn't care. With Shah Jahan's pearly dome beaming in the full moon's light, sleep was an afterthought. This is how we remembered the city of Agra, as one more of the last places we were kids together. Love was effortless then, play came easily. We were more than ready when we found ourselves overtaken by Holi, an Indian festival known for the spreading of colored water, usually delivered in great buckets, splashed over anyone and everyone within reach. What great sport that was, especially once the half a million kids from all over town found out two white hippies were willing to join in the give and take. Gangs of nine-year-olds flung themselves out from hiding places and ground the colored powder into our hair (magenta and chartreuse were popular), shoved it into our ears and eyes. By noon we looked like five years of Fillmore East light shows had blown up in our faces. Then, that night, back on our roof, the dome of the Taj seemed to be rising along with the moon until it hovered over our little bed, like a luminous silken ship, a flying funhouse of devotion, ready to whisk us off to anywhere lovers liked to be.

Too bad Holi wasn't happening when our family pulled into Agra. The kids would have dug that messy mayhem. But it was summer, Holi comes in the spring, and I remember no tears shed as we walked through the red sandstone gates to behold the Taj.

India was weighing on us, the dust, the heat, the million touts, their faces way closer than the western sense of personal space deems polite. For days we'd been charting our individual SLs, or "serenity levels." It was another travel ritual, one more running game. "SL," one of us would call out, and each would reply with a number between one and ten. One was the lowest, a near oblivion of the spirit. Ten was tops, defined as the highest conceivable state of relaxation and willingness to mesh one's existential being with our ever-changing bizarro surroundings. Many factors went into the declaration of an ambient SL, such as Rosalie's persistent claim that Billy's very existence caused a perpetual 20 percent drop in her struggle for well-being, making it impossible for her ever to achieve an SL higher than eight. This meant, she argued quite cogently, that if any aspect of Billy, including the memory of his nattering personality or a remnant of his smelly T-shirts, remained in the universe (a virtual certainty, since what has lived will always be remembered by someone), this disproved the possibility of perfection, because nirvana could only be reached with a perfect SL, not simply an eight. Whether or not this was the ontological proof of anything, we did not know, except that upon hearing Rosalie's argument, Billy commenced an extensive catalog of his most annoying barnyard noises, which sent his sister into the usual tirade.

Even so, throughout Nepal our collective SL quotients hovered in the thirty-five to forty range, which averaged out to somewhere between seven and eight, well above the fours and fives recorded while in Cambodia. There had even been an instance of nines across the board while staying at the highly copacetic Shiva Lodge in Bhaktapur, outside Kathmandu. India, however, sent the SL into a near-terminal tailspin. Nothing was as grim as the trip to Agra, the bunch of us crammed into an Indian Ambassador sedan. Lurching along the roadway, stuck behind painted lorries emitting copious clouds of black smoke, our driver leaning on the horn for five hours had plunged SL levels dangerously close to zero, which, according to the unofficial scale, was "dead."

It had been a rough couple of days, especially after arriving in Delhi from Rishikesh, where The Beatles spent part of 1969 sitting around playing songs like "She'll Be Coming Around the Mountain" and "Jingle Bells" and dreaming of inventing a solar-powered guitar. They bailed out upon learning that the Maharishi, their temporary spiritual master (Ringo, who brought cans of pork and beans from London, didn't dig him), had allegedly put the moves on Mia Farrow, who was then between dating Frank Sinatra and Woody Allen. Originally we'd planned to stay at one of Rishikesh's large mountain ashrams. But the SL-raising potentiality of these massive lodge-like structures was shattered by the booming loudspeakers that blared Hindi chants twenty-four hours a day. Plus, what was to be made of the sign hung at the Omkarananda Ashram exhorting believers not to "hate the evil-hearted, the jealous and the selfish because it is they who promote your salvation"? Did this mean you should be happy that there were rotten people in the world, since their hideousness served to advance, the ostensible good person, ahead of them on the rungs of heaven's ladder? The children thought this not very compassionate, or even democratic.

It was the arrival at the Delhi train station that really put things around the bend, however. The electricity must have been on the fritz, because the surrounding area was pitch dark. The touts were like bats, operating on another kind of radar. In they closed, a hissing gaggle of clamping hands and pairs of blood-shot eyes. Their hotel was a good one, their rickshaw the best, sir, madam, please come.

No thanks, we declared. I'd picked a hotel out of the Lonely Planet guide, some dive no doubt, but right around here. "The name?" came shouts. What was the name of our hotel? It was an old trick: you say the name and they tell you the place has been closed by the police, or flooded out, or overridden by rats. "The name?" they yelled again. The name? It seemed as if I'd forgot-ten the name of the hotel. I thought it was the Namaskar, or the Amakar. Thinking I'd better check, I pulled out the guidebook, which I couldn't read in the dark. This only egged on the crowd. The cheapest and best hotels are not in books, they shouted.

Of course I should have reserved ahead. I had broken my own first rule of family travel, or any travel: never arrive after dark with-out a plan. But I hadn't expected it to be dark. The train was delayed, for hours. I was winging it. Not a good idea, not at all.

Around us, the catcalls were starting up. Until now the wolfish behavior of the Indian male had been more of a joke than anything else. At Clarke's a gardener asked the girls why they wore one-piece bathing suits. It was his understanding that everyone in the United States, in fact all women outside of India, "were fond of the two-piece, or perhaps wore no pieces at all." Now, however, on the dark streets outside the train sta-tion, the graspers were closing in. One put his arm on Rosie's shoulder. Rae got pushed. Billy freaked out, almost ready to cry. In an alley, I was trying to read the guidebook, now with a lit match, still parroting idiot lines about the "ambiance" and rough wonder of the road.

There is a moment, a shift beneath the feet, when suddenly you feel things are about to get out of control. In New York, I would have known what to do. In New York, I know when to walk faster, when to stare back, when to say something, when to fight, if it comes to that. But this was not New York.

"Hey, get away," I yelled. I haven't hit anyone with my fist for several years. Not for keeps, anyway. But I am the Dad, the Protector. Anxiety translated to rage and I was ready. It was only the look on the kids' faces that stopped me, the contempt behind the panic, like: "Okay, asshole, you got us into this, now get us out." It is a look that only makes me want to smack them instead.

Finally, totally by accident, we managed to find the hotel that Lonely Planet said had the "really helpful and friendly management." But it was late. The lobby, such as it was, was filled with sleeping men. One, who had been lying on a couch with his pants half undone, got up to let us in. Yes, he said, they have rooms, would we care to see? No, we are sure they are fine. Up the four flights of unlit stairs, we slammed the door, sat there in the dark and seethed.

This was the basic mood as we arrived in Agra, the city of the Taj, where love once reigned. The place had changed since my wife and I were last here, that was obvious. It was always a two-day tourist burg at most, full of hucksters and bereft of the seamy vitality found in most northern Indian cities. Now, the town appeared to have folded in on itself, held prisoner by the presence of its great treasure. Pollution was eating away at the marble dome, endangering the structure. The building had to be closed for regular cleanings. Stricter controls on auto emissions and wood cooking fires had been implemented. But since Taj tourism is the main generator of capital in this otherwise impoverished area, and much of the pollution comes from the idling engines of excursion buses and the exhaust of factories, many of them engaged in the manufacture of Taj souvenirs, the environmental situation is seen as a vicious cycle.

"It is a matter of the gander and goose's egg," said one local observer.

The fact that Yanni, the world's most annoyingly innocuous pop star, had recently been allowed to play a concert inside the Mumtaz Mahal's tomb could not have helped stem the degradation. In any event, the problem may soon become moot, since several measures recently discussed in the Indian parliament called for obscuring the Taj under a metal scaffolding, lest the national symbol become a target for Pakistani fighter planes. Indeed, that very day the headline of one of the English language newspapers read, "THE TROUBLE WITH PAKISTAN IS THAT IT STINKS."

Poor ol' Shah Jahan; once he might have ruled the Moghul world, but he ended his days inside the jailhouse at Agra Fort. The king had four sons, and the one he liked best, Dara Shikoh, was defeated in the fight over succession by his jealous brother, Aurangzeb. Aurangzeb consolidated his power by locking up Shah Jahan for the rest of his days. He did, however, grant the old king's request to be given a cell with a view of the Taj Mahal.

Shah Jahan's cell block diary on the vagaries of love and family might have made interesting reading, considering that his beloved Mumtaz died in the midst of giving birth to his jailer, Aurangzeb.

Only days before, I'd traced the outline of a bodhi leaf, and despaired my inability to further my children's potential enlightenment. Now the heart-shaped dome of the Taj offered a similar canvas, this time for the contemplation of the limits of love. Once my wife and I lay here under a full moon, just the two of us, lost in this one pure thing. Now, there was this overload, this cacophony of need and desire. Love—was there ever enough of

it? Five people, including myself, five people to love, that didn't
seem like much. Some people had ten children, even more. Five
people—certainly the human heart, my heart, could stretch to
cover that canvas. I could love five people, couldn't I? Jesus loved
the whole world.

How fragile everything seemed all of a sudden. The Taj was
being eaten away by car exhaust. Buddhas in Afghanistan were
blown up by people who never knew the Buddha. Planes crashed
into buildings. What seemed solid melted to air. Once I had this
idea that every baby was a product of all the other babies who'd
ever been born. A man and woman came together sacred and
unique, but not alone. They came from a line as long as the species and the other species that had mutated over millions and
millions of years to create the first humans. This was what was
behind every act of love, this unmatched, immeasurable power.
It was a power as vast as the universe itself, and like the universe it was always expanding, a ripple through the galaxies.
Gravity, which held things together, harnessed this infinite
power. Love was a kind of gravity, a sacred force field.

But you couldn't count on it. One false move, intended or
not, could wreck everything, make things fall apart. Eventually,
because you were brother and sister, husband and wife, or father
and child, you made your peace with the space that remains between. I suppose that is what happened between my father and
me that afternoon out on Long Island Sound: we finalized our long
surveyed deal, built our fences, made ourselves good neighbors,
waved as we went by every so often.

This is my nightmare: to be lying in my pine box, looking
up through dead eyes and see them there, peering down. They
will kiss me then, one by one, as I kissed my father, because we're
not Navajos and even if we're not crazy about it, we will touch
the dead, if only for an instant. But this isn't what I want for
them. I don't want them to be haunted by the seeming endless

passage of their lips through empty space, before they land on my refrigerated forehead, and pull away, for all time.

I don't want to be lying in my grave, out there under all that Queens dirt, in Beth Israel Cemetery not so far from the Belmont Race Track, for nearly seven years and have them come to visit me exactly once, which is exactly how many times I've visited my father's grave. No, I don't want that, not for me, not for them.

The next morning we drove back to Delhi in our trusty Ambassador, each one of us sucking on a foot-long stalk of sugarcane. This time the five hours of Indian "superhighway" motoring, with its usual overturned haywagons, side-swiping lorries ("horn please!"), seemed a breeze. The great ordeal was ending. We would be on a plane out of India the very next morning.

Also, it was Lord Krishna's birthday, a fact we noted while passing Mathura, birthplace of the god, on the Agra-Delhi road. Just like parents affix party favors to apartment house buzzers to designate where the party is, some pink-and-blue balloons were taped to the U.S.-style freeway marker, which said "Mathura—Birthplace Lord Krishna—Exit Now."

Back in Delhi, the party was on. In the god's honor, the late afternoon sky was filled with hundreds of homemade kites, a fabulous array of color across the pale blue sky. In the spirit of our coming liberation from the subcontinent, the children ordered a couple of pizzas from Domino's. As with the homeland version, the food chain's Indian affiliate offered a free pizza should their delivery man arrive late. No specific minute limit was noted, the free pie deal being good only if it did not arrive "in timely fashion." Not that any of our group was in a mood to split hairs. They didn't even seem to mind that the "cheese" on top of the pizzas was actually *paneer*.

Pizza was perfect for Krishna's birthday. Krishna is most often shown as a child, the adored mischievous prankster. He flew his kites, made music with his flute, looked like a boy and still got to have sex with many beautiful maidens. No wonder he gets top bill in the Gita. The authors knew a teen idol when they saw one.

After all that business about Shiva the destroyer, and the yellow-decked, club-holding Vishnu, the kids were into Krishna. They liked that his name means "black" or "dark as a cloud." That gave him that brooding yet virile punkish thing the girls find so irresistible. Finally getting a chance to employ the portable Gita I'd dragged around the planet, I read through Krishna's declaration of his own godhead.

"I am the conscience in the heart of all creatures." I delivered these words with hiphop inflection in the style of Run-DMC's "(I Am) The King of Rock":

"I am their beginning, their being, their end/ I am the mind of the senses/ I am the radiant sun among lights/ I am the song in sacred lore/ I am the king of deities/ I am the priest of great seers. . . ."

"Well, HAR-ray!" the kids said. "Hare! Hare! Hare Krishna! . . . oh radiant sun among lights."

Years ago, when they were babies, we'd push them in their strollers in Tompkins Square Park and often see bunches of sallow-faced, orange-robed Hare Krishnas. It was always a moment that gave me pause. Those days, like now, Tompkins Square was full of people you really hope your kid does not grow up to be. The park was a veritable Ed Sullivan variety show of parental nightmares. There were the junkies, the tattooed squatters, the homeless. But of all these people you didn't want to see your kid be when you ran out for a container of Tropicana in the middle of the night, at least the Hare Krishnas seemed to be having fun. Far more doleful and beaten down than their ram- bunctious Godhead, at least they still acted like kids, singing their little song, beating on their drums.

For now, that seemed enough. "Hare . . . Hare Krishna, Krishna, Krishna, Hare Rama, happy birthday to you," we sang, shouting out the window, praising the God of children everywhere.

Talkback/Backtalk #3

by Rae Jacobson

Day 37, New Delhi.
"*Everyone is shaken up I think. In many ways it's worse than any-where we've been, all these guys looking at me and Rosie with the worst kind of undisguised lust. It's the kind of thing that makes you feel helpless and small, like you can't do anything no matter how bad the circumstances get. And it's true, repulsively and angrily true. I would never walk through the streets here day or night, which brings me to another disturbing thing; I've become bizarrely reliant on my parents, way more than I have been on anyone at any time for the past three years. I guess it's because we just follow them everywhere, but now it's a safety thing, too, I don't want to go anywhere without one of them with me. It's like being a little kid again, asking for fifty glasses of water just so I won't be left alone in the dark.*

I have no independent urges like I do back home. I just want to fol-low them and let them take care of me and protect me. Everything I won't let them do when we're home, I give into now. They're the only familiar thing I can find. I never knew I was so scared of everything. It could be-come a syndrome, like jumping at your shadow and loud noises. Like now, I'm really hoping my mother will come over and give me a hug, but in a moment of arrogant stupidity I snapped "I'M FINE" when she told me to stay close to her to avoid the creepy skanks that were staring at me. I yelled out of a stupid jibe for lost independence when in actuality I really,

really wasn't fine. Not fine at all. Sometimes I think this is what it is being me, faking bravery, knowledge, trying to be cool. Truthfully I was very grateful for the offer but I did it anyway and offended her and now she's sort of ignoring me."

Throughout all this I was dealing with that other matter, my father. By the time we left, he and I had reached the age where fathers and daughters come undone. Suddenly I had breasts and boyfriends, I felt like I had become unrecognizable to him. It seemed that most of our talks ended in screaming so most of the time we just stayed out of each other's way. Seemed easier that way. We'd never had the typical dad-girl relationship, but to me that was a good thing, we shared the same sense of cool, reporting to each other. If there was some especially beautiful light falling across the buildings, we wanted to share it. I don't know who else likes driving to fantastic places like Red Hook, which is this beaten-up neighborhood not too far from our house in Brooklyn. We'd drive out to the end of this deserted street and there was a broken-down trolley car, just sitting there. They haven't used trolley cars in Brooklyn like for fifty years. But there it was, with "Ebbets Field" written in the destination window at the front. It was like when we were in New Orleans. I was so happy to see that there really was a streetcar going to "Desire."

We loved the same things about life it seemed, and he noticed things I never would. He'd pay me a compliment on a well-written sentence in an otherwise boring school paper and it would make my whole day. Our sense of humor was always similar. When I was about five we made my mom a present for Mother's Day based on one of our favorite sayings (rules I have learned to live by): Never take the top paper, never play cards with a guy named Doc, and never eat at a place called Mom's. Our present was a menu; at the top was the saying, and then below it in huge letters, it said "WELCOME TO MOM'S!" The dishes included such delicacies as "booger pie with a side of earwax" and "bread and toejam." She liked it.

I guess that's what I'm trying to get out of this trip, a way to recontact my dad. I wanted to go exploring with him again, and I wanted to make him smile. As bad as things had become between us, though, there was still a connection—even when I was buried under a haze of confusion so thick that sometimes I couldn't see anything, the connection endured. It was in our blood somehow. No matter how hideous I became and how dense he was, it flew between us like sparks. I keep a collection of collages that I've done, one of which I found not long ago. It was an old picture of me and my dad hugging in a Pizza Hut on one of our road trips. Around it I'd drawn branches and underneath was written, "Sometimes we get lost but I still love him." I can't even remember making it now, but that describes it better than anything, the connection. Dad and Rae. And now I had a chance to be there again. Here in the middle of nowhere, we had no choice but to speak, and once again despite the multitude of problems that arose, we were able to talk to each other, to explore together the way we were meant to. I think this is our chance to repair the damage done and finally find each other again. I was kind of hoping, anyway.

The Holy Land

When we got to the Holy Land, the fighting hadn't started yet. It would be some months before Ariel Sharon would appear on the Temple Mount, and the bricks would begin flying once again—bricks that would shortly give way to bombs and debates over whether those who blew themselves up on buses and in restaurants should be called suicide or homicide bombers. Palestinian nightmare followed Israeli nightmare, one after another, a "cycle of violence" newscasters said threatened to become endless, as "eternal" as the Holy Land itself.

Like so many other parts of the world where children died every day, the Holy Land was no place for kids. But we'd managed to catch a lull, a little break in the action. It was better than running the risk of being in the wrong place at the wrong time, and better, way better, than not going at all.

Our entry to the Middle East came through an unexpected door. The soggy tickets we carried in our sweat-drenched money belts said Delhi to Cairo, with a half-hour stop in Amman, Jordan. But we decided we wanted to see Petra, the fabulous "lost city" south of the Jordanian capital. Might it be possible to break our trip in Amman? The Gulf Air representative didn't seem to know. No one else seemed to care, which we took as a yes.

In the Hashemite Kingdom of Jordan after less than ten minutes, the children had already declared their preference for the tidy, nonrepresentational monotheism of this new Holy Land over the multiarmed, blue-faced clutter of the one we'd just left. Suddenly, cleanliness and godliness became an immutable couplet for them, no matter how high the pile of unwashed clothes they'd left on the floor of their rooms back home. Order—railed against, shirked and belittled, now beckoned like a consoling snuggle. Imagine: a whole airport, spanking new and full of buffed chrome, without a single cow turd or splatter of betel spit against the wall!

As we dragged our bags across the glossy granite floor, a man came over to ask if he might assist us. Twenty-four hours earlier, well-exercised hackles would have risen. But here, in this blissful oasis of hygiene, there was no need to preemptively shoo suitors aside. In Jordan, a country we once joked to be the only land named after a sneaker, as Manila was the only city to be named after an envelope, assistance approached not in the form of a desperate rickshaw driver or clutching rug wallah. Speaking a charmingly Arabic-inflected English, our would-be helper told us his name was Basil and he spent his days teaching Shakespeare at the university. His goal seemed nothing more, or less, than to extend the venerable hospitality of his homeland.

The professor was meeting his mother, a robust woman who arrived in a full black chador. We were about to bid them goodbye but Basil would not hear of it. Expressing regret that he could not put us up at his house where his sisters would cook all our meals, he insisted on at least dropping us at our hotel. As we rode into town, Basil quizzed the children on their Shakespearean acumen and was gratified to find them well-acquainted with several of the Bard's masterworks, most notably *Julius Caesar*, *Macbeth*, *A Midsummer Night's Dream* and *Romeo and Juliet*, especially the soundtrack of the Leonardo DiCaprio version.

Happy to hear that Rae liked *Othello*, Basil said the play was also a favorite with his students. "It is resonance of the Moor" that accounts for Othello's popularity, said Basil, who admitted to "a preference for Iago."

"He's creepy, all right," Rae said.

"Completely creepy."

What a relief! Finally a place where things made sense, where actual conversation was possible with reasonable strangers.

Amman, an ancient site reinvented as a desert-modern sprawl of stucco apartment houses, supplied one more hit of familiarity. The place might as well have been a hillier Phoenix, Arizona, aside from ubiquitous pictures of the recently deceased King Hussein, the father of the nation, monarch for forty-six years. The country was still in mourning. Hussein's son, King Abdullah, was showing promise. But more prominent, at least in our minds, was the continued presence of Hussein's fourth wife, Queen Noor, a one-time American deb and Princeton cheer-leader. Noor looked "very queenly," declared Rosalie. Ever the Hitchcock fan, Rosie said the ice-blonde looked much more like Grace Kelly, the epitome of all things royal, than Princess Di.

We thought Basil, being an urbane professor, would offer some even-handed critique of King Hussein, some insight into the politically erratic leader who supported Saddam in the 1991 Gulf War and four years later appeared totally distraught at the funeral of assassinated Israeli prime minister Yitzhak Rabin. But no analysis was forthcoming, other than, "The king is our hero. Here everyone loves him. We are sad he is dead, but this makes us love him even more." As proof of his fealty, the professor kept a framed picture of the Hussein in his car. Everyone did.

This was fine with us, considering that among Middle Eastern monarchs, King Hussein has always been far and away number one in our family. This owed to the fact that my grandmother's cousin Ruth had once purchased one of the king's many houses, in Palm Beach, Florida. How Ruth, who grew up in the coal-furnace tenements of Williamsburg and Sheepshead Bay along with the rest of the immigrant crew, had managed to buy a Palm Beach mansion on the same street with Estée Lauder was another one of those family things you weren't supposed to ask about, like the demise of my uncle Hymie, the diamond cutter who was whispered to have become wealthy in the employ of various mob families and then had a heart attack while waiting on the cashier's line at Aqueduct, which was too bad because Hymie's horses rarely came in.

Family lore said Ruth had barely turned seventeen when she left with a clarinet player to go to California. Once there she got lucky in a number of marriage settlements, which were parlayed into investments in San Fernando Valley real estate. Always called "Ruth from California," she rarely appeared at family functions. So I was surprised to find that, in her early eighties and sickly, she'd heard I was in Miami and wondered if I'd drive up to visit her. She'd heard I looked like her cousin and my grandmother, Laura, and wanted to see for herself.

"When we were in Sheepshead Bay, Laura was my best friend, we did everything together," said Ruth, a tiny lady in a housecoat sitting on the edge of a giant couch in the middle of the mansion's living room, which must have been seventy-five feet across. With its ceramic tile floor and twenty-foot-tall potted palm trees, the place had a 'Rick's Cafe American' feel, the wheeze of Ruth's oxygen machine only adding to the noirish ambiance.

"Sit closer to the light," Ruth said, moving her glasses farther down her nose. She stared at me without speaking. Then, finally, as if in a trance, she gripped my hand and said, "Yes . . . Laura . . . I see you in there . . . I do . . . well I suppose I'll be seeing you soon."

It was weird, channeling my barely remembered grandmother who died of Parkinson's disease when I was seven for this distant cousin whom I'd never met before that night. But this is the faith humans place in the magic of familial blood. Soon enough, Ruth snapped back and, much flintier now, said I'd better go. Stay too long and the other relatives, whom she was certain watched her every move and couldn't wait to collect her fortune, would get the wrong idea.

As for King Hussein, Ruth held him in the highest regard, recalling a "gracious personal letter with a royal seal" he sent her around the time she purchased the house. She had hoped to meet the king at the closing, but "he sent some woman lawyer instead." Nonetheless, as a sign of respect Ruth kept several of the king's official photographs. They were all over the place, in the kitchen and in the bathroom, too, just where he, or his minions, had left them.

Indeed, I recognized one of these same pictures, of a younger, smiling Hussein, in the lobby of our hotel in Amman. We'd been directed to the place, located on a hill in a pleasant residential neighborhood, by a friend of a friend, an Arab-American videographer named Walid, whom I had never actually met at that time. No matter, we understood, Walid's family ran the hotel and we should simply mention his name upon arrival. We did this and were immediately whisked into a back room where an elderly gentleman in a starched white short-sleeved shirt sat behind a desk simultaneously going through a stack of receipts and playing a hand of solitaire. Hearing the name "Walid," he rose from his chair and strode toward us with the unmistakable air of a patriarch.

So glad we could come to see him, said the eighty-seven-year-old, who identified himself as "the famous Walid's grandfather."

Speaking in a gruff but eminently passable English, he shook hands with Billy and me, bending his still fit, six-foot-tall frame to kiss the hands of the girls and my wife. Had we really come all the way from New York? By way of India? A roundabout routing, no? Of course he could accommodate us. It was time for his daily swim, so he would have the desk clerk set us up with some rooms. Then we could relax. Tea would be forthcoming. After that, if it suited us, we might like to join him for dinner. Several other members of Walid's family were coming by and since we were such good friends of his grandson, he was certain they would be anxious to meet us.

This was, of course, a very gracious offer, but by the time we closed the door of our pleasant room the panic was in full throttle. Clearly the opportunity to confess that we'd never even met Walid had passed and now we were booked in to discuss our great friendship with his whole family. Plus, there was the usual table manners problem. Judging by the bearing of Walid's grand-father, these were clearly cultured people, an educated, worldly elite. Palestinian Christians exiled during the war in Lebanon, they had scattered across Europe and the United States, where they'd all done exceedingly well, becoming doctors, lawyers, pro-fessors. People like that knew how to carry on witty conversa-tions, which fork to use. Once seated at their table, we would be exposed as the Cro-Magnons we so obviously were.

As predicted, the various cousins, aunts and uncles of our unencountered friend were the soul of cosmopolitanism. It was like a dinner scene from a more animated early Antonioni movie, with three or four political and artistic discussions, in three or four different languages, going on at the same time. Not quite the quintet of *homunculi* we feared we might be, we held our own. After a cautious start, Rae and Rosalie soon commandeered a conversation about New York shopping. If you really had to, Rae said, you *could* go to Prada, Bergdorf, and those two thousand-square-foot places in Soho where hilariously affected sales people lorded over three impeccably placed pairs of ostrich-hide shoes and a straw pocketbook or two. But the real fun was to be had scouring the racks of Trash and Vaudeville and the other teen emporia of St. Marks Place. Why, Rae reported, she bought a long velvet coat at Religious Sex back in ninth grade and she was still wearing it (despite our best attempts to burn the thing). So the stuff really held up, as well as being hip. Rapt, Walid's cousins soaked up this ground-level account.

In the end it was simply two families eating dinner with each other. Us, the tight little moving nuclear model, and them, the brilliant, far-flung refugees, here together for a day, then gone again. We had our differences and our similarities, something we often noted when comparing ourselves to other families. These were not necessarily comparisons of who had more money, a bigger house, more kids, or even whether they seemed happy or sad. These things came into it, of course. But it was more a matter of the Tao of the thing: what the family seemed to be *about*.

It was a big lie about all happy families being the same, we thought. In this day and age, it seemed the other way around. Once you heard about trouble, you could more or less fill in the blanks, from the hockey dad, to the restraining orders, and the alcoholic mom forgetting where she put the kids' Ritalin. All that shoddy behavior was on TV every night and in the dumb teen literature. Happiness seemed a less standardized, more elusive and creative state.

We thought of the families we knew. Every one had their own little thumbnail. There were the Greens (these names are changed because you never know who'll get mad about what) who liked to be physical, and were always rowing and canoeing, throwing each other around in karate studios. There were the Blues, marvelously detached and scholarly in their European way, chess champions every one, each more romantically spaced out than the next. And the Reds, on the surface the most middle American, but who were actually stone gamblers who gloried in high risk. And the Silvers, from damaged backgrounds, caps desperately set for success, which incurred its own sort of damage.

In the blather about so-called family values, family identification did not appear to carry the same weight in the popular mindset as it once did. You rarely heard people say things like, "Oh, he's an Amberson, you know what *they're* like" or "She's one of *those* Buchanans all right." People nattered on about football teams and corporations being "families," at least until they got traded to the Bengals or fired. Being a Blood or a Crip inspired more loyalty than being a Hatfield or McCoy.

But at the end of the day, the nuclear family, for all its manifest defects, remained the most viable container for bunches of people. We were lucky. At least we could stand each other. We were an entity unto ourselves. But what was the nature of that entity? Who exactly were we? What was our thumbnail? Through all the vague ambivalence with which we conducted our daily lives came a burning need to *represent*, as the rappers say. If we were us, we should be *us*, a distinct unit about which people could say, "Oh, those Jacobsons, you know what *they're* like."

Throughout dinner Walid's grandfather sat at the head of the table, saying little. The discussion of bargains and various musical favorites did not appear to interest him. Then, as we finished our dessert, he finally weighed in.

Perhaps it was just "an eighty-seven-year-old man talking," he said, but he had a problem with this rootless business about going here and there, traveling from one end of the earth to the other. If he had his life to live over again he would not have gone anywhere. He would have just stayed put, never left the town where he was born. Because even if he had been to Europe, America, on both business and pleasure trips, much of this moving around, *most of it*, in fact, was not his idea.

"We were chased," he said. "Always chased. We ran businesses in Jerusalem, and the Jews chased us out. We ran businesses in Beirut, and the Muslims chased us out. Now they will likely chase us from here, too . . . they do this because of *who we are*."

This was what it was like in this part of the world, Walid's grandfather said matter-of-factly. People immediately knew where you were from, where your father was from. There was no hiding it. Middle Eastern people had a special antenna. They could detect the slightest gradations of clan and belief. If they didn't want you around, they let you know. This was one way you found out who you were, through the people who wanted nothing to do with you, who hated you, for good reason or not.

Americans did not understand this, the old man continued, pointedly. Americans thought they could go wherever they wanted. It didn't matter if they were unwelcome, because they were too full of themselves to know any better, or because people wanted their money enough to hide their dislike. Americans had no sense of who they really were because they did not know where they did not belong.

This willful ignorance couldn't last forever, Walid's grandfather said. It was something he understood from his own life, from the days when he felt himself as cosmopolitan as anyone, living in Lebanon before the war. "Everyone was from everywhere else there. It was like a movie. People told lies about their past and no one cared. You could be one thing one day, something else the next."

Those were good days, he said. "Now they are looking under the sheet. People are being sorted out. If you do not feel like being a Christian, Jew or Muslim anymore, that is too bad. Nothing is up to anyone anymore. It is out of your hands. Because no matter what you say, or feel, the other people, *they know who you are*."

*   *   *

Petra had been a myth to us. We first caught a glimmer of the place while reading *The Red Sea Sharks,* a most excellent adventure of our beloved, cowlicked comic-book hero, Tintin. To travel with Tintin, who was supposed to be a journalist but never seemed in a hurry to make a deadline, was like going through the atlas. Wherever Tintin, his friend the crotchety Captain Haddock and the grand mutt Snowy went, we wanted to go, too. A Kiplingesque purveyor of the nineteenth-century style of supposed colonial high-mindedness, Tintin was often thwarting the evildoing of nefarious sultans and gangster sahibs. This retro noblesse oblige was occasionally remarked upon by our kids' teachers, who felt Tintin's particular questing spirit, especially when accompanied by the drunkard Haddock (whose stream of colorful, often racialist epithets we always understood as a foil for Tintin's tender-spirited ecumenicalism), did not suit the "inclusionary" curriculum.

Not to fall prey to the too easy lampoonery of "identity politics," but this is one of the problems of so-called progressive education. *Treasure Island,* with all its pre-Conradian provincialisms, will always make for more thrilling and uplifting kids' literature than the drearily "realistic" housing project or crummy suburb survivalist sagas (Great! Mom's off crack again!) that my children have constantly been handed through grammar and middle school.

This doesn't mean kids shouldn't confront the harsh realities of urban life. Rosalie, for her part, refused to return to the sweet (some might say prim) little private school we were paying through the nose to send her to. Why did she want to leave, the headmaster asked her, she was doing quite well, on the honor roll. "Well," Rosie said, "I'm a political person and there's not enough . . . *realism* . . . here for me." The headmaster was somewhat nonplussed. "Not enough *realism*? Never heard that one before," he said. Was she intimating that the school wasn't liberal enough? It was *very* liberal, in a *sensible* way, of course. Sticking to her position, Rosie now goes to a giant high school deep in the bowels of Brooklyn, with four thousand students, a sizable percentage of them Russians from Russia. This offers much realism, which makes her intermittantly happy, about as happy as teenagers would ever admit to being.

We didn't exactly need Edward Said to give us the subaltern deconstruction of Tintin, to tell us that colonial adventure was adventure only for the few, like Indiana Jones, the rapacious Leopold, king of the Belgians, and his agent, Henry Morton Stanley, finder of Livingstone, murderer of thousands. No, we didn't need an Earth Firster to tell us that humankind's supposed heroic triumph over nature only sowed the seeds of the wheezing prune of a planet we live on today. We know people suck, that our extinction is the earth's only chance.

It's just that when you have children, you need a little optimism, some cool places for them to play, and patience when they break a couple of things along the way. This is why we like Tintin, who, after all, never dug a single offshore well, made no gold miners live in hovels, stole no artifacts, and sought no profit beyond the expansion of his imagination. When you're with him, the world is still big.

This said, the saga in question, *The Red Sea Sharks*, started to get good when Tintin, Snowy and Haddock, in the mythic land of Khemed to aid their friend, the unfairly deposed Emir Ben Kalish Ezab, crash-land their plane in the desert. Chased by minions of the bad new ruler, they take refuge in the hills, eventually hiking through a narrow pathway and coming upon an astounding city carved into soaring sandstone.

"Thundering typhoons," Captain Haddock says, "a Roman temple, hewn from the rock! Incredible!" On the bottom of the page, in a large panel, is a drawing of a fabulous columned structure. Obviously huge, it might have been hundreds of feet high.

Back in Brooklyn, the edifice caught our attention. But since Hergé, Tintin's sublime creator, had not seen fit to identify the structure (which only appears in that one panel), it entered consciousness as a fantasy, something made up. It wasn't until years later, thumbing through the far more staid pages of *National Geographic*, that we learned such a place actually existed and was called Petra.

Wow. That's what everyone says after they emerge from the Siq, the narrow, mile-long corkscrewing canyon that serves as the entryway to Petra's ancient city, and come upon the Khazneh, a.k.a. the Treasury. The Treasury is not like the Taj or Angkor, iconic postcards that you place yourself in front of and behold, in one great gulp. Built by goddess worshippers, the Treasury reveals itself more slowly, flirts with expectation. You know it is down there, pink and massive, but it plays hide and seek, until the Siq completes one last teasing coil.

Not "Roman" as Captain Haddock said, but *romanesque,* the Treasury is the work of the Nabataeans, a vanished tribe of brilliant engineers and draftsmen (their cursive writing would become the basis for modern-day Arabic), who came to what is now called Wadi Musa, the Valley of Moses, some twenty-three hundred years ago. Nor is the Treasury a temple or a bank. It is not quite a building at all, but rather a façade, a mask carved into stone. Archaeologists have never determined the function of the structure (there are some dark, tomb-like rooms gouged deeper into the rock but they are unimpressive, almost afterthoughts). The Nabataeans, forgotten ghosts in their own fossil city, seem to have constructed the structure for no other reason than to amaze the senses.

This was a place to play! Hidden away so whole conquering armies passed by unaware of the vast potential plunder on
the other side of the surrounding hills, it was a world apart, a
kid's perfect fortress, a magical private castle. Here you could
be anywhere, at any time. The Bedouins on horses looked no
more or less at home than the Mars lander being used by the
film crew taking advantage of Petra's pink sandstone's ostensible resemblance to the Red Planet. Even if the movie guys
were carrying around giant papier mâché boulders (a world of
rock and these bozos cannot resist the urge to make fake ones),
it was easy enough either to relocate yourself in the Old Testament, or be lost in space. Emotionally, the place had that kind
of range.

Inside Petra's surreptitious fortress a grand thing happened. We formally acknowledged we were having *a good time*.
Before, in those other countries, there were stretches when
some of us were having *a good time*, even *a really good time*. But
others claimed to be having *a bad time*, or even *a really bad time*.
Sometimes, maybe four of us might be having a *really good time*,
but there'd always be that other one who said he or she was
having *a really bad time*. It was hard to get in sync. If Billy was
happy, this precluded Rosalie from happiness, or so she said.
His *really good time* translated into her *really bad time*. At Petra,
our planets lined up in a harmonic convergence; SLs sky rock-
eted, registering steady nines and tens. It was the land of *the
really good time*.

The biggest news was Rae. Feigning the lost grumpy soul
no more, at Petra she walked past the Temple of the Winged
Lions, where the Nabataeans worshipped the fertility goddess
Atagartis, and pronounced herself to be "remembering where I
am supposed to be and what I'm supposed to be doing."

This was how it was with her. She has always been drawn
to antiquities, digging fossils from the ground, thinking about

mummies; it is as if the past is her place, the more removed from now the better. From her days as a baby, those who fancied themselves knowing such things said she was "an old soul." There was something about her eyes, even through the Dracula makeup—a special, endless empathy. I'd seen it at work, several times. Once, when the two of us were in Florida, an elderly woman sat down next to us at the beach. In a few moments Rae, solicitous of older people, started up a conversation with the woman, who looked to be in her eighties. She'd recently lost her husband and had come to Florida to be with her sister. The idea was a Florida trip, the supposedly magic elixir, might cheer her up. But it hadn't. She didn't want to go back to Michigan, but saw no reason to stay where she was. She didn't know what to do.

She and Rae spoke for a while, about several things. I didn't pay attention; I was reading a magazine. Later, when Rae ran down to the water to stick her foot in the waves, the woman started crying. I asked her if she was all right, and she said, "yes," especially now. It sounded crazy, she said, she knew she would die soon, but didn't feel "so afraid" anymore. Talking with Rae made her feel a lot better about it.

Being "an old soul" had its drawbacks. We sometimes thought the problem—her increasing inability to click in and do what she was supposed to do, like get good grades, show some initiative, not lose her keys, not pick at the candle wax, et cetera, came from a temporal dislocation. Like Brian Wilson, it seemed as if she just wasn't made for these times. It was a poetical affliction but a maddening one, mostly for her. For an old soul, Petra offers refuge. Indeed, Rae became an instant oracle of the place, rattling off much detail, such as the location of the Byzantine portion of the city, and the dates when the Romans had taken control of the Temple of Dushara. How she knew these things seemed a mystery, but then again Rae's way of knowledge has always been baffling. Teachers were constantly telling us that she never appeared to be listening, even that we should get her hearing checked. Yet somehow, if you happened to ask her, she could recall everything that was said.

Listening to Rae explain how ancient cities like Petra were often built on the site of even older cities, the ruins of which were used as the foundation for the next place, Billy was both pleased and suspicious. He rarely got to hear his older sister go on at such length, or so authoritatively, at least pertaining to something he was actually interested in.

"How do you know that?" Billy demanded, after hearing one of Rae's tour guide lectures. "Did you read it in a book?"

"I just know it," said Rae, our priestess of the rocks. It was like the long-gone Nabataeans, their legacy not likely to be on any mainstream test aimed at getting you into a good college, had opened their ledgers to her.

On the way back up the hill, we encountered a group of young German tourists. One of the women, maybe a little older than Rae, was dressed in a black short skirt, black ripped T-shirt, black spiked doggy collar, purple-streaked hair—the whole goth getup. Had we been back in New York, this might have been the girl dancing beside Rae at The Bank. They would have been sisters, bonded through the dark will of their all-encompassing rejectionism. But here, fused with the spirit of the Nabataeans, Rae had little use for such fuzzy nihilism. Who would show up at Petra wearing platform boots? At Petra, black was not cool; it was an affront.

We went south from Petra, into the Wadi Rum. Twenty million years ago tectonic plates tore apart here, leaving behind these craggy hills, the world's best backdrop for viewing the silhouette of a Bedouin riding a camel across the horizon at twilight.

We'd seen the Wadi Rum, or its facsimile, before, in *Lawrence of Arabia.* In fact, in retrospect, you could say our trip began the night we saw the movie on the giant screen at the Ziegfeld Theatre in Manhattan. It wasn't that the kids were so crazy about the picture or were so mesmerized by Peter O'Toole's rousing, deeply fruity portrayal of T.E. Lawrence (somehow, when I first saw the movie in 1962, I did not notice how, like, *into it* Lawrence seems to be while being whipped by the nasty Turk Jose Ferrer). No, what got to the kids was the steadfastly old-fashioned Brit refusal by director David Lean (Sir David to you) to allow himself the smallest wink to the audience. Watching Lawrence, you gave up control. For what seemed eons (Billy's review: "really sandy, really long"), there were no channels to change, no escape from the clunky drama, the far-flung yet claustrophobic sweep of mood. The usual cues for audience participation were removed. You were trapped in Lawrence's world, an experience not all that different than being thrust into the alt. world of another culture like, say, India. This wore the kids out. When we got home, they immediately got into bed and slept until well into the next morning.

Several months later, in the real Wadi Rum, the shadows moving beneath the full moon, no one was asleep. We were wide awake, turned on. New ground was being broken. In this desert, our journey had come about, experienced a sea change. Until we landed in Jordan, with the exception of a few spots, we went nowhere that my wife or I hadn't been before. Every place had a past, its own well-chewed memories, expectations. At any moment I might go into Dad-bore mode, spieling out a heavy-thumbed balance of then and now. It is a short haul between empiricism and a one-way ticket to Poloniusville. Petra and the Wadi Rum arrived free of such windy constraints. Discovery was on an even footing.

Deeper into the Rum, a million stars fighting for space in the sky, Adel, whom we'd hired to drive us around in his Toyota van, said it was getting late. We should get something to eat. Food was of paramount importance to Adel, a stout, bearded, thirtyish Jordanian with a rakish sense of humor. Trained as an economist, he really wanted to be a chef. His relatives in Chicago kept telling him to bring his wife and daughters to America where he could open a restaurant. Once they packed him up a piece of Chicago deep-dish pizza as a sample of the cuisine in their new homeland. Adel said his wife and children were very excited. From what they saw on TV everyone in America ate pizza constantly. Pizza was the king of American foods. But, even allowing for the long-term take-out status of the pie, neither Adel nor his family had cared for it.

"Jordanian food is much better," Adel declared, getting no argument from us, since after a lifetime of consuming falafel and gyros on St. Marks Place, the local fare proved a huge step up, especially the lamb and chicken *shawarmas*, which cannot be beat, anywhere.

Talk of food made everyone hungry, so Adel pulled off the road into a Bedouin camp. It was like driving into a truck stop, except the parking lot was full of camels. Under a tented canopy lashed together with goat hair sat a large group of men. In the middle of the group, in a position of importance, sat a young man wearing a shiny silken *jalabiyya*, which is the name for the long robes the Bedouins wear. Around his kufiyya head cloth were two strands of newish-looking *agal* ropes, indicating an upgrade in the young man's responsibility in the group.

"Good luck, we've arrived at a wedding," said Adel, "now the food will be very good." Immediately we were given seats of honor in the assemblage. Any notion that we might be intruding was set aside. As Adel informed us, despite their dwindling numbers, the famously hospitable Bedouins continued to adhere to their custom of *diyafa,* which entitled any visitor, even an enemy, to three nights and days of food and lodging.

We were sipping tea from clay cups when two young men got up and started playing what appeared to be one-string violins. Two others blew into foot-long metal flutes. The music, slow-paced and mournful, rose like smoke through the tent ceiling and up into the desert night. We sat there, watching the bridegroom. He looked kind of nervous, but that might have just been a cultural thing. However, his family seemed pleased with the dowry, which included horses and a Toyota pickup truck.

This was an experience not available in Brooklyn, at least not in any part of the borough we were welcome in. We turned to each other with widened eyes, amazed half smiles. We were thinking the same thing at the same time. That thought was *"Look where we are."*

This is the best part of getting anywhere, one more way to esteem the chance booty. Going around is not just a matter of having your picture taken in front of the Grand Canyon, or collecting trophy stamps in your passport. The idea is to be truly transported, to *be somewhere.* Sitting in a goat-string tent with Bedouins eating charred meat listening to a one-string violin was *being somewhere.*

Plus, the Bedouins liked us. They liked that we traveled as a family, the way they did. They liked that we carried our possessions, everything we had, on our backs, like they did. "You travel like the Bedouin," one older man said. We should leave America and come to live with them, they joked.

"Don't go back to New York, don't go to Amman," one man said, with a large smile. "Stay here. You will like it."

"But are you still nomadic?" Rosalie asked, considering the proposal.

"No . . . no mad . . ." This word was not known to any of the assembled elders.

Adel explained and everyone broke out into laughter. "Yes!
Nomadic! Come, you can be nomadic, too."

And why not? Nearly ninety years after Lawrence first came
to the Wadi Rum, past the fall of the Ottomans, the discovery of
oil and the disaster of religious politics, it was still clear why an
Englishman, or anyone, would want to chuck everything back
home, put on a snow-white burnoose and be like a Bedouin. Their
world might be disappearing, but they'd done a good job of coming to terms with what was left of it. If we were to go native, this
was as good a place as any. The Bedouins could homeschool the
kids. These were the quirky little experiences guidance counse-
lors said colleges were looking for these days. Deficient SAT scores
would be more than compensated for by the notation, "I have
working knowledge of Bedouin lifestyle, including camel-riding,
saddle-making and tent-sewing, gained during a several year, total immersion into a fully realized culture antithetical to everything this university is supposed to turn me into."

Yes, *look where we are.*

After one last cup of tea and much ritualized leave taking,
we were back on the road again, heading toward Aqaba. Adel,
the driver, said he would be happy when we got there. "Because
then," he said, "you will maybe no longer shout *Aqaba!*"

It was so; we had been screaming *"Aqaba!"* a lot. It was
another Lawrence thing, the rallying cry to his Bedouin troops
as they crossed the supposedly uncrossable desert to attack the
back side of the old Ottoman fortress where all the big guns were
in fixed positions facing toward the sea. Swell place, too, *"Aqaba!"*
a perfect sort of working waterfront town, full of bustle and low-
slung intrigue. Too bad we were only going to be there long
enough to watch *The Fifth Element* on TV at the hotel where the
clerk wondered why my (replacement) passport was green, since
"everyone" in the Middle East "knew" that only CIA agents carried green passports.

The next morning we were on a boat, heading across the impossibly blue Gulf waters for the Sinai. The Egyptian crew really had the sound system cranked up, the Arabic pop music drowning out the sound of the engine drone. But perhaps we might like to hear some different music, offered the captain. Did we have any tapes? Well, actually, we did. Fats Domino, the Ramones, Swamp Dogg, John Coltrane, lots of stuff. We even had the Smiths, Morrissey's feyish voice booming out of the loudspeakers.

"Nature is a language, can't you read?" the singer sang, the ladies in chadors shaking their heads along to the beat.

In 305 C.E., Roman Emperor Maximus, angered that the virgin Catherine of Alexandria had converted several members of his family from paganism to the faith of Jesus Christ, declared that the young girl should be put to death. Maximus had Catherine strapped to a moving slab that passed through a series of whirring bandsaw-like metal blades and a second set of horizontally mounted wheels outfitted with axes rotating in opposite directions. Much to Maximus's dismay and the joy of the followers of Christ, the mechanism broke, leaving the pure-hearted Catherine untouched. Resorting to a less fanciful form of execution, the emperor had Catherine's head chopped off with a single blow. But God so loved Catherine that He sent His angels to fly her remains to the summit of the highest peak in the Sinai desert. Two hundred years later, the Roman emperor Justinian, a Christian, ordered a monastery to be built to honor Catherine near the base of Mount Sinai, where Moses is said to have received the Ten Commandments.

Home to one of the great collections of Byzantine iconography, St. Catherine's is the world's longest continually inhabited Christian monastery. And, as is often the case with places where people come to dedicate their lives to the Spirit, it is no breeze to get to. Once we got off the boat from Aqaba, our first task was to convince one of the haughty cab drivers on the dock to drive up into the mountains. This was not easy, since compared to the frantic, life-or-death fervor of the Indian cab driver, the Egyptian driver is an aloof figure. Attired in his coffee-stained, powder-blue robes, he stands with his hand on the fender of his battered black and yellow Peugeot station wagon warily awaiting entreaties.

None of the drivers wanted to go to St. Catherine's, which was far, accessible only by bad roads, and offered little chance of finding a return fare. If fate had sunk him to such an abashed station that he was forced to serve as a chauffeur for *khawagas*, which is what foreigners are called, the Egyptian cabbie would much rather drive to the sinpots of Dahab, the hippie hangout/ disco land down the coastline. Dahab is a place where fools come to lose their souls, so let them, because they usually spend a lot of money doing it.

The cabbies were also willing to take us to Sharm el-Shiek and Na'ama Bay, the famous Red Sea diving resorts. This was one place my wife and I wouldn't have minded going. Diving used to be one of our things. We spent our honeymoon in the Caymans, where the underwater visibility approaches 150 feet and the sea turtles fly over your head like UFOs. Too bad that was one of the last times we dove. We keep talking about renewing our certifi-cations, teaching the kids to buddy-breathe, but it never happens. It wouldn't now, either. The schedule was tighter than we would have liked; there was no time for a four-day detour.

Besides, as I noted while in an Amman cyber cafe, The Wilsons, our bête noire fellow globe circumnavigators, appar-ently with all the time in the world, had just spent a week checking out the Red Sea corals. There was a long entry on their website describing their two-a-day series of "family dives" (all *their* kids, even the six-year-old, knew how). Down about forty feet, they encountered several sharks that approached them in what Tom, the webmaster Dad, called, "an alarming manner."

"We were scared. But were we really in danger?" wrote Tom. "I couldn't truly say. You'd have to ask the sharks. . . . Later on, after we were back in the boat and calmed down a little, we all agreed that it had been a great experience, being on the sharks' turf. It brought us closer in touch to the real balance of power in the universe." Of course, examples of The Wilsons' children's interesting, well-made paintings of "life beneath the sea," along with several similarly accomplished poems, abounded on the site.

Well, so much for diving. St. Catherine's sounded more like our kind of place, anyway.

But we needed to go now. It was already late afternoon; we'd been told that arriving at the monastery after nightfall made it difficult to find a place to stay. Speed, however, did not prove to be a problem. It might be difficult to convince an Egyptian cab driver to get behind the wheel, but once he gets going . . . zam—only the stout of heart can bear to look. Our *Let's Go* guide, with its usual Harvardian snideness, described the horn-honking code of Egyptian drivers, noting that one long beep means "I quickly bear down on you and will soon run you over." One short beep signifies, "I do not have enough speed to run you down but if you do not move I will run over you slowly." Still, nothing could have prepared us for the homicidal zeal of our unspeaking taxi man, swerving his Peugeot pellmell toward every breathing thing, human or animal.

After this, it was a chill comfort to find the gaunt, stooped figure of a solitary monk standing in the St. Catherine's courtyard at the base of the bell tower of the Church of Transfiguration. Hood of his habit covering most of his stark-white face, the monk, who said his name was John, led us down the gloomy stone steps to our quarters in the monastery hostel. It was a spare, high-ceiled room with several cots arranged in a barracks style.

This was a very good room, John said. Monks had lived between the stark walls since the days of the Crusades and throughout the time of the Ottoman Empire. Monks would always live at St. Catherine's, "until Kingdom Come," John said with a sober monotone. The monastery had often been attacked, but always survived. There were many reasons for this, in addition to its twenty-foot-thick, hundred-foot-tall stone walls. A gold-leafed handprint of the Prophet Mohammad, guaranteeing special protection, marked the main entryway. Beside that was a letter promising safety signed by Napoleon. But more than this, John said, St. Catherine's continued due to its proximity to "the mountain of Moses. God watches over this place."

With that, John nodded and left, clanging behind him a heavy metal door, solid except for the small cutout of a cross.

We sat there silently for a moment as the yowling of several cats in heat grew louder. The room was small, but our beds seemed terribly far apart, so we pushed them to the middle and cuddled together like a jumble of cats. "Is this what a mental institution looks like?" Billy wondered from under the covers.

Touristically speaking, the Burning Bush, which is said to be a direct descendent of *the* Burning Bush, is St. Catherine's number-one attraction. Nearly eight feet high, the thriving plant grows out of a stone enclosure outside the chapel of the Burning Bush. It is a powerful experience to stand before it, tracing the patterns of the twisting branches and narrow, elongated leaves, especially if you happen to be reading aloud the Book of Exodus, chapter 3, verses 1–5, as we were.

It tells of how Moses led his flock to *"the backside of the desert . . . to the mountain of God, even to Horeb"* where the angel of the

Lord appeared to him *"in a flame of fire out of the midst of a bush."* The bush *"burned with fire"* but *"was not consumed."* Moses turned aside and God called to him from the center of the flame. *"Moses, Moses,"* God said, *". . . Draw not nigh hither: put off thy shoes from off thy feet, for the place whereon thou standest is Holy Ground."*

We'd stood on "holy ground" before. From the Yucatán to Mount Rushmore, four stone faces chiseled into one of the Lakota's most sanctified sites, holy ground was a staple of our various itineraries. But this wasn't one more point of abstracted anthropological interest. The Burning Bush wasn't in the Gita, or part of a Hopi creation myth. It was in the Bible, the core text, for better or worse, of our particular version of the world. The Bible was something you dealt with every day. It was about belief, but it wasn't only about belief. There were those famous phrases, all that common knowledge that both spurred and bound the imagination. This raised the stakes.

But could this *really* be the Burning Bush, or, as St. Catherine's faithful insist, the most recent offering of the original plant's root system? "The back side of the desert" mentioned in Scripture is not what you'd call a pinpoint location. Then again, this was the true challenge of faith: believe it or not.

The question of the bush's "physical reality" came up a few moments later as we did what we usually do, which is tail along with the tour groups because we like to hear what's said but are both too cool and too cheap to sign up. The guide, an English-speaking German professor of comparative religion, said if the bush were to be the real bush, it could only be the real bush to Christians, since Orthodox Judaism "did not accept the corporeality of things." To the Jews, the professor said, "the idea of the objectified image is controversial . . . the object has meaning more as metaphor . . . a symbol of the Almighty's inexhaustible ability to sustain and light the world." Christians, on the other hand, the professor said, tended toward "more literalistic

interpretations." Christians were very concerned with iconography, the guide said, which connoted a "more identifiable reality . . . so close to reality as not to make a difference."

"What's he talking about?" Rosie wanted to know.

"He said," Rae told her sister, "that if the bush is a Jewish
bush it's a metaphor, and if it's a Christian bush, it's a Bush."

Rosie reached up, plucked a leaf from the plant. "This is a
leaf. I am holding it in my hand. Is it a leaf or a metaphor?"

Rae, a vet of logic class, looked at Rosie's leaf and said,
"Better say both to be on the safe side."

The Burning Bush has supposedly never been transplanted.
Popes and kings are said to have taken cuttings from the shrub
and attempted to root them in their homelands without success.
This brought up the obvious comparison to the bodhi tree in the
Sarnath Deer Park, the alleged spawn of the Buddha's tree of
enlightenment. Rosalie's Burning Bush leaf now tucked between
the pages of *The Inscrutable Americans* along with the ones from
Sarnath, we contemplated the botanical and spiritual implica-
tions of transplantation. Which plant was more holy—the one
that could not *or would not* reproduce itself and therefore existed
as one single undying entity, or the one that might take hold,
given the proper conditions, in any soil?

The girls weren't sure. The idea of the singular One, the
indivisible monotheist argument, was impressive. But so was the
notion of the spreading, moveable meme.

Billy, not the phenomenological sort, did not regard the
Burning Bush in this manner. Instead he was trying, unsuccessfully, to stifle a guffaw. Sometimes it seems like Bill spends
half his life unsuccessfully trying to stifle a guffaw, and the rest
of it cracking up. The way he looks at the world, he seems to
find more things funny than does the usual individual. Sometimes he'll just giggle, a short chortle, but then he'll be falling

off his chair, snorting and gagging. "What? What's so damn funny?" everyone yells. Sometimes Bill is so amused, he can't speak, only point. Such was the case during the tour guide's talk on the "physical reality" of the Burning Bush. Bill directed our attention to the wall where the plant grew. There, on the ground, was a bright red fire extinguisher.

"You never know," Billy finally said, catching his breath and drawing his eyes skyward.

The next night, shortly after midnight, we were supposed to climb Mount Sinai where God is said to have given Moses the Ten Commandments. No visit to St. Catherine's is supposed to be complete without an ascent of the holy mountain. The big problem is you're supposed to leave in the middle of the night, so as to have time to return before the following afternoon, when, this being July, the temperature would be pushing 115 degrees. This schedule was at odds with our internal clocks. When it was time for us to get up and make our way through the chilly night toward the 3,750-step stairway leading to the summit, we rolled over and went back to sleep.

A couple of hours later, suddenly awake, I was thrown into a dense spate of misgiving. Walid's grandfather said the Middle East was where people could not escape their identity. Was this not the case with us? Being too lazy to climb Mount Sinai seemed to embody the true lassitude of our familial ethos, go to the heart of our flaccid underachievement.

If the Wilsons were here, for sure they would have climbed Mount Sinai. They would have knocked on God's door. I could imagine the account on their website right now. They weren't going to brag about it, of course, not wishing to separate themselves from other travelers less fortunate or marvelous than themselves. But you knew it would be there, hidden away like the kabala code deep in the HTML: an eight-by-ten-inch glossy of flame and fire, too bright even for the eyes to behold, and at the bottom, the following: *"To the Wilsons—Finally Someone Worth Talking To. Keep on Truckin'—G-d"*

But, as Rosie pointed out, so what if we didn't climb Mount Sinai? The mountain had plenty of customers. Every other tourist in the hostel was making the trip. A tour bus from Dahab had pulled in about midnight with forty more pilgrims. One hundred Bedouins and their spitting, crouching camels waited in the moonlight; for $25 they offered to take out of shape or inappropriately shod seeker-tourists to the mountaintop. On any given night as many as five hundred people would ascend Sinai. It wasn't like God, if He was up there, was getting lonely. We were probably doing Him a favor by staying in bed. In fact, by what power were these tourists assigned the spiritual self-entitlement to assume that they should be allowed to go to the mountaintop without actually being summoned? Who needed all these would-be Moseses? Someone had to stay down at the bottom of the mountain. Or else who would there be to give the Commandments to?

We were The People and without us Moses was just another chest-thumper pushing a bullying screed of thou shalts and thou shalt nots. In the end we would decide whether or not the idea/revelation/bill-of-goods brought down from on high was worth listening to.

Besides, we didn't need Sinai; just being in this room, where monks have slept since the Crusades, was intense enough. Between these four walls people experienced absolute, unvarnished faith, the highest possible achievement of the human mind. Also present here was the echo of some of man's most far-fetched dictums, wrongheaded notions that had been the bane of rationalist thinking for a millennia and a half, leading to who knew how much intolerance, pain and suffering. But this was cool. The room was a scene of huge thoughts, and we wanted these kids to *think*. Wasn't that the goal of this entire endeavor, to get things moving between those waxy little ears?

In the middle of the night at St. Catherine's, the moonlight hard on the hills, it was possible for me to see my children not as canny lawyers for international relief organizations (my current vision for Rosalie), teachers/ever concerned shrinks (the usual choice for Rae), or NBA stars (Bill's plan), but rather as prophets, biblical figures, arbiters of the sacred.

The inspiration for this reassessment could be found in Exodus 32: 7–14, immediately following the Lord's tirade concerning the Israelites' reversion to idolatry through the fashioning of the golden calf. Calling the Jews "a stiff-necked people," God makes ready to have his "wrath burn hot upon them."

Moses protests. "*Lord,*" Moses says in verse 11, "*why doth thy wrath wax hot against thy people, which thou hast brought forth out of the land of Egypt with great power, and with a mighty hand?*" Did God want the Egyptians to think that He'd gone to all the trouble of leading the Jews from bondage just "for mischief . . . to slay them in the mountains"? How would that look, "to consume them from the face of the earth," his so-called chosen people?

In verse 12 Moses ventures a grand, Promethean gambit. "*Turn from thy fierce wrath and repent of this evil against thy people,*" he tells God. In its way, this straightforward entreaty reveals a greater show of faith in the Creator's innate goodness than Abraham being willing to kill his own son on Mount Moriah. After all, Yahweh has been acting a little hotheaded. He isn't one to tolerate much backtalk. Moses could not be certain of the often intemperate Creator's reaction when properly reprimanded.

Yet, Moses' faith wins out. God backs off. In verse 14 it says, "*And the Lord repented of the evil which he thought to do to his people.*"

When I think of my children as mythic heroes, I cannot see them leading the tribe for forty years in the desert, or harrowing hell like Gilgamesh, Orpheus, Aeneas and the rest. But they could do what Moses does in chapter 32. Calming down the Old Man, getting him to repent his rage through the use of canny argument, with the faintest hint of a mocking guilt trip thrown in—the circumventing of authority, yet somehow remaining in its good graces—this was something my children could do. As well as any prophet.

The next morning we had no choice but to get up early. The taxi we'd booked for the twelve-hour trip to Cairo was arriving at four in the morning. We filed into the courtyard of the Church of the Transfiguration as the bell tower was in the midst of pealing thirty-three times, as it has for the past one thousand years. Monk John was there, his thin, stark frame leaning against the chapel wall like a haunted Modigliani trapped in a DiChirico painting. We'd run into him the day before and he recommended we visit the monastery ossuary. All the skulls of the monks who had lived and died at St. Catherine's were piled in there.

"Thousands," he said. We might find it interesting. The kids said they thought they would give it a pass. Piles of skulls kind of gave them the creeps. Plus, we'd already seen Tuol Sleng.

"Tuol Sleng?" John inquired.

The kids gave a short-form description of the Khmer Rouge torture chamber and the room where hundreds of skulls were nailed to the wall in the shape of a map of Cambodia.

John seemed stunned by this information. Evil haunted the world, it was important to remain ever-vigilant against it, to learn its ways, to better stand fast in Christ. But John was not familiar with the Khmer Rouge and the killing fields. This spate of twenty-five-year-old bad news shook him. He swallowed hard, then, drawing a deep breath, he said what happened in Cambodia sounded very, very terrible. But, in the end, Good would always triumph over the forces of Evil, otherwise life would cease to exist. This was the very nature of faith. Then, seemingly recovered, John again suggested we visit the ossuary. He understood not wanting to see a room full of skulls, but these were not just ordinary skulls.

"These are *monks'* skulls," he said.

It took a day or two, but after one more cardamom coffee at Groppi's on Talaat Harb in Cairo, we'd pretty much nailed down the plan. We would rent the house in Brooklyn, put everything in storage, ship the dog out to the sister-in-law in Texas, enroll the kids in the American school, and move to Egypt for a year, maybe two. Finding the new place had always been an underground agenda of this trip, an unspoken teaching point. We were New Yorkers, always would be, but to become truly "worldly," you had to stretch the definition of the word "home." A citizen of the world should feel at home in the world, in whatever corner of the globe they find themselves. The true life traveler had to walk an unfamiliar street, climb a strange set of stairs, get a job and pay a funny-looking electric bill. The magic was in the routine, the dissonant delight of adaptation to a separate normality. On that account, Cairo, older than dust yet chock full of modernist panache and hassle, would do quite nicely.

For the most part, talk of relocation—changing anything, for that matter—drove the kiddies into a frenzy. In our house you could barely mention the name of a continent, like, say, South America, without someone yelling, "Forget it, we're not moving there." Games of Geography could easily turn into full-scale panic attacks, as if "D is Dime Box," "X is for Xanadu" was really secret code language aimed at having the Mayflower mov-

ing van pull up at the door. Their bodies in constant transfor-
mation, the kids loathed external change, clung to the familiar,
generated formidable nostalgia for events that seemed to have
happened only yesterday. The girls had never forgiven us for
moving from St. Marks Place to the far-off wilds of Brooklyn. It
was as if we'd ripped them from their roots. For years I had to
drive both Rae and Rosalie back down our old street so they could
peer wistfully up at the fourth-floor window that used to be ours
and hear our former first-floor neighbor yell at her overstuffed
dogs.

So it was a surprise to hear them talk about how maybe it
wouldn't be so bad to live in Cairo, maybe even get an apartment
downtown, or perhaps out on the wide leafy streets of Zamalek
Island.

"You know," Rosie said, "just to *be* here for a while."

Strange what puts you at ease, gives the sense of fitting in
a place. Arriving late on our first night in the Egyptian capital,
we went out looking for a place to eat. The only open restaurant
was a brightly lit joint serving *koshary*, an Egyptian fast food staple
composed of noodles, rice and lentils in a tomato sauce. This was
a specialty of the house, but other things were listed on the wall,
including *taamiyya*, which is what falafel is called in Egypt. The
waiter, a brusque man wearing a white paper hat, came over with
his pad. I ordered a *taamiyya* and some mango juice, also listed
on the wall.

"Koshary and Pepsi," the man said.

"Excuse me?"

"Koshary and Pepsi," the waiter said again.

"No, taamiyya and mango."

"Koshary and Pepsi," the waiter returned once more, sharply.
What was this, some language problem, or was this his way of
recommending the koshary? It was obviously a local place; we
were the only non-Arabs there.

"I'd rather have taamiyya and mango."

Thick eyebrows rising, the waiter glowered at me. "Koshary and Pepsi."

Maybe they didn't have taamiyya. Reading from the wall, I asked, "How about hummus and a 7UP?"

"Look," the waiter said. "*Do you speak English? Koshary and Pepsi.* That's it. That is *all* we have. That is all we *ever* have! We've *never* had anything else."

"Uh, I guess I'll have koshary and Pepsi."

"Koshary and Pepsi," the waiter said, writing it on his pad.

The kids thought this was a regular riot, Dad getting chumped, like some out-of-town rube. When the waiter returned, I said, "Let me ask you one thing, okay? If all you have is koshary and Pepsi and all you've ever had is koshary and Pepsi, why do you have to write it down on a pad?"

"You wouldn't want me to forget, would you?" the waiter said with a slick, Big City smile, sending the kiddies into one more paroxysm of mirth. It was cool, a perfect New York moment, Cairo style. For people like us, stuff like that builds bridges.

There was hardly anything we didn't like about Cairo. We liked the way the hundreds of iron oil lamps hung on chains from the great vaulted ceilings of the Hassan Mosque, we liked climbing the minaret of the Mosque of Ibn Tulun (built in 876) during prayer call, we liked the Cities of the Dead, where whole neighborhoods lived inside the cemeteries, hanging their clotheslines between the tombs. We liked the taste of the hot sesame seed rings outside the Khan al-Khalili, the great bazaar, where we sat among the *sheesa* smokers at Fishawi's, the coffeehouse that has been open twenty-four hours a day for the past two hundred years.

The next day, we went out to the pyramids in Giza, because it makes no sense to come to Cairo and not look at the Pyramids. We got there at dawn, hoping to beat the crowds and

legendary armies of hucksters, which we did, except the haze
and pea soup air pollution rendered the massive forty-six-
century-old structures all but invisible. All that could be made
out was the top of the Great Pyramid of Cheops floating in the
mucky air like a ghostly eyeless triangle, as if ripped from a
dollar bill or part of a Sun Ra video that would never be shown
on MTV.

With the arrival of the souvenir sellers, none of whom got
the joke when Billy tried to trade his Taj Mahal keychain for
one of their mini pyramids, we soon retreated to the Pizza Hut
depressingly located directly across from the Sphinx. The place
was packed with a busload of Rosicrucians from Virginia. They'd
just gotten back from a private tour of the tombs. The Egyptian government granted the tour, one of the Rosicrucian ladies said, "Because they respect our knowledge of pyramid
power."

After they left, Rosalie said, "Ten thousand."

"Ten thousand what?" Rae inquired.

"Slaves. Slave labor. The Great Pyramid took thirteen years.
It is six million tons heavy. That is a lot of pyramid power."

"Don't be such a killjoy."

"I wonder what you could do today if you had ten thousand
slaves?"

"Probably make a movie."

"Yeah," Rosie said, warming to the idea. "Can you imagine
how many extras they could have had in *Titanic*."

"They could have had a much bigger boat."

"Two boats."

I didn't know what I'd done to raise such cynics.

Give or take a half dozen mosques, this concluded much
of our tourist chores in Cairo. Now we were free to indulge our
fantasy about actually moving here. Eating in a downtown bar

decked out in 1950s dark wood style that we were told was all the rage in the Nassar days, we asked our dining companion, Sharif, what he thought of our relocation plans. Marvelously urbane, a publisher and student of literature, Sharif had been introduced to us by a friend who covered the Middle East for a stateside paper.

"Moving here?" Sharif said, tickled by the notion. "Only an American would think of doing that. Just like only an American family would think of going around the world. It has nothing to do with the money. A trip around the world is only comprehensible to an American. Americans see the world in a binary way. There is America and not-America. Every place is either 'like America,' 'somewhat like America' or 'not too much like America.'"

For Egyptians, it was different, Sharif said. "Once we were the center of the world but now we are on the side, a fringe. The only country like Egypt is Egypt. If I go to Russia as an Egyptian, how am I to make sense of anything? What do Russia and Egypt have in common? Where is my reference point? I could go insane."

This was the state of cultural imperialism today, Sharif remarked. The American model was so pervasive that it was necessary for two members of wholly unrelated societies, places as far-flung as Papua New Guinea and Greenland, to think like Americans to be able to find the common ground between them. "It is a massive plot to turn the whole world into Ugly Americans," Sharif half joked.

Still, Sharif did not think it would be a brilliant idea for us to move to Cairo at this particular time. With the unloved Hosni Mubarak holding onto power due to old-line connections, aid money and the general fear of fundamentalist takeover, the political situation was far from stable. You never knew exactly what might happen next. Mostly, however, Sharif said, we'd find living here frustrating. This wasn't an open society.

We didn't understand. Everywhere we went everyone was very inviting. Egyptians were very friendly.

"They're polite," Sharif said. "We've been here a long time, we know how to act. People will listen to you speak your mind but they won't let you know what they're thinking. Their minds will already be made up about you."

Sharif, our friend, agreed with Walid's grandfather: in the Holy Land people were being sorted out, whether they liked it or not. In fact, he used almost the same words. "Here it is difficult to control one's own identity," Sharif said. "As far as they are concerned, *they know who you are.*"

It was so; everyone judged everyone else according to their own criteria. In India, a man asked Billy what his caste was. Billy replied that he "didn't have one." "That's impossible," the man replied. But here, Y2K in Holy Land, these assumptions took on a heightened relief. We'd already felt the hostility, albeit in a mild form, just a few days before, on our ride from St. Catherine's to Cairo. The afternoon had started as a grand triumph of cross-cultural fun. It being viciously hot, we'd joined forces with a few of the other passengers in our communal taxi to demand that the driver stop at the beach along the Gulf of Suez so we could go swimming. It took some doing, but finally the cabbie relented and everyone ran into the water fully clothed. When the driver, now smiling, came crashing into the sea, everyone cheered.

Soon enough, however, a man claiming to be a watchman came to say we couldn't swim there. He worked for a real estate concern that was putting up condos on the beachfront. This was private property and there could be no swimming allowed. He was sorry, but he was only doing his job.

"The keeper of the toilets," a youngish Egyptian passenger said of the watchman as we got back into the stifling van.

Wearing horn-rims, the man, a sociology student, had a serious, contemptuous look. Once he'd gone to New Jersey, to visit his cousin, but he hadn't liked it. He felt Americans were prejudiced against Arabs.

"In Sinai alone they've built five thousand new apartments," the student said. "Five thousand apartments, that means ten thousand toilets, at least. This is a desert, where will they get the water to flush ten thousand toilets? Once you came here for the sea, now you come for the toilets. . . . This is the way people think; if they have money, they can do anything."

The student paused, looked us right in the eye. "But you . . . the *kind of persons you are*, you already know that." With that the student stuck his head into the Arabic paper he was reading and didn't say another word until we reached the Suez Canal, where he got out.

It was a small incident, far from conclusive. But the attitude, the quiet defiance, the barely repressed rage, gave us a chill.

Riding out of Egypt, bound for Jerusalem, the bus attendant, a twentyish Egyptian guy, wanted to marry our daughters. Already rebuffed by Rae, he was now leaning over the vinyl seat, proposing to Rosalie.

"I would be an excellent husband for you," he said. "As you can see I am quite handsome. You have heard of Omar Sharif, the actor? He was very handsome but I am even more handsome as him and speak many more languages. I am fluent in Russian and Mandarin."

Blushing madly, Rosie said it was good to speak many languages. "But I'm only twelve."

"Yes," the bus attendant said, "I know, it is not your custom. But perhaps it is possible to *reserve* you . . . until you come of age."

Rosie said she didn't know about that, but she really couldn't talk about it now. The bus ride was making her sick. In fact, she felt like throwing up.

"I am very sorry you are ill," Rosie's suitor said, gallantly handing her a wad of tissues. "I will go to discuss reserving you with your father."

We have had our share of boyfriends over to the house during the years, mostly Rae's. These things go so fast. Once Rae had a crush on Jonathan Taylor Thomas, who had fourteen minutes of fame as the male ingénue of the TV show *Home Improvement*. While visiting Los Angeles, I managed to secure two tickets to a live taping of the program. Rae was beside herself as we lined up with the rest of the audience outside the studio. Then, for a fleeting moment, there he was: JTT, as he was called, his blow-dried little head stuck out the stage door. Obviously some years older than the character he was playing on the show and heavily pancaked, he looked like he was trying to sneak a cigarette before the taping. There was an unwholesomeness to him that made me feel like launching myself and hitting him with one of those leaping left hooks Floyd Patterson used to throw. He would have deserved it, the sawed-off faker, deceiver of my daughter's purest heart. Before Rae could turn around Thomas ducked back into the doorway. She will never agree, but I've always thought she was lucky to have missed seeing the object of her early adolescent desire. If she had, being her, she would have immediately recognized how much cooler she was than him, which is no way to feel about someone you have a crush on.

This was followed by many boys, these slurred monotones on the telephone. They noticed, early on, how sleek she'd become, the way her body glided through the air. Now history repeats with Rosie, who's also become this whole other thing recently, plush and full of attitude.

When it comes to gentlemen callers, we have standards. So far the rules require that they mention their name on the phone without excessive mumbling and introduce themselves should they happen to come to our house, not slink in the door and scurry upstairs to blast the record player like that troll A. (he knows who he is). If they are willing to eat dinner with us and actually speak, that is a plus. Beyond that, the basic policy is: if the girls like them, we do, if they don't like them, we don't. If we like them and the girls stop liking them, then we no longer like them.

It is that simple now. Kids are kids. What we worry about is that every seemingly benign sixteen-year old carries the potential seed of a closet whip-and-chain user, deep-end divorcee, failed chiropractor, self-regarding but talentless actor, teetering depressive, basketcase sympathy exploiter, secret shoplifter, public fondler, et cetera. The varieties of male sociopathy are limitless. The girls are smart but there is always the chance they'll overlook something, fall prey to the late onset of a fatal character flaw. I wish I could hand the girls a divining rod to dowse out the poison hearts (and a claw hammer to remove the offending organ) they are certain to encounter, those boys who want only one thing from them, whether they are in the mood or not.

Chances are they'll get married. That means that one of these slouching characters will become our son-in-law, just as I became my wife's parents' son-in-law. There might even be multiple sons-in-law over the years, a whole crew to tolerate across the patio barbecue. But one of these possible family additions was not likely to be an Egyptian bus attendant, even if he did speak fluent Mandarin.

"I have come to talk to you about your daughter," he said, having marched to the back of the bus where my wife and I sat. No doubt about it, he was, as he pointed out once more, very handsome, and clean, too. But his feet did not fit into his shoes. His heels hung over the crushed-down back of the brown Ox- fords by an inch or more. I asked him about this and he said, with some abashment, that these were not actually his shoes but his roommate's. He could not find his shoes this morning and feared he would be late to work.

With Rosie in the front of the bus pressing her hands against her cheeks in the style of an Edvard Munch scream, it would have been easy to say, "Well, I don't know what you do here, but in New York if you want to marry my daughter you've got to have better fitting shoes than that." But that would have been cruel. Instead, we told Rosie's suitor that she'd already been "reserved."

"Already reserved?"

"Yes."

"Then I am too late."

"I'm afraid so."

"All right, then," the suitor said, extending his hand to shake mine before dejectedly returning to his seat.

Jerusalem is the City of God but the god for whom it is named is dead. Archaeologists say people first came here in 5500 B.C. But it wasn't until 4000 B.C., with the arrival of the Canaanite people that the settlement came to be known as Urushalin, the city of Shalem, after the Phoenician god of dusk.

Since King David moved the Ark of the Covenant here from Kiryat Yearim after conquering the city in 1000 B.C., Jerusalem

has been the center of unparalleled religious and political up-
heaval. After costly siege warfare against the Samarians and
Assyrians, the city has abided the onslaught of Alexander's
army, the rule of Herod, Christ's ministry and death, the burning of the Second Temple in 70 C.E., the ascent of Muhammad
to Heaven from the site of the Dome of the Rock, the coming of the Crusaders, the Ottoman hegemony and the current
battle between the Israelis and Palestinians. Yet through these
annals of strife and transcendence, Shalem's name has been
retained.

Yet this was Y2K, the year of the millennium, a time of
reputed ultimate change, a cataclysm beyond the simple crashing of hard drives and the malfunction of cash machines. To
some, the Kingdom of Heaven was at hand, with its correspond-
ing anti-Kingdom of Hell. Should this come to be, adherents said,
Jerusalem would be the fulcrum, the vortex, the eye of the un-
blinking hurricane.

As noted above, when we came to Jerusalem, the ongoing
Al-Aqsa Intifada, which would result in hundreds, perhaps thousands, of deaths, hadn't yet begun. But people were clearly on
edge, as if cognizant of the fuse burning down. You could see it
in the body language of the old ladies selling vegetables and the
money changers just inside the Damascus Gate. It was present
on the anxious faces of the young Israeli Defense Force troops,
patrolling the ancient buildings with their Uzis and M-16s. The
tension was there in the fleeting dialogues with Arab candy sales-
men, and in the way the Orthodox priests craned their necks
before turning the corner of the narrow streets.

The millennial year (hawkers in the narrow alleyways were
already marking down T-shirts stenciled with rubrics like "I Lived
Through the Millennium" and "Y2K Go Away, Come Again Another Day") brought a spike in the incidence of the Jerusalem

Syndrome, the localized psychiatric phenomenon during which the afflicted came to believe themselves imbued by Divine mission. (In 1969, one alleged syndrome sufferer, Dennis Rohan, an Australian tourist, felt called by God to set fire to the Al-Aqsa Mosque, causing widespread rioting throughout the city.)

There are several hospital wards devoted to these people. Most think they are Jesus, but there were several Moseses and Abrahams, too. A man calling himself "King David" stood at the Zion Gate playing a lyre, talking of his visions of the new world to come. "Brother Solomon" wandered the slopes of the Mount of Olives preaching Christ's imminent return. Several African Sudanese, who called themselves "Apostles of the People," could be seen standing as stock-still as Buckingham Palace guards outside the Jaffa Gate, eyes upward, palms outstretched.

One wild-eyed bearded man, a tall, skeletal South African calling himself Samuel, saw us walk by and came bounding out of the cafe where he'd been sitting. "The cork is coming out of the bottle," he shouted, lurching forward like a spastic goalie. "Don't you feel it? The pressure?"

We did, as a matter of fact. It was the concentration of belief, the axis of three still-functional religions confined to such a small space, the overload of so much otherworldly concern. Here, people said, every step was freighted with a special gravity. The air was thicker, composed of a denser weave of molecules; you could feel the friction, the heat on your forehead.

As Rae, ardent fan of Italo Calvino's catalog of whimsical municipalia, *Invisible Cities*, would point out, Jerusalem was far from simply a physical city, with a central district and outskirts. Jerusalem was in Brooklyn, in the head of the Williamsburg Hasidim, hurrying across the overpasses of the Brooklyn-Queens Expressway in their black felt hats. It was in the heart of the church ladies underlining passages in their dog-eared Bibles on the A train. It was alive in the thoughts of the Arabic guy in the bodega on the corner where we bought milk and cat food. All these people had their idea of Jerusalem, a personal vision quite possibly as vivid as anything set down by John of Patmos, in the Book of Revelations, wherein a "New Jerusalem" descends out of the heavens, its twelve-gated walls made "of jasper, and of pure gold, like unto clear glass." The real ramparts of Jerusalem, built by Suleiman the Magnificent in the sixteenth century, could hardly contain all those dreams, that much hope, that much apocalypse. As our crazed correspondent Samuel said, sooner or later, something would blow.

We'd set up our bunker at Al-Arab, a hippie hostel nestled between several falafel and candy shops on the tunnel-like Salmuddin Street. The guidebook said it was "probably as good as any cheapie in the Muslim section." Most of the backpackers slept on the roof for a couple of shekels, but we had the big room downstairs, behind the kitchen, with five mattresses flung onto the floor. Usually the room cost thirty dollars but Klaus, a graying German longhair who seemed to be in charge, said he'd give it to us for twenty.

Klaus was heartened we'd thought to bring the children to Jerusalem at the millennium. A believer in astrology and tarot, he was convinced, like so many other residents, that "massive change was right around the corner." This did not mean, however, that this future was preordained, Klaus said. A free-thinking sort of astrologer, he did not believe the "tyranny of inevitability." As far as he was concerned nothing was fixed except the stars. Things could be changed, if people wanted them changed. Even in the climate of violence in Jerusalem, with gunfire no isolated event during the evening hours, Klaus refused to believe that "tomorrow will just be killing." Little signs, like the presence of our children in the room behind the kitchen at Al-Arab, enhanced the odds, he said; hence our $10 room discount. If we stayed more than a week, he could do better, Klaus said.

Too bad he couldn't do much about the dense stench of the tomato sauce and pasta coming from the kitchen, apparently the only things our fellow hostellers knew how to cook, and the constant replaying of the Lisa Loeb song from the *Reality Bites* soundtrack coming from the room above. But, as Klaus said, we probably wouldn't want to stay in our room much anyway.

"Jerusalem," he told us, "was full of obligations."

This was so. The place is a teeming mall of alleged divine connection. Within several hundred yards of each other, like a compact triptych of competing monotheistic narratives, are the Western Wall, the last remaining segment of the Jews' Second Temple; The Dome of the Rock, the third holiest site in Islam, and the Church of the Holy Sepulcher, where Christ was purportedly crucified. Ecumenically minded humanists, we felt it best to visit these faith-based monuments in a round-robin fashion so as not to display any overt favoritism.

The children quickly discerned basic differences in the style and substance of the various structures. The Western Wall was the plainest of antiquities, they noted, yet by virtue of the vines that had grown up between the blocks, it also gave the impression of being alive, somehow breathing. The Dome of the Rock was, of course, the most beautiful, with its spectacular inlaid walls and ceiling, but then again Islamic buildings are always the most beautiful. The Church of the Holy Sepulcher contained the largest mysterioso quotient, filled with smoke and incense, bleeding statues, with Christ's "tomb" set down like a black boat in a sea of adoration. From this cursory architectural overview, the kids drew conclusions about the people who worshipped here. The Jews were the most direct and the most artless. The Muslims were the best mathematicians but the most repressed. The Christians were at once the most dramatic and the hokiest.

But they all believed. That was the authority of the place: all that belief. None of these people were alone, or so it seemed. They all had God.

This was the thrill and the depression of being in Jerusalem. As riveting as it was to watch the Spirit play out its diverse applications, it was equally demoralizing to feel estranged from the process. Here were all these believers and we were remote from most everything they believed.

It was an old topic with me. Religious Judaism was one thing the Titans of our family had chosen to leave on the other shore. Other families had rabbis, we had gangsters and garment industry *tummellers*. Our relatives lived in Jewish neighborhoods, worked almost exclusively with Jews in "Jewish" professions, ate Jewish food and rarely spoke to anyone who wasn't Jewish, but turned up at synagogue only on High Holy Days, and then likely only if they had free tickets.

This slim vestige of the traditional faith ran out with me, on the day of my Bar Mitzvah, a lackluster coda to what had been the most desultory of religious educations. Our temple was new, recently remodeled after a successful building fund committee organized by the Hadassah sisterhood. But there weren't enough Hebrew teachers yet present in the Queens hinterlands, so they imported some rabbis from Brooklyn. The teachers would arrive in a beater station wagon, old European men, bearded and stooped, squinting into the suburban sun with watery eyes made weak from years of studying the Torah. Charged with the responsibility of imparting the ancient law as given to Moses, they stood in front of fresh green blackboards and looked out at their students. And who did they see peering back at them? Me and my friends, passing notes, laughing like fools, thinking we'd rather be anywhere but here. It was a dark joke that Kafka might have enjoyed: these men, whose way of thinking had survived the Babylonian captivity and one hundred pogroms, ending up in Queens, handing out notices announcing still another "Las Vegas Nite" or cake sale.

One day Rabbi Gold, our teacher, lost it. Considered the scariest of the teachers—mostly due to his cataracts that gave him the look of a silver-eyed bird of prey—Rabbi Gold was something of a celebrity. He had numbers on his arm. He'd been in Bergen-Belsen or Dachau, no one knew which. According to the rumor, it was only the end of the war that had saved him from the gas chambers.

"What is that on your head?" Rabbi Gold shouted at Stewie, my buddy. "That thing on your head, what is it?" Rabbi Gold said again with redoubled fury. Instead of the proper skullcap, Stew was still wearing his Yankees hat.

"Sorry, I forgot," Stew said sheepishly.

"You forgot? . . . You come to *schul*, to pray, to learn, and you *forget* . . ." Rabbi Gold took a deep breath. "You," he thundered, as Moses might have thundered before breaking the tablets, "are not a Jew! . . . None of you are!" With that, Rabbi Gold, who told us his name was not really Gold, but it was just easier to call himself that in this stupid country, walked out of the classroom. We never saw him again.

Thinking about this incident all these years later, I retain a deep and growing respect for Rabbi Gold, because I always like people who see the flow and refuse to go with it. It was a very Jewish thing to do. But he was wrong. All the boys in his class were Jews. We were Jews for the new land.

I was the sort of Jew who learned the Torah speech for his Bar Mitzvah phonetically, from a recording made for me by one of the cantors. This was well in the tradition of my family. It was no surprise to me that when he was called to the Ark of the Torah my father could not read Hebrew any better than I could. My grandfathers also knew nothing. When it was over, the new rabbi, a young college-educated American, said how proud he was of everyone concerned, that the morning's activities reaffirmed, yet again, the true vitality of the Jewish people. I was pronounced "a man" and collected my envelopes stuffed with cash like every other member of my Hebrew school class.

With this sort of pedigree, what really is there to pass on? Many parents our age and younger tell me about how having kids convinced them to rediscover their Jewish roots. They join temples and talk about koshering their kitchens. I listen to this with mixed feelings. I think, maybe I would do the same if I could, but I can't. Not in good conscience, anyway. All that has long since run its course. Our kids have expressed no interest in being a Jew (or a member of any other organized religion, either) and we haven't pushed them to do so.

In Brooklyn this is okay. In Brooklyn, no one says anything if we feel like spending our Sunday mornings celebrating the Pentecost at Hezakiah Walker's Love Fellowship Tabernacle on Liberty Avenue because they've got the rockingest choir, and that gets us closer to our notion of God than anything any of us have felt in a synagogue. In Brooklyn, if I want to burn one of those ninety-nine-cent glass-enclosed "money come" candles from a Puerto Rican *botanica* instead of a *yartzheit*—and *still* feel Jewish—no one is calling the authorities.

But this wasn't Brooklyn. This was Jerusalem, the City of God. Postmodernism hasn't been invented here yet. Thought did not move lightly over water here, the stakes were too high, the punishments too severe. In this part of the world, as Walid's grandfather pointed out in Amman, it was good to keep a close hold on who you were, because the other people, *they knew*. And, sooner or later, it was going to matter.

Now it was Friday, the sun was well past the midpoint and *shabbos* was coming. We wandered about our tourist rounds, up to Gethsemane where Judas betrayed Jesus, around to the various halls of Talmudic scholarship, and back for another look at the Dome of the Rock. Everywhere we went there was praying, prostrating. On the Via Dolorosa, the path along which Christ carried his cross, people stopped, kissed their rosaries. From the loudspeaker atop Al-Aqsa the call came again. The devout scurried here and there, following their separate God-mandated agendas, paths crossing, but never touching, closed to the fervor that consumed the acolyte standing right next to them.

You wonder how faith comes to people, the way it overtakes everything else. Did it occur in great revelations, in the way the wily Saint Paul said the scales dropped from his eyes on the road to Damascus? Or were they simply born with it, as if the faith gene was simply one more aspect of natural selection? To the extent that I was without it, that I had failed to pass it on to my children, I felt I owed them an apology. On the other hand, did we really need to be part of *this*?

Only the day before, at Al-Aqsa, Arabic men faced off with Israeli police. It was part of an ongoing protest about the excavations taking place under the Temple Mount. Muslims charged that Jews were seeking to cut off their access to holy sites. Rocks started flying. The police dispersed the crowd with tear gas canisters and bird shot. It was nothing, really, relative to what would be happening in only a few weeks' time and still goes on today. But back at Al-Arab, the incident cast a pall. "What is wrong with them? Doesn't anyone really want peace?" asked Klaus, the German. But then someone turned the techno music louder and things were okay again.

Later on, Billy and I went down to the Western Wall. On our earlier visit we'd noticed people writing messages on small pieces of paper which they rolled up and stuck into cracks in the ancient façade.

"Are they like letters to God?" Bill asked. I said some people probably thought so. "I'll do that," he said.

It took Billy a while to compose his letter. Attempting to contact God, at least in such an overt, direct way, was a new thing for him. He never spoke of prayer, except while launching a jump shot out of his range. As mentioned, he isn't a dreamy sort of kid. Even in his class-clown mode there was a sober matter-of-factness about him. His conscious communication with other-worldly forces appeared to be limited to tooth fairy missives, mostly requesting extra payment for molars. But if the cracks in the Wall were God's post office, this was something to take seriously, even if officials came by every week to remove the messages, making room for more.

"Want to know what I wrote?" Bill asked after he'd shoved his bulkily folded letter into one of the Wall's fractures. Sure, I said, if he wanted to tell me.

"I wrote," Bill said, solemnly, "'Please help technology rise up to help make a better world.'"

This struck me as a very reasonable request, an honest supplication very much in tune with the person my then-nine-year-old son happened to be. If there was a 99 percent chance he'd misspelled "technology" and hadn't left spaces between the words, as per his usual writing style, well, God could call a copy editor. It was a moving thing, Bill taking the trouble to write his letter. He can spend whole days thumbing through sneaker catalogs, but here, the Western Wall had inspired him to think, to be articulate about his concerns, to gain insight into his place in the universe. There seemed little more you could ask from a religious icon.

Yet, as we stood there, basking in the ancient ineffability of it all, we were pushed aside by a large contingent of Hasidim.

There were probably twenty-five of them, a pack of black hats. It was the middle of the afternoon then and the Wall was not so crowded. But the Hasids seemed to want to pray right at the spot where we were. Nowhere else would do. As they jostled ahead one of them bumped into Billy, knocking off his paper *yarmulke*. The fact was, according to religious law, Bill really didn't need to be wearing the *yarmulke*. He was already acknowledging the presence of the Lord above by covering his head with his Knicks' Eastern Championship hat. He had no desire to wear the remarkably uncool thin cardboard *yarmulkes* that are handed out as you approach the Wall; he likened them to "an upside-down french fry holder." But if this was the proper headgear in which to send letters to God, Bill was prepared to wear one. For him, it was a sign of acceptance, that he was willing to follow the rules, however occult. So what a drag it was that the Hasidim, in their tunnel-visioned obliviousness, had knocked off Billy's *yarmulke*, and then blocked his way, as it blew away in the wind.

These characters might sell a million camcorders in their camera stores but they cared little about Bill's entreaty for Yahweh to imbue technology with the spirit of Ultimate Goodness. Billy's hopes for the future were no concern of theirs. They had their own ways of doing things. In New York, on Forty-second Street, or outside of the Brooklyn Library, they'd come bounding off their "Mitzvah Tank" RVs, *paises* flying, and grabbed your wrist. "*You Jewish?*" they'd shout.

It was always a creepy moment, because the question was rhetorical. *They knew.* As black Muslims never tried to sell *Muhammed Speaks* to white people, the Hasidim never approached any *goyim.* Chemically, instinctively, they knew who you were. Then, knowing they knew, you would be faced with (a) lying, saying "No, I am not a Jew," or (b) snorting something like "Yeah, what business is it of yours?" You didn't want to say "Yes, I am" because then they'd be yelling, accusingly, "Did you put on *tfillen* today?" berating you for not being the sort of Jew they were.

The next day, as the sun set after *shabbos*, we went back to the Wall. The celebration of the holy day's end was in full swing. At first the crowd was mostly Hasidim, their prayer books in front of their faces, *davening* with increasing speed, like mad woodpeckers before the temple wall. Then everyone else came, the whole Jewish quarter, accompanied by great crowds of tourists and visitors swarming down the steps. There must have been five thousand people singing, circle dancing, throwing themselves at each other. It looked like a giant *yiddisha* mosh pit.

We watched from the plaza above. In all my life I'd never seen Jews party that hard. It was fabulous, totally thrilling, everything that was missing from the Judaism as served up in Flushing, circa 1960. But we didn't join in. It wasn't that we weren't invited to the revelry below, not exactly. We wouldn't have been turned away. It was more like we couldn't quite comply with the conditions of the gathering, which included the separation of men and women by a high, slatted fence. The girls weren't for that, especially since, as Rae would point out, while the scene on the male side approached mass ecstasy, the women sat quietly on chairs or leaned over the fence, wistfully watching the fun.

In the City of God, we found no common cause. As we excluded ourselves from the dancing below, we felt no kinship with millennialists pushing each other aside to enter the narrow door of the Holy Sepulcher, spouting their killing Revelations numerology of four horsemen, seven seals and the 144,000 believers who would be saved when the sky vanished "like a scroll which is rolled up." For certain we felt no bond, beyond likely displaced liberal sympathy, with the people in the more wretched Palestinian sections of East Jerusalem. When you're from New

York, you know a bad neighborhood when you see it, where boundary lines are, where to stay away from. Driving through there was like a trip through Brownsville, or East New York: a lot of people standing around in the street, contemplating exactly how screwed they are, getting madder, crazier. Who knew which one of them would soon blow themselves up, in a Sbarros on Ben Yahuda Street or on an Egged bus? None of these were our people, and this was not our place.

Peering down at the crowd below, thinking of the violence everyone said was sure to come, we came upon a collective kind of epiphany; Jerusalem reminded us of the great murals of Angkor, all the grandeur, all the madness.

Half a world away now, the Ramayana's marching armies, cosmic forces bent on unglimpsed destruction, had stayed with us. We remembered, too, how Mr. Long, our increasingly revered guide, had likened these cataclysmic scenes to his own childhood, when the Khmer Rouge had killed his mother and father. The way Mr. Long described it, the KR years unfolded as some kind of unstoppable human self-annihilation pageant. "People were swept up," he said, the tips of his fingers running over the smooth stone of the *Ocean of Milk*.

People in the Holy Land seemed to be likewise swept up. Beyond the brutal politics of the situation, the cruelty of the Israeli occupation and the desperate, murderous Palestinian response, there is the sense of an awful apocalyptic procession unfolding. Everywhere was the pungent stench of Revelations, as if that text, so ripe with violent fantasy, wasn't anything but an earlier version of what the Khmer Rouge once called the Year Zero. That was Pol Pot's mistake, Mr. Long said, the notion that the world could be totally wiped out and restarted again. There was no such thing as the Alpha and the Omega. There would always be something there before the beginning, and something left after the end.

Mr. Long believed in the continuum. His compass told him the world was round, that one day led to another. This did not necessarily appear to be the case in Jerusalem, not at the current moment. It was a town of flat earthers, people committed to pushing the drama until they fell over the edge. If they took everyone else with them, then this was fate, or God's will.

It was right then, overlooking the tumult in front of the Western Wall, that I wished my wife and I had had more kids. Not that there was anything wrong with these three. There just should have been more. After so much recalcitrance and ambivalence, I stood there, amid the frenzy of the City of God, and mourned our unborn children, the ones we should have had. Who knew how many there could have been, without contraception, miscarriage? All of them should have been our children, the way Rae, Rosie and Billy were.

My wife and I should have had twenty-five kids, fifty, maybe more. Because our family wasn't like these people here, these flat earth people. These obsessives, these tribalist believers. We were a whole other kind, a tribe unto our own. We weren't any better than anyone else, but we were modern, up with the times. We were worldly, as befitted world travelers. Like Montaigne, we enjoyed rubbing up against others. Like Odysseus, we moved around, but were fond of home. Like glue, we stuck together. The earth, which was round, was lucky to have us.

So we went out of Jerusalem, in the middle of the night. Our flight to Paris left at seven A.M. from Ben-Gurion Airport, an hour's drive away, but El Al said we had to be there no later than four-thirty to go through security. Amir, the night manager of the Al-Arab, booked us a taxi—his cousin's taxi, actually. He was supposed to pick us up outside the Damascus gate at three o'clock.

But when we dragged our packs past the shuttered money-changer offices, the promised red van was nowhere in sight.

I had feared this would happen. Maybe it was the way Amir said his cousin was "*very, very* reliable." This was a hassle; people said if you're late for baggage check, El-Al doesn't let you fly. I believed it. When we came across the border from Egypt, the Israeli security people took Billy into a small room by himself because they thought he looked older than his age in his passport. I insisted I go with him, but an IDF guy stepped forward and told me to sit down. When Bill came back he said it was no big deal. "They asked me how old I was and where I went to school about six times. . . . I think they were trying to trip me up."

Parked at the curb was one of the white vans we'd seen Palestinians in East Jerusalem using as a common taxi. A man was sleeping in the front seat. When we passed by he opened his eyes and nodded.

"Hey," I said, "want to drive us to the airport for a hundred and twenty shekels?" This was the price I'd negotiated with Amir.

"Okay," the man replied, rubbing his eyes. We put our stuff inside the van and began moving through the night. We'd gone about ten miles outside the city before our driver, who kept yawning, began to nod off at the wheel.

"Hey! Wake up!"

The driver sat bolt upright. "No problem," he said. Offering a smile, he put on the radio. *Hash-mi, Hash-mi,* one of our favorite local tunes, was playing. It was a hit, and as the girls always do when a song they like comes on, they let out great whoops of glee and began to sing along. The driver, surprised and pleased that our children would know an Arabic song, allowed that *Hash-mi, Hash-mi* was one of his favorites as well. His wife liked it, too. But then the radio signal failed and static blurred the reception.

It soon quit altogether. In the silence, the driver began to nod again.

Sitting in the front, I attempted to engage him in conversation, but received only monosyllabic responses. We were about to ask him to pull over, shout in his ear, throw water in his face, whatever, when the girls arrived at the proper solution. They started singing again. They know a lot of songs, from every age group. They sang *Skinna-ma-rinky-dinky-dink, Skinna-ma-rinky-do*, which they learned at day camp; they sang "Charlie Was a Boxer," which their grandmother taught them; they sang several numbers from their all-time favorite full-length cartoon, *The Brave Little Toaster*. They sang the theme song from *Mystery Science Theatre 3000*. It was working, too. With Rae banging her leg into the back of his seat on the downbeats, the driver was perking up.

Then the kids swung into a rendition of "Gravity Fails," a song that will always have a place of honor in our family's musical canon. The tune appears on *The Brooklyn Side*, a CD by the Bottle Rockets, a hillbilly band hailing from the resonantly named town of Festus, Missouri, on the banks of the often flooding Mississippi. The Rockets weren't exactly the Next Big Thing, but they were the sort of Americans we loved, a quartet of indigenous rednecks who sang, with subversive compassion, of "welfare queens" and poor dumb souls who died trying to heat their mobile homes because "if kerosene works, why not gasoline?" The band came to New York every so often in their battered Chevy van and we usually went to see them, except for the time my wife got cancer, which was about the worst thing ever to happen to our family. There was no way she was making it to see the Bottle Rockets. But the kids, always sensitive to such disappointments, had an idea. Maybe we could get in touch with the Bottle Rockets, have them tell my wife to get well soon, or something like that.

As it turned out, I knew someone who knew someone. "Sure thing," the Bottle Rockets said when I told them about my wife's illness. "Maybe we could sing something."

"She's kind of partial to 'Gravity Fails,'" I said. So, at the appointed time the phone rang and the Bottle Rockets, calling from a pay phone outside a 7-Eleven off I-78, did an a cappella version of 'Gravity Fails' for an audience of one stunned but very grateful fan. The chorus of the tune goes, "When gravity fails and I'm falling down, glued to the ceiling, spinning around, well, that's when I'm counting on you."

Now, our kids were singing these same lines as we rolled through the darkness of the Holy Land.

"That song," our now fully awake driver said, "it is a good one." So the kids sang it again, and soon we were all singing it, the driver, too. It was one of those perfect travel moments, getting that harmony together, especially here, where everything seemed an inch from breaking apart.

Soon enough we were turning off the road, toward the airport. We could see the terminal lights blazing about five hundred yards away when the driver stopped in the middle of the road. "Get out here," he said.

We didn't understand. We had all this stuff, why couldn't he take us the rest of the way? "No," I said, "bring us to the terminal." It was obvious the driver wanted to refuse, but we'd forged this little bond. So he shrugged, started up the van again.

Around the bend, unseen by us until now, was the security outpost, several dozen men and women in uniforms, many of them with guns. Within seconds they had our taxi guy spread-eagle against the van and were dusting the steering wheel for bomb traces. They got all of us out of the car and started searching through our bags. Attempts to play the outraged American tourist drew only hard stares. The driver, told to stand beside us in the freezing desert night, rolled his eyes, as if to say, I said you should have gotten out.

Some of the driver's kids' toys were in the back of the van, a tricycle and a couple of stuffed animals. They were searched, too. It was outrageous, but what else was there to do? If you were an Israeli security guard, charged with protecting the biggest airport in the country, used by thousands of people a day, you had very good reason to search vans driven by Palestinians and everything inside of them, silly American tourists included. This was a place where people were willing to kill themselves, and everyone else around them, where armies blew up towns according to interpretations of claims made in a three-thousand-year-old work of literature. It was a fight over land, and the right to dictate your own identity. It was war.

The driver watched the Israelis with a resigned antipathy. "Hey, why aren't they stopping those cars?" Billy asked him. As we stood there, dozens of vehicles were whizzing by unimpeded.

"The license plates," the driver said. The cars going by had different shape and color license plates. Realizing Billy did not understand what he meant, the driver added, "They're Jews. . . ." Then he looked at the five of us, and swallowed his next phrase, shaking his head instead. It was not all that difficult to fill in the words not said: "They're Jews . . . *like you.*" Perhaps the fact that we had just sung together earned us the deletion. Maybe the driver was just trying to be polite.

We imagined ourselves free of such profiling, members of a mysterious yet open-handed foreign tribe, expansive citizens of the world, just passing through. But the driver, like everyone else, knew *who we were.* Just like, if we lived here, amid the fear in the Holy Land, we would know, right off, *who he was.*

*   *   *

In 1981, on the night my wife and I got to Paris, there were a
million people in the street. It was election day and François
Mitterand, the Socialist candidate, had displaced the sclerotic
right-wing government of Giscard D'Estaing, causing the Saint
Michel neighborhood where we were staying to go crazy. Everywhere people offered kisses and another glass of wine, as if they
were characters in a Maurice Chevalier movie, rather than the
real Frenchmen. Democracy as a thrill ride, what a concept! The
fact that Mitterand would stay in power for fourteen years, setting new standards for Machiavellian middle-of-roadism, and that
the Saint Michel area would become as densely gentrified as the
rest of the town, seemed unthinkable amidst that tumult. It was
a time to rock, all night.

Twenty years later, it being near the end of the August
vacation, the City of Light was far more serene. For us, however,
the Parisian summer had a more autumnal feeling. Our trip was
nearly over. When you go west around the world, Europe is the
end of the line. This was how my wife and I felt in 1981, and
this was how we felt now, especially about France. Call me a
Philistine, cold to Gallic charm, but I've never liked Paris much.
The place is filled with fussy, squatty buildings that go on for
blocks. I always feel like I'm going to break something. Don't
get me started about the hotels, either, unless you can tell me
why a three-star place is any better than a Super 8 off a freeway
ramp, aside from the fact that the rooms are half the size and
you can't park your car out front. I don't even like the food.

My Europhile friends, most of whom have more money than
I do and send their children to better schools than I do, tell me
this anti-Parisian prejudice is another in my long list of sham-
bling, ne'er-do-well attitudes that have kept me from realizing
my true potential. If I can't get over this aging Queens streetboy

class antagonism act for my own sake, they tell me, I should do it for the children, lest one more generation of Jacobsons wind up on St. Marks Place. I guess they have a point. The history of our family in the U.S.A. has been about moving up. Who am I to say we've moved up enough?

Luckily for them, the kiddies seem not to have fallen prey to my churlish anti-Continental biases. According to them, Paris was the first place we'd visited that anyone they knew might actually go of their own free will. Indeed, we hadn't been in town more than a few hours before Rae hooked up with some of her New York friends, visiting for the summer. She'd been setting up the meeting for weeks, E-mailing from cyber cafes from Thailand to Cairo. Many pages of her journal were prefaced with items like "twenty-three days to Paris," "only nine days to Paris!"

Now the great day had arrived. Two of her buddies from La Guardia, art and drama majors, arrived at our hotel, dressed to the semi-Goth nines, and whisked Rae away. We didn't see her for the rest of the day and, of course, had no idea where she was. Asked when she planned to return, she said, "I know how to figure out a subway system, you know," which translated to, "Like, don't wait up." Rosie was on the move, too, in her headstrong, practical manner, already scouting the *arrondissements* (near the Sorbonne looked okay) for potential living quarters. She figured she could live with another girl, maybe her cousin Stephanie, when she came back here in two or three years (but no more), this time without the clanking anchor of her family to weigh her down. Her French would likely be close to perfect by then.

It was all so very familiar. The return to normalcy was fast approaching. Trip Time, that little rip in the continuum of Regular Time, was zipping shut.

But that was okay, I thought, sitting in the gondola of the giant Ferris wheel in Place de la Concorde between the Tuileries and the Egyptian obelisk. Paris looked pretty great from up top of the giant wheel, I had to admit, better than it did from the Eiffel Tower (it figured that the national symbol was just for show while my much-loved Brooklyn Bridge continued to move thousands of cars across the river 120 years after it was built). Besides, riding a Ferris wheel was a fine place to wrap up our circumnavigation of the globe, going round and round. That was the whole idea of the trip. To follow the edge of the circle, check what was different when we got back where we started.

Big things were changing all the time. Only a few weeks before we left the States, my uncle Adolph, one of the very last of the Titan generation of my family, died. Left in his apartment on Nostrand Avenue near Brighton Beach was a signed photo of Jack Dempsey, the Manassas Mauler, the famous heavyweight champion of the Roaring Twenties, decked out in his fighting togs. "To Ad, thanks for EVERYTHING, your buddy, Jack." The unspecified "everything" is underlined three times. Gee, I didn't even know Uncle Adolph was a boxing fan.

My mother, the fabulous, dynamic Grandma Rita, now eighty-two, retired after thirty years in the New York City school system, another twenty buying trimmings for my uncle Bobby, the garment center *macher*, and still running the book and movie club at her apartment building on Bell Boulevard in Queens, is the last remaining grandparent in this family. The others, my father, my wife's parents, have passed away recently. Three times in five years the kids have had to dress up and go to funerals for people they loved, their lives turned incrementally sadder. There is some solace, knowing this is the plan, that the old people are supposed to die first. It had been a good deal, after all, one more bit of luck, having the full complement of grandparents around for such a long time. Not all families had that.

Love gets whittled away, memory grows, the present turns to past. I think my father, reconfigured as the fabulous Grandpa David, was a little surprised by how much he turned out to like our children. With each birth he lingered at the hospital with his counterpart, the equally fabulous Grandpa George, looking through the nursery glass, homing in on which one in the sea of pink- and blue-swaddled squirmers was ours, all ours. The day before he died was spent at the dining room table helping Billy smash his flotilla of matchbox cars into each other.

"Blam!" my father shouted, with each bone-crunching broadside. It had long ago ceased to matter that I had no memory of him ever participating in such gleeful mayhem with me. In happy stories, things have a way of coming around. That's what makes them happy.

Should I get lucky enough to make it to the next station of family life, I think this grandpa gig could be good. There is a hint of insubordination about it.

My Grandpa Jack, my mother's father, a family Titan who was known to move and shake, getting married four times in twenty years after the death of my grandmother, showed me the ropes. He knew my mother was nervous about him driving his 1954 Dodge up from Florida by himself to New York, especially since he was blind as a bat. His policy was to arrive unannounced, argue about it later. We had a ritual. He'd call me on the phone from North Carolina, or Washington, D.C., and say "same plan." This meant that when he arrived at six the next morning and woke me up by throwing pebbles at my window, I should sneak around to the front door and let him in. When my mother got up, there he'd be, sleeping on the couch. She'd hit the ceiling, accuse me of "only encouraging him," but she never could stay

mad for long. After all, he was her father, I was her son. Whatever conflicting feelings she had about each of us (*way* more about
him than me, at least then, no doubt), she loved us both very
much.

I look forward to joining in such conspiratorial joy with our
prospective grandchildren. You could call it a little of 'what goes
around/comes around' for a lot of broken curfews, backtalk and
unwalked dogs. But I wouldn't call it that. I'd call it fun.

So it was good, soaring over Notre Dame and the Louvre's
pyramid. The ride was nice and smooth, not like Deno's Wonder
Wheel, our favorite Coney Island attraction. Deno's is big, but it
is rickety, with groaning, gear-gnashing engines that threaten to
give out at any time, likely with your car swinging precariously fifty
feet above the mucky boardwalk. The Paris wheel, being Parisian, moved quietly, in seemingly frictionless circles, one classi-
cal, perfect Greco-Roman 360 degrees after another. Whizzing
through late-afternoon air, it was possible to lean back, forget the
machinery, picture yourself at the pinnacle of another, bigger
wheel.

The time at the highest point of the curve isn't long, but
the view is wide, uninterrupted. From here, I imagine, I can
see the past and the future, what is behind and beyond. I can
see as far back as the first Jacobsons and Rahinskys and Siegals
and whatever else they called themselves before their names
were changed at Ellis Island. I can see my great-grandfather
Alfred, stuffing my grandmother into his potato sack, I can see
my uncle Larry shooting dice. I can see them all, in the ghettos
and on the farms.

For this moment, all lines pass through me. I am the hub.
As I've watched my children nearly every day since they were
born, I can see their lives unfold from this day on. High up on
my perch, I only see good things, the happy things that come to
those who are lucky and smart. My children are lucky, and they

are smart. So they grow up, have wonderful lives, their children are even more wonderful. Generation after generation, it is the same: sweet, beautiful, human. If, somewhere in this process, my wife and I become nothing more than a couple of names on some great-great-great grandchild's genealogy project, or are even forgotten altogether, what do we care? *We're dead!*

Watching the successive waves of my blood ebb and flow, the countenance of Mr. Sen, the sad, childless follower of Shiva we met at the Burning Ghat in Varanasi, came to mind. No birth or death could be possible without the opening of a *tirtha*, Mr. Sen told us as the stench of charred bodies rose above the Ganges. Every soul came from somewhere and was going somewhere else, and the *tirtha* was a passageway between these states. These were dangerous portals, Mr. Sen said; one should always pray for Shiva's unreliable aid while traveling through them. But Shiva must like our kind, I thought, because at least in my vision every Jacobson soul got to where it was going. Not one of us was ever crushed or maimed or damned, and none of us ever would be. This was how the view looked to me, from my fleeting position of the top of the arc.

The last day we were in Paris, the sun went out for two hours. In apparent perhaps ironic acknowledgment of the Church of Christ's calendar reckoning of the millennium, the heavens and earth had conspired to stage northern Europe's greatest solar eclipse. By late morning, from our Left Bank vantage point at the appropriately named Café Champs Du Mars, more than 99 percent of the sun was covered by the earth's shadow. We watched the whole thing through our *lunettes*, our special eye-protecting glasses. The French authorities were very adamant on this accord. Giant billboards warned that watching the eclipse without glasses would risk much *mal aux yeux*. Unfortunately, there weren't nearly enough *lunettes* to go around. We managed to find five pairs, but many of the others sitting at the Café

Champs Du Mars peered up at the disappearing sun with only their naked, soon-to-be-damaged *yeux.*

Being nice, worldly Americans, not the ugly, globalist kind, we felt a little concerned about this, coming to another country and seeing their once-in-a-lifetime eclipse when the locals could not. We lent our *lunettes* around a bit, to people who looked friendly, which made us feel better.

Everyone knew exactly what to expect. Scientists get very precise when it comes to eclipses. They predict them a century in advance, know exactly how long they will last. It is very cut-and-dried, like long division.

Still, the moon's shadow obscured the sun, as if a circular shade were being drawn across its surface. It was unsettling. The air temperature dropped. The streets darkened. It wasn't quite like night; more like "day for night," the shadowy fakery of the old black-and-white Hollywood pictures the French love so well. The sun looked like a dirty plate, round but flat. If the scientists were wrong and things got stuck right now, it would be a disaster. Life on earth would perish, as the dinosaurs supposedly did 65 million years ago. Humanity, what was left of it, would likely be forced underground, into giant heated caves lit by full-spectrum mood lights. It wasn't a totally impossible scenario. Those madmen promising apocalypse couldn't be wrong forever.

The five of us, feeling the collective anxiety, reached for each other. The circle of our hands was like a halo around one of those little French espresso cafe tables. When we get nervous about each other, we touch. If this really was the end of things, we wanted to go out together.

But it was just one more false alarm. As predicted, the penumbra, like all moving shadows, poor players who strut and fret their hour upon the stage mostly for the benefit of our particular amusement, soon receded. The world remained in place, and us with it. Which was, of course, kind of how we figured it would go.

So that was about it. We went over to London for a few days, complaining about how much everything cost, buying all our meals at the food stalls of Marks and Spencer, eating in the hotel room. The events of the past few months had already begun their inevitable recycling. In one of the bookstores at Charing Cross, we found a copy of *Absolutely Goldie* by Christopher Wilson. It was pretty much the usual celebrity pap, but still we were mightily put out that Mr. Wilson had neglected to mention Ms. Hawn's silk-buying forays in Varanasi. When it came to Goldie Hawn, the small silk-selling cult of "Goldie people" seemed far more important than that same old tripe about *Laugh-in*.

In Camdentown, where the kids delighted in buying the same boots they'd be able to purchase only several hours later on St. Marks Place, we ran into a guy who had been staying at the Vishnu Guest House in Varanasi the same time we were. Now employed selling organic soap, the business that had paid for his holiday, he recognized us right away but we had no memory of him. He didn't take this personally, saying it made sense.

"You know," he said, "when you bring kids to a place like that, people tend to remember."

Everyone had their own particular memories of this trip. That was part of the idea, the laying down of the mnemonic base. We remembered Mr. Sen, Lobsang and Adel. Did they remember us?

The next day at the airport, waiting to board British Airways flight 177, the kids came over together. They said, maybe they had been a little difficult at times, maybe not always the best of travelers. But still, they wanted to say thanks. Or as Rae would say, "Thanks for making me go on this trip."

"Thanks?" we said, taken aback. "All we've done for you, and all we get is *thanks?*" We gave them stern looks.

It took them a minute, trying to figure out what to say next. What more could they say? Then, they broke out laughing.

After all, what more could we really ask for but *thanks* . . . which we took, and gave, liberally.

Back in the U.S.A.—
The Mnemonic Update

W hat can I tell you now, more than two years since we got back from The World?

Well: yesterday was Thanksgiving. As noted before, our table is smaller. Both my wife's parents have died since our return. Grandpa George, still a volunteer fireman at age eighty, had a heart attack while photographing a blaze. Everyone said that at least he died doing what he wanted to do, literally with his boots on. This was a nice sentiment but it doesn't make him any less missed. His death was considered in the line of duty, so firemen from all around the state came to the funeral. Many of Rae, Rosalie and Billy's friends came, too, because Grandpa George was very popular with all age groups. Most people held it together until the firemen started ringing their bell, which is what they do for fallen heroes. It still didn't make him any less missed.

My wife's mother, Grandma Marion, died just a few months ago. Her lungs gave out. Not a follower of dull consensus reality, Grandma Marion had an elevating sense of humor. She was with us the day my wife and I drove over to the Connecticut town hall to get our marriage license. My wife and I had gotten into some kind of squabble over who knows what. I got out of the car and slammed the door, which shattered the side window. We stood there stunned. Then, with perfect timing, Grandma Marion started laughing, which was pretty generous, considering it was her car. She always had a great sense of timing. This Thanksgiving we miss her, too.

The rest of us are still here, that is the good news. This is the most up-to-date report:

Rae graduated from high school, went to college in a remote little town in upstate New York, left there before she went batty, came home, got a job in a drug store, quit it, fell in love with a guitar player from Long Island, and now figures she'll go back to college, except this time in New York, where things make a little more sense to her. Except for the fact that she remains forever beautiful and dreamy, her head always in a book, with Rae, there is always suspense. You want things to go well, yet you never know quite what will happen next. But I suppose she can tell you about that.

Rosalie has been moving along her chosen path, which is the only one she is likely to move along. She almost got suspended from high school for organizing a protest against the war in Iraq. She had fifty kids ready to leave class and "walk out" to a rally in Manhattan. When the principal tried to stop them, Rosie told him, "We believe in this, so we're going to do it," which they did. In the end, we figured she didn't get suspended because the dean, who told us "You have a brave and strong daughter there," secretly dug the whole thing. The strangest part of the event, Rosie said, "was the way everyone was looking at me, like waiting to hear what I was going to say." She is also currently working at twisting her hair into dreadlocks and listening to ska punk bands.

Billy is now our tallest child. In the seventh grade and generally attired in the Eminem mode, he just keeps growing, a good thing since he recently attained a very high social position at his school, starting on the basketball team. He also plays on our team in the local police precinct league, of which I am the coach. Sometimes he'll walk past me and mutter how "this offense sucks," but mostly he does what he is supposed to do, which is rebound, play defense and get out on the break. We're not quite thinking college scholarship yet, but he is already way better at basketball than I ever was. This makes me proud. However, he still cannot beat me in a foot race and I am willing to risk a stroke to make sure he never does. Last summer Bill went to sleep-away camp for the first time. A homebody, he didn't want to go, especially since we'd found the place on the Internet, which he said was an insult. His first letter said, "I will never forgive you for sending me here." The second letter said, "This is getting a little better but you guys are still idiots for sending me here." Eventually he wound up liking it, especially staying up late talking with his bunkmates. Asked what they talked about, he said, "You know, philosophy, mostly."

Since we got back, a place called the Tea Lounge opened a couple of blocks from our house. It is one of those joints with frumpy thrift-store couches where you can nurse a single cappuccino for three hours. Sometimes I go over there in the morning to read the newspaper. There are always plenty of young moms and dads with their toddlers—our neighborhood has more than its share of Maxes, Dylans and Emilys. It all looks familiar, the moments of total bliss, followed by absolute terror and distraction, the sharp pendulum swing between extremes. Preoccupied, the parents don't even seem to notice that the Neil Young record the Israeli counter girls play over and over again skips. Some of the kids are very cute, some aren't (although you know that the uncute ones may be cute tomorrow, and vice versa), but I can't say that I have much nostalgia for those harried days.

I like it better now. For years my wife, smart about these things, said fatherhood gave me a dose of schizophrenia. There was me, the faithful husband and father, and the *alt.me*, the unattached, the free agent image of myself I kept alive in my mind. It wasn't a devil or angel sort of thing, one on each shoulder. The djinn in me was more of a neutral figure, just there, available. He was my secret enabler, the ghost I disappeared into for one minute or ten, the refuge that allowed me the momentary psychic separation—the space between—to be a dad, at least at first. I don't need the other me as much now that I am more experienced in the ups and downs of parental love. But I keep him around, because some days . . . well, you know about some days.

As I said, I like it better now, with them growing and grown. I even have stretches when I think I know what I'm talking about. That is a good thing because there is still a long way to go. When we go out with our younger friends, the ones with the five- and six-year-olds, they treat us like wizened veterans, old pros in the kid thing, as if we're coming down the home stretch. This is wrong. Those chilling stories of the forty-five-year-olds still living at home notwithstanding, there is much parent life to come. We plan to keep the gig as long as possible.

Our trip around the world comes up fairly often; more often than I thought it would, really. The kids seem to remember everything, the names of our hotels, the airlines we flew on, the places we ate. The Siq and the first view of the Treasury is often commented upon, the Bedouins fondly recalled. At Angkor, Mr. Long told us that you could always tell which leaders in the Ramayana carvings were the most important by counting the UM-*brellas* held over their heads. "The more important, the more UM-*brella*," Mr. Long said. So now, whenever it rains, we quote Mr. Long, because why would anyone want to say "umbrella" when you can say "UM-*brella*"?

These are the details of The World, things entered into our permanent record, stuff only we know. It gives us pleasure to know them. The other night we drove out to Floyd Bennett Field, New York's first commercial airport, which has now been converted into a national park. We were hoping it would be dark enough to see a meteor shower scheduled for that night. But it didn't really pan out; we saw only a few meteors. Billy said that if we were only still at St. Catherine's, we would have seen a lot more. "St. Catherine's," Rosie repeated, and we all stood there a moment, transported. Once there, together, we could go back again.

This said, I have detected no groundswell for a repeat circumnavigation. I say, "Hey, who wants to go around the world again?" and there are no takers. They tell me to go eat some Indian food if I'm desperate for a little weirdness, and leave them out of it. It isn't, after all, a trip you could exactly take again, not as it was. Time marches on. The World is different and so are we. This doesn't mean there won't be other journeys, more circling of the globe. My wife and I might go again, in another twenty years, like a ritual. But most of the circumnavigation will be done by them, stopping in whatever parts of the planet are still open for business. There should be enough of those, as long as the earth is round and spinning.

So, in the spirit of ongoingness, it makes sense that Rae, spokesperson for *der kinder* in this particular context, should get the last word. She will—*they will*—anyway.

Backtalk

by Rae Jacobson

This is supposed to be an ending, a final chapter of sorts, I guess. But really it's my beginning. Today as I sit writing this my life is more uncertain than ever. I have been to college, last year, in the tiny town of Potsdam, New York. I never missed my family so much. When we said good-bye I was surprised by my father; I had expected some clinginess from either myself or my mother, but as they were leaving, my dad was the one lingering, shooting suspicious glares at my male neighbors and lecturing me on the evils of boys. This was all new in a way; he'd never been the outwardly protective type, having little interest in my past boyfriends. The most he'd do was hand down a spiteful nickname (Matt became Door-matt, et cetera). Usually he just ignored them. Here, though, he was hanging back, telling me to lock my door, giving extra hugs, and although it was surprising, it was welcome. Our old connection had surfaced, and as separation loomed, it held us fast. I was my father's girl again and it felt good.

College . . . turned out to be not quite what I had expected. In my eyes it was supposed to be an intellectual dream world where your classes fit your personality. It turned out to be the thirteenth grade, La Guardia all over again, except this time I lived there. My goal had always been college; now that I had gotten there, I was lost. I took classes ranging from bioethics (which I loved) to line dancing (which I sucked at) but I couldn't find anything that fit. I've always been bad at the "what do you want to be when you grow up?" question. But I never thought it would come back at me so hard. Suddenly growing up was so much closer than ever, and I still had no clue. By the end of the year I'd decided to move back to the city and figure out a new plan. I couldn't help but feel that I was wasting time though; almost twenty years old and direction-free, I was prime for a career in fast food.

On the other hand, being home again after a year away was virtually impossible. My family has a magical way of spreading themselves into every room in the house, and having grown used to my peace up at school, this was incredibly frustrating. I had decided to move out with a friend from school earlier that year, and I couldn't wait. I got a job as a cashier at a mom-and-pop-type drugstore in the West Village, hoping to save money. Never has there been a worse idea. I was the absolute most terrible cashier on earth. Making change? Nooo. Not me. My only skill seemed to be being nice to the customers as I screwed up their purchases, making unprecedented mistakes in the field of cashiering. The only thing I did right was dust.

By the end of the summer I quit my job and emptiness filled my days. For the first time in my life I wasn't going back to school. Taking another nine-to-five job seemed implausible but necessary. I searched for any alternative and then my father reminded me of this book. Going over all my old notes, reading my journal and my father's writing began to bring me back to my family. One night I went and found an old article my dad had written after the Columbine shootings. For research he'd accompanied my friends and me to The Bank. I was fifteen, dressed up, made up, and having my father there seemed so uncool. My friends had agreed to the arrangement but it still was weird.

Upon our arrival I'd shooed him, scared that the bouncers would realize I was underage. A covert kiss and an under-my-breath "I love you" and I was on my way. When the article came out most of it was as I'd expected, somewhat condescending but funny, but then I read the end. It described how my father had felt watching me walk away into the dark smoky club; betraying a strong loving parental worry I hadn't expected, he even called me beautiful. My heart broke and soared at the same time and I was overcome with the intense urge to hug him.

Then, of course, we went on our trip around the world. My memories of that time are strange and wonderful, coming back to me in odd ways. Sometimes I can pass hours recalling the beauty of the Pyramids and how small they made me feel both in size and in history. I sat for a while on one of the huge sandstone blocks, watching my family run around, fascinated by just how brief one person's time is on earth in comparison to these stones. Then I'll forget about that and think of the Pizza Hut right across the street and just how totally dumb that was. The large decal logo of the chain was pasted on the window in such a way that no matter where you sat you had to look directly through it to see the Pyramids. It seemed as though mediocre middle-American pizza was now sponsoring ancient burial tombs. Thrilling.

My recollections are in bits and pieces but they come together to form a quilt of experience. Drinking hot tea with Bedouins in Jordan touches the corners of swimming in the blue, blue water at Ko Samet. The boxes of every-color every-shape gummy candy that they sold everywhere in Jerusalem meets at the seam with pictures of the strange fruits my mother brought back to the hotel room in Cambodia. Everything is sewn together, and when I want to escape from my current life I wrap myself in it and let the dreams take hold, sweeping me back to the brilliance and strangeness of those days.

Soon I will actually be moving out, and despite my recent purchase of a button that says "I didn't like college anyway," I am hoping to return to school in the spring. Things are becoming marginally clearer, and I'm hoping they will soon shine. As usual, my family has been an annoying yet infinite help. This book and that trip, my memories and the solidarity among us back then allowed me to find a way to let them back into my life. For that I am grateful. If it works, why not stick with it? And just think, I almost stayed home that summer.

Family Shout-Outs

One super loud family shout-out to Ada Calhoun, our all-time travel fiend and big-time buddy, the greatest role model for both children and parents.

Rae's shouts: Mike Kozak, who is beautiful and fantastic in all possible ways. Mi familia: there are no real words. Amy Wolfe, Julia Carson, Victoria Monte, Dan and Katherine Ambia, Katherine Martinelli, and Megan Mendenhall—thanks from the bottomest bottom of my heart. Thanks to the Potsdammies. My Grandma Rita has been nothing but amazing since I met her and continues to be nothing but that as we grow. She has believed in me forever and I love her. Thank you Lisa Chasin for a similar feat. Much love to the kittas. And a toast to absent friends. Nancy's shouts: to Carol H. Cardozo and George H. Cardozo II. Rosie's shouts: to all my friends, past, present, and future, you know who you are. Billy's shouts: our family and my video games. Mark's shouts: To J.B. the man. Michael Daly for inspiration. Will Blythe for being Roy. Morgan E. for the dough and belief. Flip B. for the proper pushiness. Steve E. for the soundtrack. Terry B. for having the glass half full. Lucius S. for having the power. Caroline Miller for the time. John Homans for the coffee. Marianne Butler for going to The Bank. Antonin K. for the Cambodia flake-out. Chris and Mike for the space and a lot more. Big shout across Time and Tide to Mrs. B. and Mrs. C. for St. Mark's Place. And to all mentioned in this book, around The World: good wishes and peace always.